R O

Published by Other Forms

Making m : Cultural Production in Occupied Spaces

Edited by Alan Moore and Alan Smart

3

Contents

Contents

Preface

Miguel Ángel Martínez López

First of all, I want to thank Alan Moore and Alan Smart for their enthusiasm in bringing to life this book. They have displayed all their knowledge and skills to develop the initial idea while being able to connect people from different backgrounds. The work has been done within a very limited period of time which makes the effort even more astounding.

The editors, many of the contributors, and I know each other because of SqEK (Squatting Europe Kollective). This network of activist-researchers started to meet in 2009 and once or twice every year since then—in addition to enjoying a regular and fruitful exchange through our email list. It is under the umbrella of SqEK that some of us prepared conventional academic research proposals among other activities. One of them, the MOVOKEUR project, succeeded and we got some funding to conduct a comparative study of squatting in some of the major Western European cities. Until recently, I almost had no knowledge or personal contacts about squatting in Eastern European countries, although SqEK is increasingly incorporating more activists and researchers from that area. The MOVOKEUR project focused on what we called "cycles, contexts, identities and institutionalisation". Its rationale may be read extensively elsewhere[1] and we have also published some articles and one book[2] where we deal, mainly, with three of these issues -all except the 'identities'. With the present book, then, we intend to fill this gap.

It is generally assumed that social movements shake society because they question policies, governments, injustices, threats or just taken-for-granted ideas. They do so by mobilising activists and supporters while engaging in different protest actions. Movements may need either to create their own identity if they lack any, or to recall already formed social identities in order to gain visibility, legitimacy and appeal for their claims. Collective identities are thus supposed to be the cradle where the movements' demands are engendered. They also serve to unite members and bring about cohesive organisations able to endure over the time of struggle.

What is more controversial is to assure whether the movements' actions and outcomes can be directly and sufficiently explained by collective identities. Alternative approaches point to crucial aspects of the contexts where the movements emerge and develop, such as the political conjunctures and the elites' strengths. The interactive dynamics between movements, opponents, authorities and third parties, or even counter-movements, tend to diminish the explanatory power of collective identities as well. However, few social movements scholars would deny the evidence that a deep understanding of collective identities helps us to make sense of the significance of a particular social movement and the issues and values at stake.

The major problem faced by the study of identities is their blurred nature, which is consubstantial with the idea of culture itself. Almost everything we human beings do and think may be considered cultural production. From the routines of our attendance to a particular venue, to the way we dress or speak. When the MOVOKEUR project was designed, the preference was to emphasise two major cultural dimensions which we consider under-studied: a) the practices developed by squatters; b) the social networks they form. For 'practices' stands a wide range of activities beyond the conventional attribution of culture as arts, in order to delineate the different modes of communication, shapes of buildings, self-organization, protest repertoires and the like. As for 'social networks', I refer not only to electronic ways of expression and interaction, but above all to the social milieu where social movements relate to each other by creating families of movements, political cultures and fertile grounds for the promotion of radical activism. In essence, the idea was to focus on the material production of culture by adopting a broad view about all the symbols, codes, discourses and social relations that are involved in squatting. In other words, the squatting scene produces more than concerts, graffiti, or pamphlets.

One of the principal cultural expressions of squatting as a political act is the explicit announcement of the occupation of a place. By painting walls and doors, or hanging banners from the windows, the disobedient action is made public. Flags, leaflets and press conferences may also spread the word but this primary cultural creation also entails the political possibility of the opposite: to not communicate or claim the occupation, to remain silent and stealthy, just to keep living and let the neighbors guess what are the differences and what are similarities between their lives and those and those of squatters.

Things step up a level should squatters get more socially, culturally and politically active. Instead of a house just for living, the building may be transformed into a public venue open to any kind of activities. For instance, it may serve as a meeting place for different political groups and campaigns who cannot enjoy other convenient or non censored spaces for their activities. It may host workshops, or collectives or solidarity kitchens. It may help as storage for all kind of construction and artistic materials, plants, toys, books. Gardens on the rooftops and balconies are also common. Free or clandestine radio stations and do-it-yourself publications, zines or newspapers, may find adequate shelter in squats. Of course, squats are excellent venues for parties and the performance of musical gigs, theatre, films, circus, dance, acrobatics, exhibitions, etc.

All these cultural practices are not uniquely artistic, and the social networks they create go surely beyond the narrow definition of the squatters themselves. Therefore, I consider that squatting not only constitutes a valuable gesture towards opening up possibilities for underground and counter-cultural manifestations which are banned from the mainstream and commercial spaces, but is also a powerful engine to bring about wider social diversity in the various political exercises of self-management of free, albeit usually temporary, spaces. Squatters are able to trespass the barriers of the youth-radical political scene to connect with their families, friends, neighbors, sympathizers, foreign residents, minorities, and all those who wish to feel some fresh air in these creative urban spots. Obviously, these creative groups and these modes of creation differ significantly from the so called 'creative classes' and the city branding strategies that promote high-end tourism and consumer culture. In the squats you learn how to occupy, disobey, resist, protest, organise, manage, socialize, repair, rehabilitate, create, enjoy, protest, solve conflicts and many other things—unfortunately, not all positive, given the multiple contaminations with the society at large and the internal contradictions among squatters. This political socialization and culture is conspicuously absent in the dominant discourses about the creative cities.

Not the least, squatting challenges the everyday life of squatters. Domestic issues such as cleaning, cooking, maintaining the common areas, taking care of kids and those who are ill, usually defy gender relations and patriarchal patterns, not without continuous conflicts to face. Queer-LGBT cultures may also find favourable channels of expression through the squatters' networks and spaces. The development of the hackers', free-software and open-source movements has found enthusiastic support among squatters. The same may be said of the struggles in solidarity with migrants and asylum seekers, and of bicycle workshops, where can be found tools, hands, ideas and convictions to re-frame low cost and sustainable urban mobility. It is not unusual, then, that squats and occupied social centres—rather than many houses just for residential purposes—have played a central a definitive roll in a broad spectrum of radical cultural production.

10

To what extent are these identities rooted, place-attached and consolidated? How fragmented, interconnected and overlapped are they? Do they represent global concerns of a left-libertarian culture or just local lifestyles, needs and institutional gaps? Is the illegal status of trespassing and taking over unused spaces the only source of all these practices, networks and identities, or would it be impossible to imagine them without the assistance by and mutual contamination with many other third parties?

These are some of the questions I had in mind when dealing with the cultural dimension of squatting -although I must admit that they are mostly the result of many discussions with fellow squatters, friends and colleagues. SqEK members and meetings have been outstanding in this regard as a shared source of inspiration. Even more, the long-lasting efforts and great contributions made by Alan Moore with his fanzine *House Magic* provided a very eclectic example of how to collect and explore the diversity of the cultural production in, through, and by (or despite) squats. The texts and images presented in this book attempt to contribute to the history of squatting by representing an array of faces, voices, experiences, artefacts and collective breath to fight urban speculation in order to make cities more liveable, accessible, and ours.

NOTES

1 http://www.
miguelangelmartinez.
net/?Squatting-in-Europe

2 https://sqek.squat.net/
books/

Whether You Like It or Not

Alan W. Moore

Squats play a vital role in the field of cultural production. They support art forms that might wither without them, and they incubate new usages that never would have been had squats not existed. This anthology is a first step towards proving that case. There are innumerable questions to be asked about culture in squats, questions which bear on the social movement of squatting itself, the spaces squatting opens up and the uses they make possible, inquiry which will surely reflect back on the conditions and ethos of mainstream cultural production.

Squats and occupied social centers in Europe have been bastions of alternative and radical culture for decades now. They announce their presence with painted banners and murals, and their posters line the walls of the urban districts in which they arise. In the evenings and late into the night, they often exude music, and the sounds of revelry. Inside, young people, who don't work for wages to pay rent do what they want to do. And what many of them want to do is be artists, or at least be creative with their own lives, find out how to live together, and do social and political work.

Cultural production in occupied spaces and in squats is a principal concern of the activists who make these places. In fact, the very act of occupying is a central cultural fact, a condition of everything that is done and made in such a place. Visual and performing arts—mural painting, fashion (as mode of dress and self-presentation), festooning and parading (demonstrations), the traditional components of pageantry—are also the clearest statements of the positions and intentions of squatters as regards their neighbors and as projections to the public at large.

Squatting is illegal, no matter the purpose, whether it be simply for living or to make public provision for non-commercial activity, to "commons" a vacant and disused building or patch of land. As this securitized century of endless asymmetric war against non-state actors has begun, squatting has been repressed ever more energetically. In Europe, important long-lived centers of social, political and cultural life have recently been strongly attacked.

As the many and varied texts in this anthology will make clear, the wild weeds of squat culture have played an important part in some of the most significant creative movements of the late 20th and early 21st century. Today however, many states and cities are acting like gardeners who systematically cut off new growth, uproot sprouting bulbs, and mix salt with the compost, while at the same time they carefully tend languishing and long dead shrubs and trees.

The culture and cultural production of squatted spaces is that part of the growing changing city which is constituted in resistance—not covertly, like ganglands and underworlds, but overtly as integral parts of extra-parliamentary political movements. Even so, their activities and products, even their entire beings, have been regularly recuperated by governance as part of city cultural infrastructure, with varying results.[1] These incorporations are the outcome of negotiations, processes of relation usually marked by conflict, often violent, as successful autonomous projects strive to maintain themselves in the face of state antagonism and bad deals.

This is not always so. Some cities have adopted sophisticated normalization processes, as in Amsterdam and Paris. Most have not. Their policy towards squats is haphazard, and highly dependent on the politics of the day which can regularly impel state actors towards violence.

Because they are such centers of innovation, with doors wide open to (nearly) all, and ample scope for intelligence, cooperation and

Bicycle repair shop in a legalized squat, Amsterdam

13

hard work, projects organized in squats are regularly recuperated by institutions, launched into the commercial world, or spin off into a wider autonomous universe. The rhythms of rule-breaking occupation, project growth and recuperation can seem eerily similar to the establishment of successive *avant gardes* in artistic cultures. These have been recognized, and then become celebrated currents of their respective mainstreams. But squatting culture is not *avant garde*. It is, in many respects, even traditional, recreating the same features from project to project, across borders and languages. It is within this continually regenerating framework of customs that innovation can arise.

A lot of the conservatism of squatting must come from "hardening"—the endless fight with repression of all kinds, and the need of a hardy, proven model to reproduce in the face of regular extirpation. Still, as assembly-driven projects based on shared desires, open to (most usually) collective initiatives whose members are prepared to share the burdens of maintenance—someone has to pick up the bottles and unclog the toilets—the potential for innovation and change in squats is always present. And unlike hierarchically managed cultural facilities, squatted social centers are open door projects. You don't need to be trending, be recommended, to know somebody (although that never hurts!), or undergo a competitive review to qualify to propose your ideas to the assembly. Of course, there is no grant money, and no credit to be earned in the obedient world.[2]

Squatting as a movement is continually interacting with the wider economy, and with institutions of all kinds. This is because squats and social centers produce within all the major fields of artistic vocation. Music, theater and circus, visual art, literature, rap and poetry, research and study, archiving and book-making, photography, cinema, architecture, fashion, mechanics and artisanship—all are represented in squats, usually by collective working groups. Emergent fields of cultural production are represented as well, e.g. media art and broadcast, computer hacking, and creative social practice. This anthology includes texts directly relating to many of these areas of work, telling stories from the collectives that undertake them.

While squatting culture has a continual relation and interaction with the mainstream of artistic production, the publicity and marketing mechanisms of the latter almost never point to or acknowledge work that takes place in disobedient spaces. Many squatters as well deliberately separate themselves from such media circuits and economic arrangements.

Almost none of the academic institutions which undertake

the instruction and reproduction of artistic professions include or acknowledge squatted spaces as part of the purview of the aspiring professionals they train. Despite the historical constancy and special conditions of cultural production within squatted places, and despite that many important artists began to work in squats, these venues are officially off the table as prospective zones of experiment for art students.

This forbidden fruit can be particularly attractive to some. Squats have strong ideological valences which can appeal to politicized artists. Among the ideologies and ideations most commonly found in squatting contexts are classic and neo-anarchist, communist, anti-imperialist, feminist and queer positions. Entire squatting projects form around them.

Social centers have been key in devising concrete strategies and innovative tactics that, while they resonate with political ideologies, have addressed specific urban struggles. This happens continuously, and intensively at key moments. Among these are strategies of resistance to gentrification of working class urban neighborhoods, urban development projects perceived as coercive and/or corrupt, for historic preservation, for food justice, and against privatization of public resources. Squatters have also organized long-lived solidarity projects with migrants and *sans papers* immigrants, and coordinated anti-fascist struggles. Because occupied social centers are often at the center of political movements contesting top-down urban plans, they stand for urban development from below. Cultural producers in squats regularly cleave to ideas of free culture—including making work that is "copyleft," or open source (this last usually applied to computer software). Closely allied to this is the rising idea of commonsing, opening spaces for public social use that have been long vacant, or formerly public spaces that have been privatized. In fact, thinking around the commons is a major part of legal arguments for the practice of squatting itself.

More broadly, squatting has long been a key part of bohemia and counterculture, the culture of disobedience and transgression of social norms. And, like those subcultures, social centers are open to migrants, queers, and others who are socially excluded or marginalized within urban communities.

To speak about the relation between academic institutions—in particular, art schools—and squatting, is not to say so much that one ignores the other. What matters more is the exclusion of so many young people from the cultural professions which the former institutions reproduce. Squats and social centers draw many who cannot easily pursue careers in culture by reason of their class position. This is the result of the stratified education system in Europe, with its high stakes exams for public positions, prohibitively expensive private education, and deeply embedded doxa of competition along rigidly prescribed lines.[3]

In a statement that could be a platform for cultural production in disobedient spaces, U.S. art critic Ben Davis asserts among his well-known theses on art and class: "Creative expression needs to be redefined. It should not be thought of as a privilege, but as a basic human need. Because creative expression is a basic human need, it should be treated as a right to which everyone is entitled."[4] Davis' thesis is in tune with the Italian jurist Ugo Mattei's ideas of culture as a commons. Mattei was a supporter of the recent Teatro Valle occupation in Rome.

In Italy and elsewhere, a good number of occupations and squatted centers have arisen as a result of student movements against increasing restrictions on the public education systems, and more recent stringent austerities. The intention of some squats is to undertake free popular education, especially political. Historically, in Spain at least, squatted social centers trace their ancestry back to the tradition of workers' ateneos, centers of education free of church and state control.

As new generations of academics, working under conditions of austerity and restructuring, have become increasingly precarious—and in that sense, more like artists, and their engagements with social centers have also increased. Significant research projects have originated in autonomous squatted spaces, early among them the Precarias a la Deriva militant research collective investigation of conditions of domestic labor which came out of the feminist house project La Karakola in Madrid.

This project thus far has been about social and economic conditions. A key question for art however concerns the affect of squatting, the feeling and meaning of cultural production in disobedient spaces. Otherwise, everything that squats and social centers do could easily be replaced by conventional facilities as part of a normal liberal program of government social and cultural services.

In a general text, cultural theorist Stevphen Shukaitis has gone some distance towards laying out grounds upon which this affect might be understood. Working with Italian Autonomist ideas and conceptions of the classical modernist avant-garde, Shukaitis expands on Antonio Negri's suggestion of a "constructive punk realism." He describes a form of sociality conjoining aesthetics, politics and life, whose participants refuse to separate aesthetics from the social domain. (For it is in that separation that capitalist recuperation arises, and academic specializations take hold.) His notion of an "an aesthetics of refusal" unfolds within the process of collective creation, its relations and intensities. These very personal interactions in the process of production create an affective space in which particular feelings and relations can unfold. This is clearly what social centers try and often do. Shukaitis works with the Italian Autonomist notion of "affective composition," the bringing together of a class of social and political actors through cultural means. For him this is about an aesthetics of transgression, not as a crime, but as a revolutionary resistant form of action. It is also the affective composition of a new class of political actors. For Shukaitis and others, squatting and occupations are parts of a new social and political order, an imaginal machine, coming into being, rising with and through state resistance.

At the same time, everyone in this world is sensible of the perils of what the Situationists called recuperation. Innovative modes of artistic production have become vital to the forward motion of capitalism today. New imagery and creativity is vital to the continued existence of the totalizing system the Situationists called the Spectacle. This is why Shukaitis insists that "refusal" be part of the system, setting disobedient aesthetics against the forms of separation that sustain capitalist social relations and most creative production.

While simple poaching of for-profit emulation, and "dumb" recuperation goes on a lot, there are smarter ways for institutions, both cultural and governmental, to interact with the innovative political squatting movement. A small consortium of museums for some years has been experimenting with a "new institutionality" which at times aligns their programs with social movements. They seek at the least to recover the educational role of the museum, to provide a space for debate and conflict, and, in the words of Chantal Mouffe, to "oppose the program of total social mobilization of capitalism". While most of this work has been in the realm of historical exhibitions, the consorted institutions subscribing to this program have at times worked with squatted spaces.[5]

Other more flexible state-funded cultural programs and institutions work with artists' and architects' groups with ties to, or experience in squatting movements. In Madrid, the Reina Sofia museum (MNCARS), the Medialab Prado, and Intermediae in Matadero both intersect with some squats from time to time, through their discussion programs and various off-site initiatives. Medialab is what maxigas would call a "hackerspace"; these are more traditionally known as media centers, which as his essay in this volume demonstrates, have important historical antecedents in the squatting movements of Europe. Intermediae is dedicated to public art, a field that has been revolutionized by the growing interest in forms of social practice.[6]

Public art is a sibling of architecture. The traditional form of the architects' charrette, an intensive series of discussions around building projects, has grown into new modes recently. Some currents of the "new institutionality" among museums, quite apart from the stated programs of the Internationale consortium, amount to an under-the-table collaboration with groups and people with close ties to social movements and nascent and out-of-power political formations. This is a world of near-latency, where architects' groups, skilled in DIY ("do it yourself" — of which squatting is a paradigmatic example), can be hired to stimulate citizen participation in civic projects.

Other recent funded projects, like the Goethe Institut's Europe-wide initiative "Project We-Traders: Swapping Crisis for City," worked with a select group of architectural collectives, sharing strategies for developing citizen participation in cities. The BMW Guggenheim Lab was similarly motivated, albeit more of a discourse project, and more inclusive. "part urban think tank, part community center and public gathering space, the Lab traveled globally to inspire new ways of thinking about urban life." Even so, activists in Berlin virtually shut down the unfortunately branded Lab when it came to their city. They didn't want to discuss about it. For them it evoked what Markus Miessen called the "nightmare of participation."

While the process is clearly not without conflict, the inclusion and refinement by institutions of initiatives that have arisen within the political squatting movement is motivated by the widely felt necessity by nearly all thoughtful people to move smartly into the post-petroleum age. Squatting culture, and the commune movements which preceded it in the 1960s, have long been pioneers in ways of living that are urgently required for contemporary sustainable city programs. Hardy volunteer initiatives like garden squats on vacant land, bicycle activism and Critical Mass, food justice projects which build new farm-to-city relations, projects of cooking and brewing, recycling of clothes, books and more, cooperatives and solidarity economy projects have long been integral parts of squats and social centers. So it is little wonder that institutional initiatives along these lines have drawn from squatting culture.

In the longer view, this is all good. As it plays out in real time, however, it will be fraught with contradictions and contest. From both big capital and the direct action movement, every step of the way, we may expect resistance. It's going to be an interesting ride.

NOTES

1 As they are assimilated, they may easily lose their character, their vitality, because of reversion to "quality reviews" and familiar hierarchical forms of management.

2 I originally wrote "no social capital to be earned." Miguel Martinez responded: "We shouldn't offer a wrong view about squats. Money, although managed in the manner of not-for-profits, is almost always involved. And 'social capital' even more, at least if we understand that expression as just referring to the dense social networks of friends, fellow activists, unknown people, etc. you get in contact with once you attend squats. A different issue is the 'economic potential,' to transfer that social capital into economic capital."

3 Early in the last century, artist and teacher Robert Henri, a propagandist for artists' independence and solidarity, coined the rallying cry, "No juries, no prizes!" The dominance of both often betokens artistic decadence.

4 Thesis 8.9, in Ben Davis, 9.5 Theses on Art and Class (Haymarket Books, 2013); also online as a short text. The world of art today is seeing intense academicization as well as concentrated speculation on market stars in the world of art, both rising and established. Both of these positions, as scholar-artist and market stars, are virtually unobtainable without the backing and leisure to pursue them, and the luxury to risk not attaining them. They are effectively closed off to artists from the working class.

5 For the story of how this idea developed in Barcelona, see Jorge Ribalta, "Experiments in a New Institutionality," in Manuel J Borja-Villel, Kaira M Cabañas, Jorge Ribalta, eds., Relational Objects: MACBA Collection 2002-2007, (Barcelona : MACBA, 2010); the essay is posted online. Chantal Mouffe discussed this initiative as against the Negrist idea of "exodus" – (and, by implication, against the social center formations of political squatting movements) – in "Chantal Mouffe...," Artforum International 48 (2010), online.

6 Nato Thompson, ed., Living as Form: Socially Engaged Art from 1991-2011 (Creative Time/MIT Press, 2012)

7 Markus Miessen, The Nightmare of Participation (Sternberg Press, 2011)

REFERENCES

Hans Abbbing, "Why Are Artists Poor?: The Exceptional Economy of the Arts" (2007)

Florian Malzacher, et al. Truth Is Concrete: A Handbook for Artistic Strategies in Real Politics (Steirischer Herbst Festival, Graz, Austria/ Sternberg Press, 2014)

Alan W. Moore, "Art + Squat = X" (2012), on academia.edu

Alan W. Moore, Occupation Culture: Art & Squatting in the City from Below (Minor Compositions/Autonomedia, forthcoming)

Stevphen Shukaitis, Imaginal Machines: Autonomy and Self-Organization in the Revolutions of Everyday Life (Minor Compositions/Autonomedia, 2009)

Beneath the Bored Walk, the Beach

Stevphen Shukaitis

The classic 1968 slogan "beneath the pavement, the beach" was used to indicate that beyond industrial technology and mundanity one could still find a passionate drive for a vibrant life. Yet something more profound seemed to be hinted at. We do not want to abandon the inquisitiveness and joy of 'uncovering' something precious, despite that these are the very same emotions that have been mined constantly since the 1960s to fuel new shopping campaigns, designer holidays, and produce countless other forms of commodification. The point is not to ignore the commodity and its fetish, its shimmering appearance of general equivalence that is constantly denied, but rather to turn the gaze in the direction of the bored walk, and pay attention to the one who walks slowly because there is no reason to walk any faster. That is, we may try to consider more carefully the constant silent war taking place on the factory floor (or any number of workplaces), as work and domination are stealthily avoided, not through open resistance, but through foot dragging, feigned respect, or feigned stupidity. As Anton Pannekoek argues, "Every shop, every enterprise, even outside of times of sharp conflict, of strikes and wage reductions, is the scene of a constant silent war, of a perpetual struggle, of pressure and counter-pressure." Rather than focusing too much on the spectacle and spectacular forms of resistance (which risk falling into a critique of consumerism), this focus keeps the emphasis on the production involved in the labor of the social, the constant construction of the social field itself.

Revolutions in their everydayness, as movement through and of the entire social field, are nearly impossible to describe as open and constantly fluctuating processes. But how to describe them without imposing closure upon them? What do autonomy and self-organization, the substance of the compositions forming and animated through imaginal machines, mean? The problem is that both concepts are notoriously hard to pin down. There are also long and complex histories of how these concepts have developed.

20

A banner at the queer feminist squat Cagne Sciolte in Rome.

As George Caffentzis notes, notions of autonomy used within the radical Left include:

—0 The ability of workers to transcend the "laws of capital" and the confines of their roles as dependent variables in the surplus-value producing machine;

—1 The attempt by the Italian extra-parliamentary Left in the early 1970s to "go beyond the contract" into the "territory" of social life (self-reduction of rents, electricity bills, transport, etc.);

—2 Feminists who argue that women should make their political decisions independently of male organizations;

—3 The politics of the squatters' movement in Europe (especially Berlin) that reject any negotiations with city authorities and other traditional "Left" unions and parties;

—4 The politics of Hakim Bey's "Temporary Autonomous Zones" and related actions by groups like Reclaim the Streets;

—5 Negri's notion of autonomy—in Marx Beyond Marx—as the power of the working class to self-valorize through its use of the wage not for the reproduction of its work function;

—6 Harry Cleaver's notion of "autonomous Marxism".

Thus, autonomy broadly refers to forms of struggle and politics that are not determined by the institutions of the official Left (unions, political parties, etc.). In other words, extraparliamentary politics; a rejection of the mediation of struggles by institutional forms, especially since representation and mediation are all too often the first step in the recuperation of these struggles. To borrow Wolfi Landstreicher's description, autonomous self-organization is characterized by non-hierarchical organization, horizontal communication and relationships, and the necessity of individual autonomy in relation to collectivity. The last point is important for Landstreicher (otherwise there is no reason why states or corporations could not argue that they were also forms of autonomous organization). This is a key debate within radical politics concerning the relation between the realization of individual and collective autonomy, and how best to go about creating spaces for realizing these relationships. For Landstreicher, "autonomous self-organization is the development of shared struggle based on mutuality for the full benefit of each individual involved."

It is important to think critically about the notion of autonomy and calls for its realization. As David Knights and Hugh Willmott wisely remind us, the call to become autonomous can have a potentially dark side, especially when the nature of that autonomy and its emergence is not considered. For example, autonomy may function as a mechanism for the self-discipline of the subjects in question. As they emphasize, autonomy does not in itself describe or even point toward a condition or state of mind that exists within the world; rather, it is a "way of imbuing the world with a particular meaning (or meanings) that provide a way of orienting ourselves to the social world." And that is why the question of the composition, and the compositional process, is important—precisely because the point is not to fall back on the unstated assumption of the existence of forms of autonomy possessed by the enlightened subject inherited from liberal political discourse. Autonomy is not something that is possessed by an individual subject so much as a relation created between subjects; that is, it is a form of sociality and openness to the other created through cooperative relations. It is relational, of relations composed of individual subject positions in the process of emergence, rather than something that is possessed by isolated individuals before an encounter. The assumption of the existence of autonomy, whether by individuals or collectively, might well be an important precondition in creating conditions for its emergence. Autonomy is more a notion that is useful in mutual shaping and crafting of the social field, rather than something that precedes it.

And this self that is contained within the phrase "self-organization": what is it and where does it come from? Are we talking about a self-contained and autonomous individual subject or some form of collectivity? Or perhaps we are talking about a particular kind of subjectivized individual self that emerges in the process of and in relation to the formation and maintenance of a larger form of social collectivity. What are the processes involved here? Are these forms of interactions involved in the formation of our various 'selves' a form of labor in themselves, the "labor of the social"? It is these questions and queries that need to be explored, even if from the beginning we acknowledge that the territories of the question are almost inexhaustible, and that social movements by their very nature will niftily side-step our questions by constituting new arrangements by which the same questions are revisited within a different context. Perhaps the most important element here, further complicating the question, is the hyphen in self-organization. The hyphen conjoins and brings together words but also transforms the joined elements that are at the same time kept separate even as they are joined.

What conceptual tools then would be useful in furthering a rhythm of investigation toward a form of autonomous self-organization adequate to address the current social and economic transformations? Concepts, as described by Deleuze and Guattari, whose creation it is the task of philosophy to form, invent, and fabricate as combinations and multiplicities, are defined by their elements to exist as fragmentary wholes. Autonomous self-organization, as both a diverse set of practices and ideas, comprises a history of becomings defined less by spatial characteristics than by the intensive coordinates of embodied expression. The concept is "the contour, the configuration, the constellation of an event to come." Self-organization is a point, acting as a center through which vibrations of energy flow and the desires of the working class are expressed. Concepts are embodied and animated through conceptual personae that "show thought's territories." To find the right tools for this reconsideration requires creating the means to draw from and elaborate forms of practice and organizing that have congealed into autonomy and self-organization as defined terms, and to evaluate how they continue to shape the forms of practice from which they emerged.

REFERENCES

Wolfi Landstreicher,
Autonomous Self-Organization
and Anarchist Intervention:
A Tension in Practice
(Somewhereville: Institute for
Experimental Freedom, n.d.)

Gilles Deleuze and Félix
Guattari, What is Philosophy?
translated by Graham Burchell
and Hugh Tomlinson (1994)

Mental Prototypes and Monster Institutions: Some Notes by Way of an Introduction

Universidad Nómada translated by Nuria Rodríguez
illustrations by Mar Núñez

MENTAL PROTOTYPES

For quite a while now, a certain portmanteau word has been circulating in the Universidad Nómada's[1] discussions, in an attempt to sum up what we believe should be one of the results of the critical work carried out by the social movements and other post-socialist political actors. We talk about creating new mental prototypes for political action. This is due to the importance, in our eyes, of the elusive and so often unsuccessful link between cognitive diagrams and processes of political subjectivation. That is, the link between the knowledge that allows powers and potentials to be tested on one hand and, on the other, the semiotic, perceptual and emotional mutations that lead to the politicization of our lives, become personified in our bodies, and shape the finite existential territories that are channelled into or become available for political antagonism. We believe there is a need to create new mental prototypes because contemporary political representations, as well as many of the institutions created by the emancipatory traditions of the 20th century, should be subjected to a serious review—at the very least—given that, in many cases, they have become part of the problem rather than the solution.

In this respect, the anniversary of the 1968 world revolution—an unavoidable reference given the month in which we are writing this text— shouldn't be used as an excuse to wallow in amorphous nostalgia for the passing of the "age of revolutions". Just the opposite—it should be used to demonstrate the extent to which some of the unsuitable signs of that world revolution are still present in a latent state, or, to be more precise, in a state of "frustrated virtuality". "'68" interests us because, even though it didn't come out of the blue, it was an unforeseeable world event— a historical fork in the road that left a trail of new political creations in a great many different parts of the world. Ultimately, it motivates us because its unresolved connections and even its caricatures allow us to consider the problem of the politicization (and metamorphosis) of life as a monstrous intrusion of the unsuitable into history (the history of capitalist modernity and postmodernity).[2]

Over the last forty years, this latency has been subject to a series of quite significant emergences. The latest and perhaps most important, the one that is generationally closest to us, is the one in which the "movement of movements", or the global movement, played a central role. But in spite of its extraordinary power, it hasn't always been fruitful enough in terms of generating the "mental prototypes" that we believe are so necessary. At least, it's not clear that it has been able to produce prototypes that are sophisticated, robust and complex enough to generate innovative and sustained patterns of political subjectivation and organization that make it possible to at least attempt a profound transformation of command structures, daily life, and the new modes of production.[3] The articles included in the monograph we are introducing here emerge from these issues—which, in the present context, we can only summarize and reduce to a few fundamental aspects. We've decided to avoid a merely speculative approach, and to remain as far as possible from declarations of how the political forms of the movements "should-be"; rather, we try to present a series of experimentations—not to exemplify, but more in the manner of case studies, as experiences that are being tested in practice—that are currently trying to overcome the predicaments and shortfalls that we've just mentioned.

The Universidad Nómada believes there is an urgent need to identify the differentiating features and the differentials of political and institutional innovation that exist in specific experimentations. We've chosen to place the emphasis on two aspects that implicitly constitute the two transversal themes for this diverse compilation of texts, namely: (a) we give preference to metropolitan forms of political intervention, specifically looking at one of their most frequently recurring figures—social centres; by this, we don't mean to lay claim to social centres as fossilized forms or political artefacts with an essentialized identity, but to try and explore the extent to which the "social centre form" today points the way to processes of opening up and renewal[4], producing, for example, innovative mechanisms for the enunciation of (and intervention in) the galaxy of the precariat[5]; and at the same time, and partially intertwining with the above, (b) the constitution of self-education networks that are developing in—and perhaps result from?—the crisis of Europe's public university system[6]. Ultimately, "Europe", not as a naturalized space for political intervention, but as a constituent process; the production of these mental prototypes and mechanisms of enunciation and intervention as an instituent process ·

SOCIAL CENTRES AS "BODIES WITHOUT ORGANS"

For a long time, and in many cases still today, squatted social centres (*Centros Sociales Okupados* in Spanish) have used the abbreviation CSO or CSOA (the "a" stands for *"autogestionados"*, or "self-managed") as a differentiating element in the public sphere, as a kind of semiotic marker of the radical nature of their project. And inevitably, some of us who participated in them were bound to notice the virtuous coincidence between this label and the Spanish for Deleuze and Guattari's "body without organs", *"Cuerpo sin Organos"* or CsO,[8] using it to try to imagine and put into practice the un-thought and un-spoken virtualities that we believe are present in the matrix of metropolitan social centres. The considerations found in the different articles in this transversal/transform dossier are heading in that same direction, that is, they point towards the ongoing reinvention of an institutional mechanism (a form of movement institution) that has already proven its validity and, in a certain sense, its irreversibility in terms of the politics of the subaltern subjects in the metropolis. But this doesn't mean that the irreversible validity arises from a stable, self-referential, identitary "social centre form" that remains always the same as itself, but just the opposite, as set out in one of the collective texts included in this monograph.[9]

Perhaps we could speak of the need to counteract the solidification of the "social centre form" through the production of "unsuitable social centres", that is, projects of political and subjective creation based on specific powers of different configurations of the (political, cultural and "productive") make-up of the basins of metropolitan cooperation. Creations that wouldn't therefore try to seal themselves off as autarkic rather than autonomous islands, but to transform the existing context in accordance with the variable possibilities expressed by counter-powers that would then be capable of avoiding the dialectic of the antagonism between powers that tend towards equivalence.[10] This would thus open up new, constituent dimensions in terms of spatial, temporal, perceptive,

cooperative, normative and value-based aspects.

Some twenty years have already gone by since squatters first made their appearance in the public sphere. From squatters to *okupas* to *centros sociales okupados*, there has undeniably been progress, evolution; but the experience hasn't emerged from its neoteny stage, so to speak. There are obviously numerous reasons for this, and they may be complex enough to deserve to be fully dealt with in this dossier. In any case, this complexity should not be simplified by labelling the factors that delay its growth as "negative", and those that implement the model without further critical consideration of its present condition as "positive". The problem-factor of the (politics of) identity that has characterized the social centre form, with its disturbing ambivalence, is proof of this: because identity politics can be blamed for many "evils" and we can claim that this kind of politics has considerably contributed to the underdevelopment of the experiences and to the same errors being repeated; but if we don't take into account this aspect of identity (politics), it is difficult to explain why the great majority of relevant experiences arose in the first place and persist.

METROPOLIS AND IDENTITY

From the point of view of the production of subjectivity, the act of disobedience and direct reapportion of wealth ("fixed assets"- buildings, infrastructures, etc.) is and will probably remain fundamental in the evolution of the social centre form (and of other things). We should keep this in mind when we confront a relatively recent issue that is generating endless tense disputes in the heart of the social movements: the negotiation of spaces—whether we're talking about negotiating the ongoing occupation of squatted social centres through dialogue, or about approaching public bodies for new spaces to be self-managed. Basically, how can disobedience and reapportion be reconciled with negotiation? or, in other words: how is it possible to articulate the conflict/negotiation dialectic? The crucial problem is along these lines, and undoubtedly a substantial source of controversy.

There is a permanent niche of political impulses—which doesn't just affect the younger participants in social centres—that cannot do without a predetermined way of conceiving the act of disobedience and conflict as an element of political subjectivation and identity. The political function of social centres and identity, militancy and identity, and metropolitan commons and identity thus emerge as some of the permanent problematic nodes that end up deciding whether the experience is to make progress or be annulled. That is, what's at stake here is the possibility of producing a new type of institutionality of movement that can profit from the experience gained over two decades of social centres in Europe. In this sense, the last thing we need is a new "argument" or a new "program". What we need is to explicitly question the way in which we confront the "singularisation" of collective existence in the productive, cooperative and relational medium of the metropolis; a singularisation that always entails—that "normally" implies—complex processes of difference/identity. If we think there is a need to re-start a cycle of creative experimentation in relation to the social centre form, it is not because of a fetishistic attachment to novelty, but precisely because the forms of singularisation that we experience in our bodies and in our own lives are currently going through a phase of transformation in our cities, and inevitably require us to respond through the practice of risk-taking forms of political recomposition.

One's "immersion" in the metropolis of total mobilisation can't be simply a willing act. The development of aspects of political entrepreneurship—as foreshadowed in the social centres' production of services, aspects that are bio(syndicalist) and cooperative, based on public self-education projects and so on[11]— requires that we confront the dead-end streets of endemic, self-marginalized political experiences in the city. But it also implies the need to clarify what we could call the supplements of subjectivation that allow languages, value universes and collective territories to be re-founded as part of a device that can continue to be subversive, particularly on the level of forms of life. This means no longer aspiring to be subversive simply in terms of a dialectic of molar confrontation between subjects that are always pre-formed, channelling us towards a binary dynamic in the face of forces that have already been counted, with results that are already taken for granted.

GOVERNANCE AS AN ADVERSARY

Social centres' geometry of hostility in the productive metropolis
becomes fixed in accordance with the establishment of government
figures that try and combine the power of centralised command
with social diffusion of (metropolitan and transnational) powers. The
multicentric scheme of capitalist powers demonstrates the crisis of party-
like, representative forms of integration. Governance has become its
transitional mode. "Thus when we speak about metropolitan governance
we are alluding to a set of public practices that represent, in the face
of the harmonization of irreducible and heterogeneous interests, the
response to the inability of deriving decisions from an initial process of
institutional legitimation. The weakening of traditional mechanisms
of social regulation and the channelling of interests has in fact rendered
subjectivities impervious to the practice of government. Governance,
in a certain sense, constitutes the struggle to continually produce,
through variable and flexible structures, subjectivities that are consonant
with the 'administrationalisation' of life, where the boundaries between
public and private become transient and elusive".[12]
Governance is the device that opposes social centres, the
counterpart with productions of consensus, obedience and exclusion that
have to be dismantled, destabilized and sabotaged. The main objective
of metropolitan governance consists of making the shared conditions
of life productive in accordance with the concept of the city-company;
it consists of organizing the total mobilisation of its inhabitants and of
linguistic, emotional and financial flows in political and institutional terms
- a total mobilisation that neutralizes the political and existential valences
that emerge from cooperation and from communal metropolitan life; it

consists of producing a "government of difference" based on a constant inflation of statutes, segmentations, regulations and restrictions that allow the subordinate groups to be ordered hierarchically, isolated and divided. Social centres are one of the crucial operators of practical criticism of metropolitan governance (and are destined to become even more intensely so). The fight of the social centres against governance takes place in the field of practices of de-individualisation; in the reappropriation of spaces that can then be used to configure political situations that transform the conflict arising from placing a heterogeneous mix of population singularities up against the devices of urban income into a new motor for urban dynamics; in the production of new service relationships, such as those that try out a reappropriation of the relationships involved in care provision, which can de-privatize and denationalise the processes of reproduction and valorization of life that remain confiscated by metropolitan biopower institutions; and in experimentation with ways of practicing and experiencing the time of the metropolis in the face of the total mobilisation of frightened, anxious individuals.

EDUCATION, SELF-EDUCATION AND RESEARCH IN MONSTER INSTITUTIONS

Ultimately, the medley of experiences that this dossier deals with reveals unequivocal traces of the monster institutions that are necessary today in order to bring about the inevitability of new manifestations of the "frustrated virtualities" resulting from the long and unfinished sequence that followed the existential revolution of 1968: this takes us back to the beginning and closes a circular argument that considers present emergences by making the most of the virtualities of the immediate revolutionary past. Needless to say, the case studies shown here aren't exhaustive and don't inflate these virtualities. In agreement with the challenges set out in the articles (greater innovation, increased cooperation, more contagion at the European level and beyond), the Universidad Nómada is interested in tackling the possibility of constructing these new mental prototypes linked to the desired monstrosity, to the need to think and do another, different kind of politics based on education, self-education and research. We believe there are four basic circuits to be implemented, as follows:

(a) A circuit of educational projects, to be developed in order to allow the circulation of theoretical paradigms and intellectual tools suitable for producing these cognitive maps that can be used to (1) intervene in the public sphere by creating swarming points

30

of reference and producing counter-hegemonic discourses; and, in addition, to (2) analyze existing power structures and dynamics, as well as potentials;

(b) A circuit of co-research projects, to be organized for the systematic study of social, economic, political and cultural life for the purpose of producing dynamic maps of social structures and dynamics that can be useful for guiding antagonist practices, redefining existing conflicts and struggles, and producing new forms of expression endowed with a new principle of social and epistemological intelligibility;[13]

(c) A publishing and media circuit, to be designed with the aim of influencing the public sphere, areas of intellectual production and university teaching, for the purpose of creating intellectual-analytic laboratories and, consequently, new segments of reference and criticism of hegemonic forms of knowledge and ways of conceptualizing the social situation;

(d) A circuit of foundations, institutes and research centres, to be devised as an autonomous infrastructure for the production of knowledge, which would constitute an embryonic stage for forms of political organization by means of the accumulation of analysis and specific proposals. Its activities should link the analysis of regional and European conditions with the global structural dynamics of the accumulation of capital and of the recreation of the global geostrategic options that are favorable to the social movements.

In some cases, the devices that make these tasks possible are already operating, and their manifestations can be found or intuited here and there, peppering the texts in the monograph we are extending with this short introduction. To finish off: we are talking about devices that are necessarily hybrid and monstrous: hybrid, because right from the start they make it necessary to create networks out of resources and initiatives that are very different and contradictory in nature, that appear strange and even seemingly incongruent among themselves; these resources and initiatives mix together public and private resources, institutional relations with relations of movement, non-institutional and informal models for action with forms of representation that may be formal and representative, and struggles and forms of social existence that some would accuse of being non-political or contaminated or useless or absurd but take on a strategic aspect because they directly give a political and subjectivity-producing dimension to processes of allocation of resources and logistical elements that end up being crucial for bursting onto nationalized and/or privatized public spheres and transforming them; monstrous, because they initially appear to be pre-political or simply non-political in form, but their acceleration and accumulation as described above must generate a density and a series of possibilities for intellectual creativity and collective political action that will contribute to inventing another politics; another politics, that is, another way of translating the power of productive subjects into new forms of political behavior and, ultimately, into original paradigms for the organization of social life, for the dynamic structuring of the potential of that which is public and communal.

NOTES

1 The original document (in Spanish) presenting the Universidad Nómada can be found at the head of our web page (http://www. universidadnomada.net/spip. php?article139); a recent text that has become something of a summary for the new phase of the Universidad Nómada is "Towards New Political Creations. Movements, institutions, new militancy", by Raúl Sánchez Cedillo, published in Transversal: Instituient Practices, July 2007 (http://transform.eipcp.net/ transversal/0707/sanchez/en).

2 Also along these lines, see "On the Breach" (http:// transform.eipcp.net/correspon-dence/1209407525), a recent text by Gerald Raunig that – in reference to Claude Lefort and Gilles Deleuze – recalls precisely the unexpected, unforeseeable and unsuitable nature of that "event", while also vindicating the nature of its "latencies", which may still be reactivated or verified. Anti-68 "reaction" theory and nostalgic evocations of the events both serve to suspend these latencies indefinitely.

3 This is also what Paolo Virno seems to be saying, using an accurate image, when he states that in recent years the global movement was like a huge battery that had been charged in a short, vertiginous process, but couldn't find where to connect itself and discharge its power, and that it specifically couldn't manage to connect with "those forms of struggle that are necessary in order to transform the situation of precarious, temporary and atypical work into political assets"; see "Un movimento performativo", in transversal: precariat, July 2004 (http://eipcp.net/trans-versal/0704/virno/it). In any case, in these notes for (self) critical reflection, we continue to declare that the configura-tion process of the global

movement already constitutes the inalienable genetic code of the cycle of struggles that is currently in course.

4 We refer to the reflections contained in the text by Andrej Kurnik and Barbara Beznec "Rog: Struggle in the City", in Transversal: Monster Institutions, op. cit. (http://transform.eipcp.net/transversal/0508/kurnikbeznec/en).

5 Which constitutes our explicit response to the problem set out in supra, note 3.

6 How can we avoid mentioning the centrality of "the university" in the 68 world revolution, how students discerned the paradox of an institution that is in crisis in terms of its historic model, but meanwhile plays an increasingly central role in capitalist modes of production and valorisation? See, among many other recent reflections, Gigi Roggero, "The Autonomy of the Living Knowledge in the Metropolis-University", in transversal: instituent practices, op. cit. (http://transform.eipcp.net/transversal/0707/roggero/en), and the related experience described in "The Metropolis and the So-Called Crisis in Politics. The Experience of Esc", in transversal: monster institutions, op. cit. (http://transform.eipcp.net/transversal/0508/esc/en). See also two Universidad Nómada texts by Montserrat Galcerán, "¿Tiene la universidad interés para el capital?" ("Are universities already of interest to capital?") (http://www.universidadnomada.net/spip.php?article242) and "La crisis de la universidad" ("The crisis of the university") (http://www.universidadnomada.net/spip.php?article184), both n/d.

7 See Francesco Salvini, "The Moons of Jupiter: Networked Institutions in the Productive Transformations of Europe", in Transversal:

Monster Institutions, op. cit. (http://transform.eipcp.net/transversal/0508/salvini/en).

8 See "'Mil mesetas' y los espacios liberados metro-politanos. Notas para un agenciamiento" ("'A Thousand Plateaus' and metropolitan liberated spaces. Notes for an assemblage") (1998) (http://www.sindominio.net/laboratorio/documentos/milmesetas/laboratorio.htm), which contains reflections that some of us participated before becoming involved with the Universidad Nómada.

9 Pablo Carmona, Tomás Herreros, Raúl Sánchez Cedillo y Nicolás Sguiglia, "Social Centres: monsters and political machines for a new generation of movement institutions", in Transversal: Monster Institutions, op. cit. (http://transform.eipcp.net/transversal/0508/carmonaetal/en).

10 Thus the type of asymmetry between powers and counter-powers that characterises the movements in the new cycle of struggles that we've called "another geometry of hostility". See Amador Fernández-Savater, Marta Malo de Molina, Marisa Pérez Colina and Raúl Sánchez Cedillo, "Ingredientes de una onda global" ("Ingredients of a global wave") Desacuerdos 2, Macba, Unia and Arteleku, Barcelona, 2006 (http://www.arteleku.net/4.0/pdfs/1969-2bis.pdf; and http://www.universidadnomada.net/spip.php?article188).

11 One of the richest and most hopeful cases along these lines is certainly that of the oficinas de derechos sociales, as explained in the text by Silvia L. Gil, Xavier Martínez and Javier Toret, "Las Oficinas de Derechos Sociales: Experiences of Political Enunciation and Organisation in Times of Precarity", in Transversal: Monster Institutions, op. cit.

(http://transform.eipcp.net/trans-versal/0508/lopezetal/en).

12 Atelier Occupato ESC, "The Metropolis and the So-Called Crisis of Politics", op. cit.; see also Francesco Salvini, "The Moons of Jupiter: Networked Institutions in the Productive Transformations of Europe", op. cit.

13 See Marta Malo de Molina, "Nociones comunes", Introduction to the collective volume Nociones comunes. Experiencias y ensayos entre investigación y militancia, Traficantes de Sueños, Madrid, 2004 (http://traficantes.net); also published in two parts, as "Common notions, part 1: workers-inquiry, co-research, consciousness-raising", in transversal: militant research, April 2006 (http://transform.eipcp.net/transversal/0406/malo/en), and "Common Notions, Part 2: Institutional Analysis, Participatory Action-Research, Militant Research", in Transversal: instituent Practices, op. cit. (http://transform.eipcp.net/transversal/0707/malo/en). Also useful along these lines, is an overview of the texts included in the monograph Transversal: Militant Research, mentioned above (http://transform.eipcp.net/transversal/0707), in particular the text by Javier Toret and Nicolás Sguiglia (members of Universidad Nómada), "Cartography and War Machines. Challenges and Experiences around Militant Research in Southern Europe" (http://transform.eipcp.net/transversal/0406/tsg/en).

Reprinted with kind permission from the authors and the European Institute of Progressive Cultural Policy, Vienna. Published on transversal web zine at http://eipcp.net/transversal, 2008.

Squatting for Justice: Bringing Life to the City

Miguel Ángel Martínez López

Squats have to be recognized and supported for what they are: vibrant social centers at the very heart of the 'commons', actively including the excluded.

A few months ago one of the editors of an architecture magazine emailed asking me to write a short piece about squatting, squatters and squats. His request was accompanied with a few guidelines: "The argument I am interested in is that squatting, far from being harmful to cities, is an essential component of social, cultural and economic development and should be welcomed and supported by governments and local authorities. I think it is important to make the case that over time, squatting contributes to the mainstream economic and culture vibrancy of a place as well as its alternative scene."

This is definitely my own position about squatting in general, although I admit that many urban conflicts often flare up once squatting emerges. Needless to say, I felt happy with the prospect that a widespread architectural publication might cover what I consider a progressive and sensible issue. With this orientation toward providing a positive view of squatting, I started writing my column.

However, while exchanging some messages with the editor, he insisted on what I would call the "gentrifying imaginary" of squatters. "[The area] in London where our office is based was once full of squatting artists and designers who gradually transformed the area from one that was quite dangerous to one that is now home to Google, Facebook and a myriad of trendy bars. Now that squatting is a criminal offense in the UK, I suspect we'll never see such an organic and successful transformation of a neighborhood. That's not to dismiss the value of an alternative cultural movement but as many of our readers are firmly embedded in mainstream industries, it is the joining of the dots between mainstream and alternative that will persuade them to think differently."

34

Well, the challenge for me became a bit uphill by then. How could I persuade architects and real-estate managers that banning squatting is just a "bad idea" without mentioning that squatting tackles the very core inequities of the housing market? Would there be space for arguing that squatting is not exclusively about producing culture and revitalizing urban life in decaying urban areas?

Simply put, I see squatting as a great practical alternative to capitalism, although it is not always very effective in changing housing and land policies. At the very least, it provides affordable spaces for living, for politics and for social and cultural life. But, if it were to be the case, gentrification as a side effect of squatting would be a key contradiction of this urban movement. To my knowledge, in general squatters are not gentrifiers. Rather, they tend to oppose global corporations and urban redevelopment where residents have no say, as well as market speculation. It is far easier to find squatters who are more concerned about social justice, homelessness, displacement, housing prices and the commodification and surveillance of urban life than those who are blindly proud of their belonging to a so-called "creative class".

So I made an effort to emphasize these features and controversies instead of portraying a misleading sketch of squatters for the sake of the mainstream industries' satisfaction. Not surprisingly, as I had feared, the article was rejected. Perhaps, I thought, critical thinking can still appeal to other architects, planners and people interested in improving urban life beyond the stereotypes of squatters and the culturalistic approach to gentrification. So I decided to publish the original text, which follows.

TAKE CARE OF THE SQUATS

Why evict squats? This question has always shocked me very deeply. Are authorities, private owners and real estate developers right in aiming at the eradication of squats? According to their immediate interests, squats are an obstacle to their projects. Squatters, they argue, take over spaces illegally and sometimes overtly confront urban redevelopment. In this simplified, market-driven reasoning, squatting is seen more as a spoke in a wheel than as a collective effort to fulfill the right to the city.

As a sociologist and urban scholar who has been also involved in some squats, I argue that the repression of squatters is indeed a big mistake. My stance is that squatters and squats enhance cities in many ways that are not usually taken into account by politicians, judges, the mass media, the public at large and urban developers. Furthermore, their opponents tend to base the repressive measures on either weak or insufficient evidence, if not on a very narrow minded view of city life.

Let me start first with a few remarks in order to clarify concepts. My experience and knowledge stems mainly from squats in European cities, which are not slums, shanty towns or self-built houses in derelict land of the outskirts. Although all forms of occupation of empty spaces must be regarded as essential parts of urban history, and all their dwellers deserve respect and resources to improve their living conditions, their challenges are somewhat different. Hence, I refer to squats only as occupations of vacant buildings or flats without the owner's permission.

For instance, to mention a common misunderstanding, if a residence is broken into when their owners or tenants go on vacation, this is not a squat, but a distinct serious offense. A durable vacancy or abandonment of a house, factory, school, etc. is a prerequisite to setting up a squat. Only then is it manifest that the holder of the legal title of property does not need it in the short-run. His or her underuse of the property and the lack of maintenance may even ruin the building and cause damages to other residents. Therefore, while using it, squatters help to keep the property in a liveable state.

The squatters' purposes may vary between housing provision and the performance of a broad range of cultural, economic and political activities. Importantly, not all squatters use this label to identify themselves. Notwithstanding, when squatting takes root in a given urban area, it is likely to give birth to a wider movement with manifold expressions of collective identity.

FROM PARIS TO BILBAO

There are many types of squatters and squats. Their needs and impacts can be, accordingly, very different. One of the primary errors, then, is to pack them all under the same social category. At the other extreme, it is equally wrong to simplify that diversity by splitting squatters between 'good' and 'bad' ones in a manipulative manner. Leaving aside the lack of tolerance towards many squatters' criticisms of the capitalist system, the dismissive attitude facing 'bad squatters' lies on the assumption that most of the squatting projects engender typical problems—for instance, the noise that disturbs some neighbors or the spoiling of properties. This is something that can happen everywhere and is not necessarily due to the presence of squatters. Quite the contrary, what I have observed more often is a great effort by squatters to take care of the places they occupied, to promote communal ways of living, and to share their ideas with their surrounding neighbors. Is all of that so insignificant as to put our focus exclusively on the not-granted legal right to use a private or public space?

It is not difficult to name famous squats in Europe because, occasionally, they obtain media coverage due to the massive protests that their eviction, or threats of eviction, ignite. This is the case of the recent public outcry against the city of Hamburg after evicting the Rote Flora, a social center occupied in 1989. After several days of demonstrations and clashes, a truce was declared that will prolong the activity of the squat. But one wonders why the media did not pay the same attention to the impressive 25 years of continuous exhibitions, concerts, workshops, talks and sociability fostered by the voluntary work of several generations of activists and thousands of visitors.

Less successful was the defense of another long lasting squatted social center, the Kukutza Gaztetxea in Bilbao, which was evicted in 2011 after an overwhelming wave of mobilization and support coming from all the social angles—neighborhood associations, university professors, architects, lawyers, political parties, artists... almost everybody except the mayor and the proprietor of the former factory. This was not a squat only for young radicals, as the pervasive stereotype of squatters leads us to think, but also a place open to all who wanted to practice sports, learn foreign languages, create art, launch cooperative enterprises, organize meetings and engage in political campaigning.

Let's look at Paris as well. There, when squats are above all about artistic production and granted some favorable governance conditions, squatters may achieve legal status and even access to munificent public funds. At the core of the city's commercial center, 59 Rivoli (nowadays called an "aftersquat") is a well-known example. Nonetheless, when migrants, homeless people and poor youngsters squat just for living, their struggle to reach a secure tenancy is always hindered by a fierce attack from the powers that be.

Again, the hot issue for the decision-makers is why they prosecute those who find an affordable means to house themselves while there are abundant empty apartments and a scarcity of social housing. A proof that squatting is closer to legitimacy (the right to decent housing) than to legality (the prohibition against trespassing on a private property) is that in cities such as Berlin, Amsterdam, London, New York and Rome, it was feasible to negotiate and legalize many of the former squats.

Authorities praise the artistic squats over others, and they are more prone to tolerate or subsidize their continuity because they are conceived as city landmarks for the so-called creative class. They also appeal to tourists. However, they forget that low-paid and precarious artists need an accessible place to live, too. As a consequence, the housing question is often ignored. And it is also misguided to think of squats as a simple temporary solution, since cases like the three above were able to last for more than a decade.

THE OUTSTANDING QUALITIES OF SQUATS

You may disagree, as I do, with some squatters and dislike the way they manage a building. This disagreement may also occur with any social movement. Take, for example, a controversial environmental action or policy—some are so single-issue oriented that you might think they do not address the core source of ecological problems. Regarding squatters, their economic troubles—daily survival, academic obligations if they are enrolled in university, or just their easy-going way of living—may result in a low level of activities or social and cultural vibrancy in the eyes of those who conceive of the city as a permanent growth machine. It is this framework of standard expectations and its associated prejudices which prevent a careful consideration of the particular circumstances of every squat. The central or peripheral location of the squat, the speculation and gentrification processes surrounding it, and the more or less conflictive relationship between squatters and authorities, may determine the outcomes. In fact, the utopian, heterotopian and liberated natures of these urban spaces are also constrained by those and similar conditions.

I prefer to highlight the outstanding qualities of most squats. First, squats are built by squatters, active citizens who devote a great part of their lives to providing autonomous and low-cost solutions to many of the city's flaws (such as housing shortages, expensive rental rates, the bureaucratic machinery that discourages any grassroots proposal, or the political corruption in the background of urban transformations). Second, squatters move but squats remain as a sort of "anomalous institution", neither private nor state-owned, but belonging to the "common goods" of citizenship, like many other public facilities.

Third, since most squats have a non-commercial character, this entails easy access to their activities, services and venues for all who are excluded from mainstream circuits. This is a crucial contribution to social justice, equality and local democracy. Fourth the occupation of buildings is not an isolated practice but a collective intervention in the urban fabric that avoids further deterioration in decaying areas by recycling materials, greening the brown fields and the sad plots of the urban void, and not least, by building up social networks and street life. There are palpable social benefits, though they are not easy to measure with official statistics.

There is a long tradition of legal regulations that granted rights to the inhabitants of abandoned properties after a certain number of years of occupation. However, in recent years neoliberal politicians have worked hard to sweep these old rules off the table. Squatting might also make deep social conflicts explicit, but given the above arguments, it is evident that there are very effective and positive urban contributions derived from this well-rooted practice. For these reasons, instead of suppressing the squats, I'd rather recommend giving them a hand and recognizing their valuable strengths and contributions.

This text was posted May 13, 2014 ROAR Magazine, an online journal of the radical imagination, at roarmag.org.

Nether

40

ands

41

Creativity and the Capitalist City

Tino Buchholz

Creativity is fancy, glamorous and desirable. Who can be against creativity? At the same time it is used selectively for normative purposes and consists of precarious and hard work. When it comes down to social and economic development the concept becomes ambivalent, involving the contrast between commercial and non-commercial innovations, creative destruction, self-exploitation, which can be summed up with the "paradoxes of capitalism" (Hartmann and Honneth 2006). In this sense, creativity and affordability are crucially interconnected. The struggle around affordability is a pre-condition for creativity; and one has to be very creative these days to be able to make a living in a creative capitalist city. The advantage is that creative working conditions are on the political agenda today—even though in need of progressive movements and radical democratization.

While the hype around the creative city began about a decade ago (Florida 2002), the discussion around creative industries is already 30 years old (Andersson 1985). After clusters and networks, creativity advanced as the dominant urban development strategy of the past decade. Nevertheless it is more of a "vehicular idea" (McLennan 2004, Peck 2012) that travels the world and may soon be replaced by another vehicular catch phrase as the emerging discourse around "smart cities" signals (Caragliu et al. 2011). Though engaging with new technology the normative potential of creative or smart development remains under-explored and serves as a "rather elastic, feel good policy that absolutely fits with orthodox development strategies" (Peck 2011).

Absent substantial arguments distinguishing creative city development from Schumpeterian creative destruction, it is not clear what is new about Florida's contribution. Creative activity today is to a large extent co-opted by an economic logic. Florida is clear: "rising inequality stems mainly from the very nature of the emerging creative economy" (Florida 2003) when re-describing socio-economic class relations in the name of creativity. In his critique of Florida's American dream, Jamie Peck (2011) says:

> *It actually provides a justification for social inequality. It says, it is the creative class who are the winning one third of the society and the losing two thirds must learn to live like the winners. And so it does nothing other than to tell the working class or the serving caste they should pull themselves up by their bootstraps. That is in the end a recipe for more of the same. It legitimizes inequality.*

Legitimizing inequality via the achievement principle is one thing; reaching out for democratic legitimacy is another. For democracy, social conflicts and social movements are crucial reference points for the recognition or mis-recognition of a social order (Honneth 1995, 2003).

In this text I follow my documentary *Creativity and the Capitalist City: The Struggle for Affordable Space in Amsterdam* (2011), and address the question of creativity as a matter of struggle. In cities, this means especially the struggle for affordable housing. (All quotes, unless otherwise indicated, derive from this project, online at creative capitalistcity.org). I concentrate on two drivers of the creative city: (a) the role of urban social movements (i.e. squatting) and the co-optation by neoliberal urban policies, and (b) the role of the real estate market and the provision of temporary housing in the form of so-called Anti-Squat contracts, which replace squatters and accommodate low-budget initiatives with no housing rights whatsoever. I briefly discuss the implementation of the Dutch Anti-Squat concept, then conclude with a call to reclaim creativity from the capitalist city.

The Handbook of Creative Cities (Andersson et al. 2011) gathers key proponents of the discourse of human capital to highlight the subsequent emergence of human creativity as a stimulus for economic development. Here I draw mainly on the critique by economic geographer Jamie Peck (2005, 2007, 2011, 2012), the narrator of my film.

THE ROLE OF URBAN MOVEMENTS

The re-description of the city in terms of creativity, and the corresponding shift in policies can be studied in Amsterdam (Mayer and Novy 2009). Here, Richard Florida's story was introduced in 2003. "Everybody was a bit inspired by his book and theories. But in Amsterdam politicians and opinion leaders said: 'Interesting story, but luckily we do already'", city official Jaap Schoufour says.

The Dutch breeding place program (described at bureaubroed plaatsen.amsterdam.nl) can count as good practice, a creative flagship project that clearly reflects prior conflicts and later transformations, i.e., the legalization of squats. Here, people in need of affordable space have left established paths and helped themselves to housing and working space. As Jaap Schoufour, the director of the program, puts it:

The breeding place program is based in fact on the squatting movement, which popped up in the 1960s, 1970s, 1980s ... In fact, these squatting groups were wiped out of the warehouses at the end of the 1990s in Amsterdam ... In these warehouses all kinds of cultural and creative initiatives settled ... [so] they addressed themselves to the city council by saying: 'well, look here, you can wipe us out. We know, we will lose this battle, but beware—we contribute to this city as well. Even economically we contribute to the city.

Today's breeding places, then, mirror the housing struggles and squatter movements of the past. The past 10 years, however, have seen the squatters' do-it-yourself logic re-articulated in the language of the creative industry. In this context, squatters do not represent a threat, but rather an asset to the political economy. Even when choosing a deviant path squatters can hardly leave the economic framework, and are likely to create alternative products and markets (Uitermark 2004).

Urban movements often play a crucial role as pioneers of processes of redevelopment or gentrification. Hans Pruijt (2013) has differentiated various types of squatters in Europe, where besides 'deprivation-based' and 'political squatters', 'conservational' and 'entrepreneurial' squatters follow different strategies. This differentiation is helpful, since squatting initiatives in Western Europe today should not be confused with revolutionary movements that seriously contest the capitalist production of space.

"There are a lot of people running around in the squatters' movement thinking they're the Spanish anarchists and they're going to win some revolution soon. I don't really have the illusion that we can change anything with direct action, but I believe that we can motivate and educate people. It's like a propaganda operation, that will as a side-effect, provide housing for the people that perform it", said Momo, an Amsterdam squatting activist.

Progressive activists, like the Amsterdam art-squat Gallery Schijnheilig ('hypocrite gallery'),[1] are aware of the struggle for creativity, and of their role and the range of their activism. For Momo, the problem of many squatters and activists is that they believe their own propaganda: "You have to be very realistic and materialistic in order to survive in such

44

Luxury lofts in the Kalenderpanden (Calendar Building), former site of a squatted cultural center that was evicted in 2000.

a context. If they say: you are the nice guys, because you are the artists, then you have to take their word and turn it around in their mouth: 'Of course we're the artists. We are the only real artists, you are the fakes. So give us everything, if you don't give us anything, we will riot.'"

VACANCY MANAGEMENT BY ANTI-SQUAT

Since squatting was banned in the Netherlands in 2010 (Buchholz 2009), the struggle for affordable space has shifted from a user's logic (tolerating squats when vacant for more than one year) to an owner's logic (property protection + vacancy management = Anti-Squat) and allowance for temporary use. The idea of Anti-Squat (Anti-Kraak) comes from the perspective of real estate and security agencies. They realized that 'live-in guardians' were a more effective and cheaper form of property protection than guard patrols. Buildings are maintained and secured from squatting and vandalism. Affordable housing is a temporary side effect.

While Dutch Anti-Squat guardians were paid for their services 30 years ago, today the agencies have capitalized on the shortage of affordable space in contested housing markets. They ask for rent-like payments but refuse to call it rent. This legal twist is crucial, as the Anti-Squat offers its temporary users, or 'live-in guardians', no tenant protections or legal rights to stay put.

The permission to use opens the doors to former schools and rundown houses awaiting renovation or demolition. Anti-Squat is promoted as a creative market solution to make interim use of speculative vacancy in the housing or office market. The conditions of use are heavily restrictive—no pets, no kids, no parties, no smoking, no candles, permission required to go on vacation etc.—and can be cancelled within four weeks. Anti-Squatters are caretakers, cleaners, and security guardians but not tenants. While prior to the squatting ban 2010 Dutch squatters enjoyed housing rights close to tenant protection Anti-Squat is more of a job, which conflicts with privacy and housing rights. However, it seems to work for some 50,000 people in the Netherlands; ironically, this is also the estimate of the number of Dutch squatters from 1964 to 1999 (Duivenvoorden 2000).

So far, these agencies have been very careful with their profiling. They primarily target young people, students, artists, single people and so on. So far, conflicts are still not a major issue. Some Anti-Squatters even hold more than one site for living and working purposes.[2]

Anti-Squat started to provide temporary working space for flexible individuals (students and artists) in the early 1980s. It has developed into a serious business strategy for interim housing in the 1990s, and even more so since the squatting ban in 2010. In this sense, users demand Anti-Squat in order to enter an upscale property market. It is used as an alternative to inaccessible regular rental contracts that would come with housing benefits and tenants' rights. Market leader Camelot was the first agency to expand its services from the Netherlands to Western Europe in the early 2000s. Camelot CEO Joost van Gestel explains:

If you look in the last five years in the Netherlands the number of these so called live-in guardians increased up to 50.000. We have 16 million Dutch people, so three out of thousand are living in a temporary accommodation. And I really feel that those numbers can be applied to England, France or Germany. Which means several hundreds of thousands of people travel between homes, schools, churches, MOD complexes and offices that are temporarily empty making creative affordable spaces.

In short, Anti-Squat is the most flexible instrument for property owners today—though it is in need of greater social recognition. Under the Camelot slogan of "make space pay ... while your property is vacant", it may count as the high point of private property-led urbanization. The right to civil squatting, on the other hand, delivered benefits to the

"Your Laws Not Ours!" A banner at the demonstration protesting the passage
of the kraakverbod legislation criminalizing squatting. Amsterdam 2010.

47

Dutch creative field for three decades. It was a simple but fundamental difference from global business as usual. The revanchist roll-back of post-war social democratic achievements (Brenner and Theodore 2002, Piketty 2014), and the Dutch squatting ban of 2010 reverse the picture.

CONCLUSION

The instrumental conception and paradoxical effects inherent in creative class policies can be seen in numerous projects in Western Europe and beyond. For example, when the Ruhr Valley in Germany was announced as the Cultural Capital of Europe for 2010. That summer two art-squat initiatives took up the promise of creative urban renewal and appropriated abandoned spaces in Essen (freiraum2010.de) and Dortmund (uzdortmund.blogsport.de/medien/). Despite the Florida logic, they were evicted immediately.

While such repression does not come as a surprise, Richard Florida himself did support the precursor of these actions, the Hamburg art-squat Gängeviertel in 2009, arguing it would fit in nicely with a creative city strategy. Earlier, Florida also advised tolerance of long-haired hashish users who may be programmers. What's the problem?, he asked, if they do their job well (Peck 2007). Such a discussion signals an ambivalence in the normative power of the concept, and its varied implementation by left and right wing professionals and policy makers.

In the Ruhr Valley the activists later formed a Network X (netzwerk-x. org) rejecting the selective achievement principle of creative economy and its language. They have continued to take action emphasizing the grassroots of creativity and supported a 2014 Right to the City manifesto entitled 'Learning from Detroit'.[3]

In any case, the role of social movements remains crucial to the democratic legitimacy of creative urban redevelopments, as the discussion around the instrumentalization and co-optation of movements by neoliberal urban policy shows (Pruijt 2003, Uitermark 2004). "The situation we face at the present time is a sort of internal crisis of the neoliberal project but not an alternative project waiting to fill the vacuum or contesting the space in the same kind of way ... There are a thousand alternatives to neoliberalism, not just one" (Peck 2011).

It would be silly if creativity was damaged by Richard Florida and his merely economic interpretation. Creativity is not an end in itself but aims for something. That is a normative issue—to be defined. Creative upgrading processes in neighbourhoods are not necessarily the problem, if they benefit local inhabitants. The problem usually is that any improvement is seen and functions as an investment to stimulate real estate prices, and serves property-led displacement, i.e. gentrification.

Interventions, however, always need to be a community issue requiring a wider discussion, mobilization and local democratic decision-making. The creative class can surely show commitment here, as the struggles of Gallery Schijnheilig and 'Not in our Name' Hamburg have made clear. Even further, creative people need to look for their return in this. Creativity has a lot to do with self-exploitation and self-destruction. Endless accumulation, competition and struggle are neither admirable nor healthy. In this sense, today's challenge rather is to focus critically on the selective working mode of the capitalist achievement principle (Piketty 2014, Honneth 2014), and a capitalist class movement that has been very successful at claiming property rights (Purcell 2008). Nevertheless, private property rights are "claims not trumps" (ibid.) shot through with moral expectations in their use (Heins 2009). Co-operative solutions like the new Soweto housing association in Amsterdam (soweto.nl) or the German tenement syndicate (Horlitz 2012), on the other hand, bear the creative power to rethink property relations and greater claims for redistributive justice (Honneth 1995, 2003), recapturing democratic procedures and reclaiming creativity from the capitalist city.

In Peck's words: "If we are talking about what a real strategy for cities ought to be in the present time, it clearly needs to deal with issues like working poverty, inequality, ecological sustainability and the caring economy. There is a broad raft of questions which need to be addressed urgently on a Rights to the City kind of framework or Reclaim the City for its citizens."

NOTES

1 Extra footage from the film Creativity and the Capitalist City is posted as "Schijnheilig and the right to the city" 2011, 4:13; at: https://www.youtube.com/watch?v=oGtrRKtBGgk

2 One explicit critique of Anti-Squat was mobilized by housing activists who changed locks and took back basic privacy rights. See the Dutch Union of Precarious Dwellers at: http://bond-precaire-woonvormen.nl/2012/04/inspections-no-more-change-the-locks-on-your-door/.

3 'Learning from Detroit', at: http://www.rechtaufstadt-ruhr.de/von-detroit-lernen/.

REFERENCES

Andersson, D.E., Andersson, A.E. and Mellander, C. (eds.) (2011) Handbook of Creative Cities. Cheltenham: Edward Elgar.

Andersson, A.E. (1985) Creativity and economic dynamic modelling. In: Batten, D.F., Casti, J. and Johansson, B. (eds.) Economic Evolution and Structural Adjustment. Berlin: Springer: p. 27 – 45.

Brenner, N. and N. Theodore (eds.) (2002) Spaces of Neoliberalism – Urban Restructuring in North America and Western Europe. Oxford: Blackwell.

Buchholz, T. (2011) Creativity and the Capitalist City – The Struggle for Affordable Space in Amsterdam. DVD 55min. published online http://www.creativecapitalistcity.org/.

Buchholz, T. (2009) To Use or Not use Urban Space. Paper presented at the Ifou conference The New Urban Question in Amsterdam and Delft. published online.

Caragliu, A., Del Bo, C. and P. Nijkamp (2011) Smart Cities in Europe. Journal of Urban Technology 18 (2): p. 65 – 82.

Duivenvoorden, E. (2000) Een voet tussen de deur (A foot in the door: the history of the Dutch squatting movement 1964-1999). Amsterdam: Arbeiderspers.

Florida, R. (2002) The Rise of the Creative Class. New York: Basic Books.

Florida, R. (2003) "The New American Dream". Washington Monthly, published online Hartmann, M. and A. Honneth (2006) "Paradoxes of Capitalism." Constellations 13 (1): p. 41 – 58.

Heins, V. (2009) "The Place of Property in the Politics of Recognition". Constellations 16 (4): p. 579 – 592.

Honneth, A. (2014) Freedom's Right. New York: Columbia University Press.

Honneth, A. (2003) The point of recognition. In: Fraser, N. and A. Honneth (eds.) Redistribution or Recognition – A Political-Philosophical Exchange. London. Verso: p. 237 – 269.

Honneth, A. (1995) The Struggle for Recognition – The Moral Grammar of Social Conflicts. Cambridge: Polity Press.

Horlitz, S. (2012) Housing beyond profit: A comparison of U.S. and German alternative ownership models. American Institute for Contemporary German Studies. John Hopkins University. published online

Mayer, M. and Novy, J., "As Just as it Gets? The European City in the Just City Discourse," in "Searchingfor the Just City," edited by Connolly, J., Marcuse, P., Novy, J., Olivo,

I., Potter, C. and Justin, S., London,Routledge, 2009. McLennan, G. (2004) Travelling with vehicular ideas: the case of the third way. Economy and Society 33 (4): p. 484 – 99.

Peck, J. (2005) "Struggling With the Creative Class". International Journal of Urban and Regional Research 24 (4): p. 740 – 70.

Peck, J. (2007) "The Creativity Fix". published online, eurozine. com

Peck, J. (2011) Interview in Amsterdam 26 July 2009. In: Buchholz, Creativity and the Capitalist City

Peck, J. (2012) Recreative City: Amsterdam, vehicular ideas, and the adaptive spaces of creativity policy. International Journal of Urban and Regional Research 36 (3): p. 462 – 85. published online

Piketty, T. (2014) Capital – In the 21st Century. Cambridge: The Belknap Press of Harvard University Press.

Pruijt, H. (2013) The Logic of Urban Squatting. International Journal of Urban and Regional Research 37 (1): p. 19 – 45.

Pruijt, H. (2003) Is the institu-tionalization of urban move-ments inevitable? International Journal of Urban and Regional Research 27 (1): p. 133 – 57. published

Purcell, M. (2008) Recapturing Democracy – Neoliberalization and the Struggle for Alternative Urban Futures. London: Routledge.

Uitermark, J. (2004) "The Co-optation of Squatters in Amsterdam and the Emergence of a Movement Meritocracy: A Critical Reply to Prujit". International Journal of Urban and Regional Research 28 (3): p. 687 – 698.

Improvised doorbells at a squatted art studio complex in Amsterdam

The Autonomous Zone (de Vrije Ruimte)

Vincent Boschma

Amsterdam, Dec. 2009:

> *Dit is de vrije ruimte. Veel mensen zijn vergeten, wat dat betekent, vrij te zijn. Vrij zijn is de natuurlijke staat van de mens. Vrij zijn betekent dat je autonoom bent, je door niemand laat leiden. Je bent een tijdelijke, ruimtelijke, autonome zone.*
> (This is a free space. A lot of people forgot, what that means, to be free. To be free is the natural state of the human being. To be free means to be autonomous, that nobody is leading you. You are a temporary, spacious, autonomous zone.)
> Simon Vinkenoog, fragment of the poem 'Here m'n tijd' (Oh Lord, my time)

I am an artist living in Amsterdam where I paint and do media work and also work at the W139, an art space that began as a squat in 1979. I lived in New York between 2003 and 2007 during which time I began visually documenting autonomous zones in New York and Amsterdam in relation to past and present initiatives in art and activism. I focused specifically on the free zones ABC NoRio and Bullet Space in New York and W139 and Vrieshuis Amerika in Amsterdam. From the 1960s on, a great deal of art has been created by artists living and working in squats and many places that began as squats have become important cultural spaces that still exist today in both cities. ABC No Rio, founded in 1980, is a collectively-run center for art and activism at 156 Rivington Street, New York. Begun by members of the art collective Colab, ABC No Rio began with the Real Estate Show at 123 Delancey Street in 1979, in which Colab artists took over an abandoned building and used it as a gallery space. The Real Estate Show was a collective project open to all artists and exhibitors that envisioned a new kind of interactive,

Anton Van Dalen standing by his mural in the CHARAS social center, El Bohio, early 1980s

53

collective art show. Despite receiving support from such prominent figures as Joseph Beuys, the show was soon closed by the police intervention. After negotiations with the city, the Real Estate Show was relocated to Rivington Street. At this location, from 1980 on and to the present day, ABC No Rio seeks to facilitate cross-pollination between artists and activists. In June 2009 ABC No Rio has been awarded $1,650,000 in City funding for the planned construction of a new facility at 156 Rivington Street.

Bullet Space, located on 292 East 3rd Street, between Avenue B and C, was founded as a squat and still exists as an autonomous art space. "Bullet Space is an act of resistance and a community access center for images, words, and sounds of the inner city." The center was founded in the winter of 1985 and was part of a larger squatter movement then taking place in the East Village and the Lower East Side. The name 'Bullet' was taken from the brand of heroin sold on the block known as "bullet block" and reflected the American ethic of violence: 'Bullet Americana', translating it into a framing of art form as weaponry.

In 1979 Guus van der Werf, Marianne Kronenberg, Martha Crijns, Reinout Weydom and Ad de Jong squatted a building at Warmoestraat 139 in Amsterdam. They were interested in creating a place in Amsterdam to show their artworks and those of their friends, stage concerts, and do performances. For the first ten years, the large, public spaces of W139 were a free state, run by a series of artists collectives. As first director, Ad de Jong, with Kitty van Roekel, worked to make W139 into a space organized by the dynamism and the energy of artists. This informed a decision to appoint a new director responsible for W139's artistic policy every two to four years. Now, a staff of five employees, some interns, freelancers and volunteers, supports the director. So far, W139 has hosted over 450 shows by more than 1,700 artists, which have attracted roughly 10,000 visitors a year. "Thanks to the unremitting dedication of many, W139's do-it-yourself mentality has been instrumental in buying, expanding and renovating our building." In 2005 it became necessary to renovate the building and, seeing this as an important step towards autonomous functioning, the W139 collective decided to acquire the building. The financing took place by way of an estimated 50% financial aid and 50% bank loans. Eventually the construction took 15 months. W139 wants to function as autonomously as possible but also wants to pay attention to the surroundings. The Warmoestraat is a rough street, just around the corner from the Red Light District, Dam Square and world's first Stock Exchange, where local residents mix with, business people, prostitutes, junkies, students and tourists. Despite cultural upheaval and transformation, the built fabric of the area has changed little in over two hundred years. The 'Blaauwlakenblok' buildings are very close to each other and have historic exterior facades. W139 has constructed a "new box" inside the old, existing box of the building it occupies. The entrance has been opened up to invite the public inside and the interior of the new spaces have been fitted with new soundproofed walls, so artists can not only work during the day, but also at night.

Over the years, W139 established itself as an important center for contemporary and experimental art in Amsterdam. Since 1979, it has been a space for continuous production and presentation of Contemporary Art, dedicated to risk and experiment and taking as its public mission to shape a new, living unity between works of art, space and the public.

Between 1994 and 1997, Vrieshuis Amerika was an important squat and autonomous zone in Amsterdam. In its heyday, the old meatpacking factory accommodated large exhibitions of contemporary and experimental art, music, performances, readings, theatre groups, cafe 'IJburg', a restaurant with punk concerts on Friday night, an indoor skate-hall, a small movie-theatre with nights for independent filmmakers, a club for dance music, an art & music festival, studios for art, music, performance practice and programming of TV and radio shows, etc. Vrieshuis Amerika was closed by the city in 1997 during a period in which more than half of all free spaces created since the 1970s disappeared. A number of these free spaces, like the Vrieshuis Amerika and the Silo had been significant elements of the cultural landscape in Amsterdam who's loss was greatly missed. The city government had long ignored the importance of autonomous zones for Amsterdam as an artistic free city. Free spaces were mostly marginalized and perceived as a zones of political resistance and as a threat to the order in society. In 1998, a number of developments resulted that free spaces became a hot topic on the political agenda. After several of free spaces were evicted and many more threatened artists and squatters decided to get together. Twelve free spaces formed an assembly, the Gilde van werkgebouwen aan het IJ (Guild of workspaces on the IJ) that represented the autonomous zones of Amsterdam. Both Vrieshuis Amerika and the Silo were located on the IJ. Both groups played key roles and had intensive discussions with the city about the need for and the importance of autonomous zones. They protested and warned that they would leave and work and live in other cities, like Berlin or Barcelona as they had nowhere to go in Amsterdam and rents were becoming unaffordable. A lot of support came from the popular media and action committees, and a turning point became noticeable as policymakers realized the important part that these places have played in the cultural and creative life of Amsterdam generally and in launching the careers of emerging artists in particular. They even came to value the anarchistic nature and temperament in these autonomous zones.

In May 1999, the city responded with the establishment of the 'Broedplaats Amsterdam' (Breeding Places, or "incubators," Amsterdam) program that gave space to individual artists, preserved existing free spaces should be preserved and set up new 'broedplaatsen' (breeding-places). A project group was setup by the city and currently acts to distribute city funds to broedplaatsen projects. They also work to negotiate between groups of artists who want to start a breeding-place and the city. The aim of this project was to secure living and working space for artists. The city wanted to create 1400 to 2000 affordable workspaces for artists in six years. However, in exchange for this subsidy, the city wants to control the organization of artists and even make demands on their income. How much is left of the freedom and autonomy of squatted arts spaces? The Broedplaatsen program imposes many regulations and many artists cannot afford even the subsidized rent that they require. Most spaces go to young and hip graphic design and digital media companies or agencies focused on commercial, market driven products and popular media. Also, hardly anything experimental or interesting is taking place in breeding-places. Instead the focus tends to be on affirmations of mainstream society and working within the confines of already existing culture rather than the radical immediacy the free spaces committed to experiment and the creation of new cultural forms. Even as it has preserved the physical buildings and some of the institutional structures, the city's response to the disappearance of free spaces in Amsterdam has been in many way a seizing, cooptation or annexation of the true anti-culture of the autonomous zone. In the Broedplaatsen they only copy or mimic the life of free spaces. These legalized 'free' spaces are subsidized and under the control of a city-board, that often includes former squatters, but it is impossible to create a real underground within these limitations and controls.

In both New York and Amsterdam autonomous zones will always exist under the radar. Buildings are still taken over to show interesting experimental art, music, theatre, performance, readings and exhibitions. These buildings and the true free zones that they represent are very important since, in absence of external rules and high rents, interesting and unexpected artistic things can still come into existence. These places create the signs by not following them.

56

The Grain Silo in Amsterdam Harbor. This disused silo and customs house
was squatted in the '90s and used for parties and art installations. It
has since been converted into luxury housing and *broedplaats* office space
mostly occupied by design and media start-ups.

Squatting and Media: An Interview with Geert Lovink

Alan Smart

This interview with theorist and media activist Geert Lovink was conducted in February of 2011. Lovink is currently the director of the Institute for Network Cultures at Amsterdam University of Applied Sciences. Lovink was active in the Amsterdam squatter movement throughout the 1980s and 1990s. In 1979 he co-founded of the Amsterdam biweekly, city center squatter 'zine *Grachtenkrant* and, in 1981, and the national weekly *Bluf!*. He has been involved in free radio beginning in 1987, with Radio 100 and then, from 1989 onwards with Radio Patapoe. He was also co-founder of the movement publishing house Ravijn in 1988. Beginning in the '90s Lovink has been an organizer of media and internet activism in the Netherlands and internationally. As a member of The Foundation for the Advancement of Illegal Knowledge (ADILKNO) he coauthored Cracking the Movement: Squatting Beyond the Media, that documents and theorizes the squatter movement in the Netherlands in the terms of media and culture.

Lovink's work has followed a trajectory from media production in support of activist movements to activism in struggles for media autonomy. This evolution from activist media to media activism defines a central dynamic in political struggles from the 1980s to the present as the relations of immaterial production and the infrastructures of the "information economy" have become sites of resistance and contestation. In this interview we discuss how the squatter movement developed from conditions in the political-economy of physical urban space and became increasingly a hybrid struggle engaged with issues both of the brick-and-mortar materiality of the city and the virtual spaces of media and information networks.

Alan Smart

You recently organized a project called Winter Camp.

Geert Lovink

Yes, we brought together twelve networks that are virtual networks of activists who collaborate a lot but cannot afford to meet. Bringing together people who work together is difficult. It's a luxurious thing to do.

Alan Smart

What kind of networks were they?

Geert Lovink

They were mix a of technical/ media people who work on free software and open source, people who work on different campaigns, labor issues, people who focus on precarious labor; twelve different groups. They did a lot of coordination stuff. They sort out the things that are sometimes hard to deal with when you are online. Online collaboration is sometimes a bit scattered. It can be focused but usually it's spread over more time, so if you work together especially for a long period of time you tend to speed up, so it's quite difficult to really make decisions, and to wrap up a project is really hard.

Alan Smart

Was there also institution building or organizing?

Geert Lovink

Organizing, yes, but institutions are a difficult question that is always in the background.... There are some people who know how to deal with that but for others it remains very,

very difficult because they don't want to create a new center of power. This is why they opt not to go for the NGO model. They don't want a headquarters.

Alan Smart

Right. Where do the networks come from? Are they affinity groups that form in different online forums or people who meet and keep in touch?

Geert Lovink

Usually it starts with individuals who meet and then set up something online. Then more and more people get involved, and the group grows and grows, and you end up having a lively but virtual network.

Alan Smart

I am interested in the urban implications of these kinds of either radical or activist practices in the '60s, '70s and '80s so I wanted to talk to you about the work that you did leading up to when you got involved with ADILKNO. I've been talking to people who were in the group Eventstructure Research that was involved in staging happenings and doing inflatables, and expanded cinema projects while also involved in the Nieuwmarkt movement. I feel like—depending on how one imagines the squatter movement as a thing—these kinds of things predate the squatter movement but involve a lot of the same ideas and, in some ways, lays the ground work for it.

Geert Lovink

Yes, that is how I see it.

Alan Smart

When did you get involved in urban space activism?

Geert Lovink

1978. I kind of grew into it. I'd been out of Amsterdam for a while but I came back in '77 when I started studying political science here, at the University of Amsterdam. Half a year into studying I moved into a big squat, Grote Wettering, which was across from the Rijksmuseum. It was a couple of weeks after the squat was squatted. Then, in October of '78 we kind of came together and we squatted our own place - a really beautiful baroque house on Singel that is still squatted, or not squatted but social housing.

Alan Smart

So that was just housing whereas the other was more of a social center?

Geert Lovink

Well that was just much bigger. Grote Wettering was, one, two, probably four houses in one. It was quite diverse. I came later and I didn't know a lot of the people there and I didn't have so much of an attachment to that group. So to have our own house was important and well, that house became important in the struggles of early 1980. So, the so-called "press group" and a lot of the coordinating facilities for the Groot Keijser were done from our

house. Our house itself was also attacked a few times, also the guy who owned it tried to get us out through court cases, so our house was a bit known. It was not really a symbol for the struggle but certainly it was one of the more active houses. We all studied political science at the time. For me the whole year of 1980 was extremely turbulent. We also squatted another house, a smaller house, then that was evicted. I came back to the *Singel*. I had to move a lot of times, and that year so much stuff happened.

Alan Smart

1980 was the year of the big evictions on...

Geert Lovink

Vondelstraat and everything—the whole list. That year ended with the eviction of Grote Wettering, which was also a big riot, and in-between you had the Kroning [coronation] April 30 with the biggest riot. So that year was very turbulent. It probably was the height of the squatter movement anyway.

Alan Smart

So why was this happening? Why were there so many people interested in squatting? Why did it work as well as it did, and why was it being attacked right then?

Geert Lovink

It was just a unique way that things came together, not only in Amsterdam, I have to say. We were in close contact with squatters in London and we were actively involved with when the squatter movement took off in Berlin. So Berlin was pretty big. They had fewer houses there but the houses were bigger so the number of people they had there was greater and the groups were bigger. In Berlin they had about 150 occupied buildings, but the buildings were huge, so just in terms of the number of people it's considerable. Zurich was important too, but the unique thing about Amsterdam was that there was a very large amount of young people and there was no housing for them so the need. The absolute need was there, and probably exists right now as well. The need was really there and also the political motivation. The political climate was there for people to say, "we are going to join the movement." The main thing was that a few things in the urban policies came together right in that moment.

Alan Smart

And what were those?

Geert Lovink

It was kind of a unique thing. People like my parents were moving out of the city, so a lot of people left. Just in terms of the population, the second half of the 1970s was a time when most people moved out of Amsterdam.

Alan Smart

So, the middle class?

Geert Lovink

Yes, but everyone, across the board: the rich, the middle class

and the lower class. Then all the factories closed: the last factories inside the old town, then everything related. A lot of the companies occupying office spaces moved away and opened larger headquarters outside the city along the highway. That was combined with the renovation of the late 19th century industrial areas that were knocked down. This, I think, created the critical mass. Other things were also important, but the question of why Amsterdam, and why was the movement so big, it was because the late 19th century areas were knocked down, and there was this huge delay in reconstruction everywhere. The old people moved out. They went to Purmerend, they went north, they were housed in the *Bijlmermeer*,[1] or in the new suburbs that were built. Then, to knock down old buildings and build new houses there was an average delay of three or four years.

Alan Smart

So there was lots of empty space that was either empty houses or else industrial space?

Geert Lovink

Ya, you name it. When you went through town all you saw was empty spaces everywhere.

Alan Smart

And yet there was a housing shortage because you had to go through the housing list?

Geert Lovink

And also because there was no

real rental market. So, just add the two and then you also had kind of a progressive political climate. Now we don't have that progressive political climate.

Alan Smart

Also now there is a rental market, and there are things like *antikraak*,[2] and there are developers who build housing.

Geert Lovink

None of that existed then.

Alan Smart

When did that develop? How did there come to be a more liberalized real estate market?

Geert Lovink

That really only changed substantially in the second part of the '90s. So this meant that it took the whole system about fifteen years or maybe even twenty to really substantially change.

Alan Smart

What were the terms of those links to London and Berlin? Did people move back and forth?

Geert Lovink

That was important. There was a lot of exchange of ideas, of symbols, of music, stories, tactics, all sorts of things.

Alan Smart

How were these ideas exchanged? I've seen handbooks and guidebooks and stuff.

Geert Lovink

Books, magazines, but especially also people traveling; hitchhiking of course.

Alan Smart

What was the difference between Amsterdam and places like Berlin and Zurich? It seems like the German context is much more political?

Geert Lovink

Yes, more political. I mean, we just didn't have that kind of political background. For the simple reason that the history of the country was so different. I mean coming to Berlin, they still struggled massively with the radical left, the autonomous left and the whole legacy of the armed struggle. We had none of that here. None of the more radical left, they never participated in the squatter movement.

Alan Smart

So, politics in the Netherlands were kind of more local and less ideologically intense?

Geert Lovink

I would say so.

Alan Smart

In the Nieuwmarkt movement one of the important elements was the Communist Party of the Netherlands (CPN).

Geert Lovink

That was less so five years later.

Alan Smart

At that time, the CPN was in the city government and there was that moment where they ended up at odds with the activists.

Geert Lovink

Well, we grew up with that legacy but the squatter's movement had

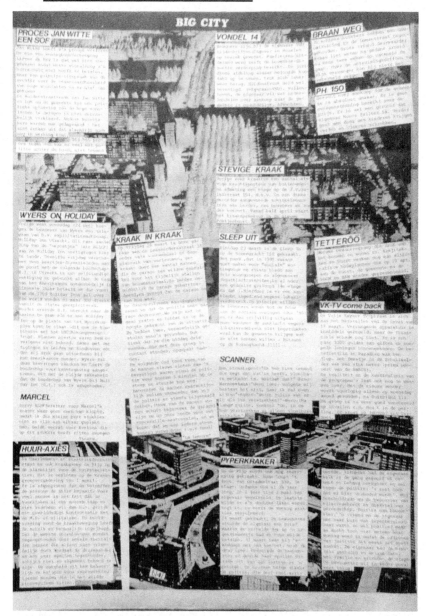

Updates on various Amsterdam squats in **Bluf!** Magazine

less to do with them. There were even communist squatters. But don't forget, though, that in the 1980s these parties themselves were very rapidly declining and falling apart. We couldn't really sense that at the moment, but retrospectively it was very clear that the fight happening in the Nieuwmarkt was kind of the last battle where they had some kind of substantial power

Alan Smart

It seemed like in the Nieuwmarkt the Communists end up being with the unions and then they have this kind of a modernist orientation that called for big housing projects and mass transit.

Geert Lovink

Yes, very much so.

Alan Smart

So that in the end they were on the opposite side of the people in the street.

Geert Lovink

In the 1980s, although there was not a link as such to the Communists, the situation was not as antagonistic as it was in the early and mid '70s.

Alan Smart

So they were neither adversaries nor allies?

Geert Lovink

I think if you look at on a practical level they were actually more allies, among the young people. But this is because, at that time, the party had already begun to split, more openly, between the young people

who were still members but shared many of the values and agendas that we had, and the old guard. So, it was turning into a generational conflict, within the Communist Party. Whereas, five, ten years before that just didn't happen.

Alan Smart

Were both the old guard and the young members both unionized industrial workers, or was it more kind of intellectuals or urban leftists at that point?

Geert Lovink

That was also the problem. At the moment this was also changing.

Alan Smart

The factories left and the workers left with them, and there wasn't anyone to be in the unions?

Geert Lovink

Exactly, these two things are directly related of course.

Alan Smart

What then were the forces that the squatters' movement was against or was wrestling with? Was it the real estate market?

Geert Lovink

I think that was really quite an important struggle. Also, a struggle for housing for young people, social housing, and also maybe what we would consider more as creative industry type issues that are now completely incorporated inside the system. At the time they were completely outside so what people were fighting for was to have small workshops, theaters, facilities for smaller shops and stuff like that. It was a do-it-yourself movement, very strong, although a certain element in the [squatting] movement was about that and another wasn't. For some it was just housing whereas for others it was more of a lifestyle movement. That was quite a clear split.

Alan Smart

That was about finding a way to live in the city after industry and after the old model of urbanism?

Geert Lovink

Yes, big factories, big offices and so on. The things we struggle with nowadays as well.

Alan Smart

What were the projects that were involved in that? What did people make? What did you end up having to build to make the project work?

Geert Lovink

Well I think what made the movement so different from now is that, unlike many other places, there was mass unemployment. It was a time of economic crisis and it was a crisis that somehow didn't seem to end, which I think, retrospectively... it kind of started with the decline in the '70s, after '73. In Amsterdam, it was only in the second half of the '90s that things started to pick up again substantially. So that's a long time. It's my whole youth basically. And it wasn't just me. It was a whole generation or even more. But the big difference from now is that a substantial amount of all the young people were all living on the dole.

This is the late cold war period. It's the period of the welfare state. In the case of the Netherlands, that was financed through gas. Gas exploration was the big money motor behind this. So that, in effect, had a big influence on the type of economic activity that happened within the movement.

Alan Smart

So when you were young there were people who worked for oil companies and for banking, kind of yuppies, and everybody else was out of work or were involved in marginal things. So making your own workshops and things was a way of imagining a new model to replace the old model of industrial labor?

Geert Lovink

Absolutely.

Alan Smart

Were there other sites or events that were particularly important or interesting?

Geert Lovink

Well, we have written the book *Squatting the Movement*,[3] our version of the growth and the decline of the Amsterdam squatter movement of the 1980s. I think what defines that movement, especially here in Amsterdam, is that it was extremely local and organized around neighborhood and suburban groups who were all so different; socially different, with different compositions, and other kinds of emphases. So it was possible to be in a lot of different kind of bubbles, small scenes of people. The movement itself, at its height, consisted of a substantial number of people. I would say anywhere between ten and fifteen thousand people—and that is a lot—who were all organized and had their own kind of shops, cafes, theaters, ways to distribute their own information, with their own kinds of discussions and discussion groups.

Alan Smart

So this is how networking became so important in the movement? Because this is both how these groups were made and also how they communicated?

Geert Lovink

Yes, for a very short while, in 1980 at the height of the movement, an attempt was made at least to create a city-wide decision-making structure. That didn't last very long.

Alan Smart

I see. That was based at Groot Keijser?

Geert Lovink

Yes, and that lasted for the year basically, but then after that, no.

Alan Smart

And it didn't work because there were just too many diverse interests?

Geert Lovink

Yes, and also politically. A lot of the groups were really more politically focused on tackling the labor government—the city government. Others were less focused on the political level itself,

and more focused on growing the base of the movement: squatting more buildings, and maybe also diversifying squatting in the sense of not just squatting apartments for small families. There were some attempts to even make squats for refugees and for migrant workers, especially in the area here, in the east and there were a few in the west.

Alan Smart

So there was one impulse that went towards expansion and stability, and the other that went towards confrontation?

Geert Lovink

Yes, the other one certainly was looking for political confrontation. This tension, or these two influences, you also find inside the Nieuwmarkt movement, because there were the same people there then. You have to understand, we were really young when we came on the scene in the 80s', so the real drivers of a lot of the events were people with a lot more experience. They were usually people who had their first experiences in the Nieuwmarkt movement. A lot of the more radical people, like Theo van Giessen, came from the Staatsliedenbuurt. Also, the most active group here in Osterpark came from Niewmarkt as well. They were more like the German *Sponti*—meaning "spontaneous." So they took more anarchist approaches.

Alan Smart

These were confrontation oriented?

Geert Lovink

Yes, mostly all of them were but coming from different directions, some of them a bit more towards the Marxist analysis where as others of them had a bit more of an anarcho-libertarian agenda... one was really organizing towards a confrontation while the other was really wary of centralization.

Alan Smart

In the Nieuwmarkt movement they picked up these notions of making events, and then as the events get longer and larger, they became things like a mail system and a phone network.

Geert Lovink

We copied all that, so that was a given. When we arrived on the scene that was the way you did it. The whole structure of the Nieuwmarkt was just laid out across the whole town.

Alan Smart

So you had newspapers then. You had your own mail?

Geert Lovink

We had everything. That was why the movement was so big—because it was tried out in one area around '73 to '75, and then all the people from that generation moved across town to many different areas. Then when the movement picked up, they immediately organized it along those same lines, Except that they did it in 10 or 15 different suburbs.

That was why the movement could grow so fast.

The *kraakspreekuur*[4] is the very basic unit, where people just go and then others help you. Then around that grows a network of the telephone snowball system in case something is wrong, or there is an incident, or the police show up. People immediately show up. Then that just grows towards the bigger events. Once it covers the whole city you can imagine that you can mobilize a lot of people.

Alan Smart

And radio stations?

Geert Lovink

Radio and newspapers. I was involved in founding one, the *Kraked Krant*, that started in '79. This was when I was part of the squatter group of the center—the *Grachtengordel*, canal zone. That's where I lived for most of the time. It was only one of many and was not particularly political or anything. It was, of course mega, mega weird to squat all these 16th or 17th and 18th century buildings. What can I say? It will always stay in your dreams. It's such an intense experience.

Alan Smart

Because it's hard to work on them and inhabit them?

Geert Lovink

Oh it's absurd, why would you live in an 18th century palace. I mean, sorry, when you are 21, eh?

Alan Smart

[laughs] It could be nice, but yeah.

Geert Lovink

It could be nice? Yah, it was, but it was completely absurd.

Alan Smart

You spoke of the darkness of the '80s. It seems like in the '60s even when things were confrontational and hard it's in this kind of happy, playful prankster mode. Then in the '70s there seems to be a kind of troubling of that, and by the time it's the '80s it's heroin and no jobs and desperation.

Geert Lovink

I certainly agree with that. In that sense it's no fun.

Alan Smart

But then maybe in the politics or the social aspects within the movement it's different. In the '60s there was a rhetoric of sexual liberation, and then later on it becomes more of a conflict...

Geert Lovink

... between the genders.

Alan Smart

Right, but then you have the queer movement.

Geert Lovink

Certainly. That certainly was very important at the time.

Alan Smart

How did that manifest?

Geert Lovink

In concrete struggles. Maybe much more then than now, when there is no radical feminist movement at the moment. But the politics at the time were completely defined by that.

Alan Smart

There were squats that were kind of social experiments in terms of being all women or queer or other things?

Geert Lovink

They all existed of course. They were strong. There were also lesbian squatter groups. Of course, yes I knew quite a few of them. Some of them are still really good friends. Maybe at the time it was more separate than it is now. Recently I looked at my masters thesis that I wrote about Bluf!, the weekly that we ran. I ran it for about one-and-a-half, two years and then after that, together with my friend Evelyn Levers. We wrote this thesis *From Groot Keijser to Weijers,* and the text "The Radicality of the Everyday," that raise questions of ideology, counter ideology and one's own autonomous media; our own media.

This is the question of money and how to run things, the perspective of a counter-economy, the schizophrenia of alternative management. Then, you know, a very important discussion was whether the weekly is the weekly bounded by the movement, or is it independent. If you ran a weekly did it have its own policy, or was it the weekly of and by the movement. Then there is the history of it, the internal power struggles and so on inside the editorial group, and the issue of the network that *Bluf!* and the other alternative projects were produced by: printing, radio and so on, to put this in more perspective. Then, the struggle between the sexes: "the personal is not political enough." Then a kind of discourse analysis of what we were writing about. And a report about threatened houses, which was always very important, because a lot of houses were not only newly squatted, but also, all the existing squats had to be defended. So how to deal with them, and how should a weekly newspaper deal with that. Then we discussed about the aims and the goals, and about the tactics and the strategies of the movement, because the movement was constantly debating its direction.

Alan Smart

So with the kind of network-making, when do computer networks become important. How does that show up?

Geert Lovink

Computers were kind of part of certain activities people did, particularly in '83, '84. Especially in a number of projects where people started to discover what you could do with databases, and search when you had a lot of data. Also, PCs became common. I bought my first one in '87. A lot of the writings of ADILKNO, maybe the first books and so on were still done on typewriters, but quite soon after, from '87 on, we wrote on computers. I was involved in the first big computer

hackers' conference where I got to play around for the first time with the Internet and other kinds of BBS and CompuServe and all the others. That was in August '89, and it was in Paradiso. It was called the Galactic Hacker party, but then '89 is quite late.

Alan Smart

In the '60s and '70s there was a certain interest in social structure, and these different anthropological arguments for different kinds of housing. It was sort of an experimental thing, but it does seem like that kind of becomes more routine in the '80s?

Geert Lovink

Yes, but there is something else that you see happening. Especially in the 1980s, the kind of theories about social control through social housing and a kind of more Foucauldian reading becomes more important. That's how I got into it. Funny enough, the first time I really started reading about French philosophy was in Delft, through social housing and its interpretation, but not so much in Amsterdam. That struggle was still very much happening in Rotterdam. If you are talking about the very tough ideological clashes in terms of the makeability of the social, as they call it, that is Rotterdam.

Alan Smart

Maakbaarheid is the Dutch word?

Geert Lovink

Maakbaarheid. That's where most of the architects and most of the struggles in the 1970s and '80s all happened.

Alan Smart

Bluf! magazine began when?

Geert Lovink

It started in late '81 and then became a really functioning weekly in January of '82. It took a while to figure out how to do it because to run a weekly is quite something. It still is

Alan Smart

Yes, and also with the magazines it seems like in the '60s it's quite an effort to get them printed and distributed and everything.

Geert Lovink

That was not an issue in the '80s.

Alan Smart

Was it that, with the photocopy machine, it becomes easier to make magazines in the 80s but then, with the Internet, they become something of a retro thing.

Geert Lovink

It was in particular because the distribution points started to vanish. There were no bookstores, no more groups that would distribute them in the '90s. There was more and more possibility to reproduce ideas but there were fewer and fewer distribution possibilities, until the Internet came and kind of reversed that. There is a gap there though, in the '90s, when the Internet is still small and growing but the movement and the distribution point of paper material is declining. This is why so much kind of disappeared in the '90s. There is a real gap between the two.

Alan Smart

so the Internet was enough to kill off the bookstores but it wasn't open enough and pervasive enough for everyone to be on it.

Geert Lovink

At the time, yes, exactly.

Alan Smart

Excellent, this seems to bring us back to where we started so let's end here. Thank you very much.

NOTES

1 The *Bijlmermeer* is a large housing development constructed in to the south east of Amsterdam beginning in 1966. It was intended to house middle class, automobile-owning commuters but came to be occupied mostly by poor immigrants, many from newly decolonized Surinam. In the 1970s, the *Bijlmermeer* came to be commonly sited as an example of the failure of modernist mass housing and master-planning efforts.

2 *Antikraak* ("anti-squatting") is a system where by temporary tenants are placed into vacant spaces by companies contracted to by building owners to prevent the occupation of their properties by squatters.

3 ADILKNO, Cracking the Movement, Squatting Beyond the Media, translated by Laura Martz (Autonomedia, New York, 1994). Online at: http://thing.desk.nl/bilwet/Cracking/contents.html

4 Literally a "Squat Speaking Hour" a *kraakspreekuur* is an open discussion session organized by squatters to exchange information and advise new people interested in becoming involved in the movement.

Masked squatters giving a press conference. From Bluf! Magazine

71

The Emerging Network of Temporary Autonomous Zones (TAZ)

Aja Waalwijk

An Autonomous Zone or free cultural space is a topographically open space, be it landscape or building, a *Freiraum* or "free space" embedding counter-cultural traditions and values like the ones promoted by Provo (happenings), the Situationists (Power to the Imagination), Woodstock (pop-festivals), Rainbow Gatherings, Trance Parties (Boom), Squatting Movements (Christiania, Ruigoord, UfA-fabrik), Goan hippies, the Burning Man Festival, etc. Autonomous Zones, sometimes called Liminal Zones, are places of self-realization, places where ecstatic energies flower. Liminal Zones lie between defined areas without belonging to any of them, like door thresholds (limen in Latin). They have a topographical as well as a psychological connotation....

In Holland in the early '70s the Kite Company of Den Bosch and the Amsterdam Balloon Company introduced Kite Flying festivals. These took place at the four cardinal sides of the city of Amsterdam, open sandy areas where new city districts were planned. In the early days, no permission was required to inaugurate a festival in no-mans-land. Admittedly, free space is sparse in Holland. But even the sky is now no longer off-limits for those who endlessly invent regulations and prescriptions. So planning free cultural space becomes our logical next step, planning places where nothing should be planned. *Freiraum* is a German word used to designate free space. It stands for all places where behavioral constraints are suspended. In theory all public spaces are *Freiraums*. Behavior constraints in public places are exercised though through, for example, one-way traffic signs, or bans on drinking alcohol, smoking joints, making music, sitting in the grass or laying on a park-bench. Public space is definitely no longer free space ...

City nomads, who travel in the tradition of the gypsies, witness

Tents, windmills and harbor infrastructure at Ruigoord

hard times. In England the Caravans of Love are under constant threat. Bureaucratic regimes have a fundamental problem with nomads, and display characteristic patterns of repression against them. There were nomadic restrictions in Mongolia during the communist period, NATO troops killed Balkan nomads trespassing over new Greek national borders in the '50s, and Nazis massacred gypsies during World War II. When you have no fixed address you are said to be hard-to-find and you don't belong anywhere. However, gypsies are in a way the perfect earthlings, since they have never drawn borders around themselves and have never sought a fatherland. (Recently, to get some form of autonomy for themselves, the Roma in Hungary accepted a "minority self-government system.")

In Amsterdam new forms of nomadism are taking shape. The so-called "City Nomads" once clustered together in caravans as the Human Garden behind the Animal Garden (as we call the zoo in Amsterdam).

73

After the authorities dismantled this wonderful free-space, groups of city-nomads spread to the margins of the metropolis. These wanderers are not simply victims of circumstance. In their urge to be free, many have deliberately said farewell to a fixed abode, financial benefits, identity papers. They've relinquished everything except a caravan, accepting the possible consequence that today in the government's eyes such lack of status might transform nomads like them into illegal foreigners.

The squatting movements in such centers as Amsterdam, Copenhagen and Berlin opened many temporary and permanent free cultural places. Sometimes temporary became permanent and vice versa. In Holland squatting is outlawed now (as a result of a law passed in 2010), though there are still social and cultural squatting traditions in Holland "social" for those who need housing, "cultural" for those who need space for cultural activities. Of course they are interwoven. Social squats and culture squats often developed into complete cult spaces. The ADM, a squatted industrial complex, is a true mini-society famous for its *Robodock* festival, among other things, and is still organizing festivals free of control and the supervision of authorities. Most of these free cultural spaces have been "cleaned out" by the government. Squatted military complexes like the one in Baarle in the south of the Netherlands had to be vacated because of the "need" for golf-courses and other money-based planological projects. In the '60s, '70s and '80s, Amsterdam flourished as a place where youth culture took the initiatives. As a Magic Center, Amsterdam was a free cultural space, a real free-town. You could find people sleeping in the parks, making music in the streets, etc ...

"Act first, then legalize," is an old Amsterdam saying. In 1972, a group of artists and writers squatted the village of Ruigoord. Because of planned expansion of the Amsterdam harbor the village had been almost emptied of inhabitants. In the same year that Ruigoord was squatted, the Amsterdam Balloon Company was created, organizing four kite-festivals around the city before finally settling down in the village. Many actions and festivals have since taken place in Ruigoord, tens of thousands of trees were planted, creating a beautiful forest on the empty plains surrounding the village. Around 2000, the authorities moved in. The forest was destroyed, though hundreds of green-front activists tried to save it from total destruction. Police forces arrived, surrounding the village with barbed wire fences. But in recent years the village has been legalized, and now Ruigoord is a green island surrounded by industries, paying a modest rent to the harbor.

During its many performance tours, the Amsterdam Balloon

Company (ABC) created Temporary Autonomous Zones throughout Asia, Europe and Northern Africa; and, of course, in Ruigoord, which remains their home-ground, where many festivals still take place. In Goa, from the late '70s till the '90s, the ABC held yearly performances. When the Balloon Company performs everybody is a participant, borders between the public and the artists dissolve. In 1972, the ABC published the following statement: "The ABC is a floating movement in pursuit of freedom in airspace. Anybody who loves balloons, kites, birds or other soundless heavenly vehicles (sun, moon, earth, stars, comets etc.) can consider him/herself as a member." The implication was that during moments of action everybody is a member of the ABC. In the early '80s, I decided to join them.

If you want something done, do it yourself. You can create your own free cultural space by being (or getting) involved in festivals and cultural free-havens as a dreamer, thinker, doer or celebrator. To create a temporary or permanent free space all you need are companions, friends who want to lay some creative eggs too, or who know places where things can or should happen. But free cultural space is only possible when there is room or space for it. It's all about territory.

When a Temporary Autonomous Zone turns into a permanent one institutionalization may strike. Institutionalized Autonomous Zones or Institutionalized Free Cultural Spaces are under constant pressure. Direct action on non-institutionalized autonomous space brings about conflicts with the authorities, as we have seen in Germany, Holland, Denmark, Belgium, France, etc. In Ruigoord, which is now officially part of the city of Amsterdam, we held a yearly Temporary Autonomous Zone on the open grounds beside the village, our yearly *Landjuwel* festival. In the beginning, just artists and activists attended. We made works of art out of our tents, statues and sculptures out of what was lying around, had an open stage for poetry, music, etc. Seeing it all happen, I suggested creating a sculpture route for the full moon night, when we traditionally also launched a balloon. The sculpture route became a theatrical interaction that included performers, acrobats, drummers, etc. This sort of initiative is necessary to provide free cultural space with substance. Form and content are inseparable. Of course, my initiative was related to and only became manifest because of hundreds of other individuals who contributed their own ideas, like Hans Plomp's open poetry stage (you might have heard his readings here), the Insect Sect conjured up by Theo Kley, Max Reneman and the Hippie King Poet Leo van der Zalm, Montje Joling's Why Not Circus, Rudolph Stokvis's balloon ceremony, Henk Spitteler's *Freiraum* concept, etc.

75

In 1991, the discovery of America bounced back across the Atlantic. As a reaction to the upcoming 500-year celebration in the U.S., the alternative circuit in Amsterdam participated in the international counter-culturally organized "Discovery of Europe," involving representatives of indigenous peoples from all over the world. After talking it over with the community at Ruigoord, I wrote the following manifesto:

America was inhabited by the Indians, New Zealand by the Maori, Australia by the Aborigines. Europe was the robber that disturbed domestic peace. The invaders built themselves a home and now celebrate their 500-year occupation. Ruigoord, a squatted village, in solidarity with the destitute tribes of the world, hereby symbolically offers its grounds as an anchorage for positive energies, a place for rituals, in short, a stamping ground. We declare Ruigoord 'Stamping-Ground Holland.' We hope that this initiative will be followed by a reaction of our governments in enlarging the natural grounds for indigenous people all over the world."

In 1992, a Stamping Ground festival took place on the open space surrounding Ruigoord. South American Indians and Mongol shamans visited us and blessed the festival grounds with ceremonial dances and other events. In 1993, I initiated the "Dream-time Awakening" festival, which was opened by the Australian ambassador. With the help of some Australian Aboriginal artists, a simultaneous ritual dance was performed in Holland and Australia, creating a Temporary Autonomous Zone on opposite sides of the globe. Our Stamping Ground is now covered with industrial buildings. What was meant to be permanent became temporary. And with that our festival grounds disappeared.

During recent years we have organized our Landjewels within the village boundaries, but the space is cramped and the authorities exercise more and more repressive control. That's why in 2010 we visited the Boom festival instead of organizing our own big festival. We still hold our thematic festivals: poetry, solstice, percussion, I-Ching, reggae, trance, didgeridoo, etc. "You've got to row with the paddles you have," is an old Dutch saying. But our liberty is constantly at risk. Admission fees are sky rocketing. For many it has gotten too expensive. The authorities' demands for guards and fences make freedom fade. In Portugal, Boom [Boom Festival, "the gathering of the psychedelic tribe," July 28-August 4, 2012 in Idanha-a-Nova, Portugal] provoked the Anti-Boom Festival exactly because of this. But an unorganized mass-meeting of 10,000 people, like Anti-Boom, can cause a total mess. No infrastructure often means no toilets, polluted water, dangerous drugs, police confrontations, etc. Total Freedom can easily turn into disorder, chaos and crime....

Festivals have become an industry. Besides hiring crowd control, one can rent tents of all sizes, musical and electronic equipment, generators, stages, tribunes, dance floors, bars, projection screens, etc. The core values and ideas of the alternative circuit are taken over and commercially exploited as mass manifestations. Just to mention one example, the relatively new mega manifestation, Dance Valley, takes place not far from the village of Ruigoord and copies everything we do....

Cultural free-havens, be they permanent or temporary, periodical or one-off, can become institutionalized. Organization within a free cultural space takes place on two levels, one deals with internal programming and infra-structure, another turns its face towards the outside world, mostly on the governmental front, be it local or national. If too much is given away to the official control system, autonomy fades. Institutionalization may lead to government control on many levels: police at the entrance, civil police among the audience, firemen controlling every prescribed fireplace, sound regulations and control, obligatory official medical assistance, controls on electricity, food quality, the use of drugs, etc. All this costs loads of money, turning the free cultural space into an unfree one based on consumption. And then it's not free or autonomous anymore.

In Denmark two important Permanent Free Cultural Spaces were created: in 1970 The New Society appeared in Thy-leijren, and in 1971 squatters transformed a former military complex in Copenhagen into Christiania. They did not appear out of the blue. Gunnar Hjelholt, one of the professors at the University of Copenhagen, experienced his first "international mini-society," as he called it, in a German concentration-camp and wrote a booklet about the positive aspects of the experience. Based on his work at the university, teachers and students, especially in the psychology and sociology departments, started new programs of therapy. Initially, empty villages in Sweden were used for their first experiments with these so called "mini-societies." The best houses were given to the rich, the poorest houses to the poor, an arrangement that naturally brought about conflicts. The rich were confronted with the poor, the old with the young, etc. But as a community they talked and their fantasies about the different social classes faded. Some of the students involved in the experiments were members of the New Student Society, which went bankrupt. The name was changed to the New Society, and since democratization was part of the program non-students were invited to enlist. In Denmark this led to a fusion of the student and hippie movements.

HIP, as an acronym for Housing Innovation Project, implies the search for different forms of living, being and working together. So in Thy-leijren the students and hippies started with a festival organized by the New Society. Temporary became permanent. Many visitors to the festival stayed to build a real New Society. A year later, Christiania was squatted. Though squatting was banned by Danish law, the Danish public largely sympathized with the projects, so the 1990s saw the creation of special legislation. For this reason, people in Thy-lejren and Christiania were not supervised by a government housing committee that set standards for how habitations should look and their lifestyles weren't policed. In Thy-Leijren one could live in a cardboard box, a tent or build a hand-made house. Following the same principles of free exploration, Christiania became a permanent autonomous community for many sub-cultural and counter-cultural groups. Residents there include the Inuit, bicycle freaks, communes of all sorts, alternative architects, the green front and hash-dealers, natural healers, artists, etc. Common ground (a permanent temporary autonomous zone) is centered at the Field of Peace (*Fredens Eng*), Christiania's place for ceremonies, happenings and festivals. But there are also many halls in the community available for such collective purposes as exhibitions and cultural manifestations. About 1,000 people actually live in Christiania, and each day hundreds, sometimes thousands, of visitors come there to seek inspiration or to be themselves, to be free, to act freely. "You are now entering the Common Market" proclaims a sign over one of the gates as you leave Freetown Christiania. Actress and culture coordinator Britta Lillesøe's biggest concern is to keep Christiania a free cultural space, to keep it a real freetown outside the control of the government. The "official" political and planological machine has worked non stop to get a grip on the place.

Just as the Amsterdam Balloon Company operates from Ruigoord, Christiania has its Sunwagon (*Solvogn)* theater troupe, which organizes manifestations that blur the borders between life and theater. In one event I witnessed that took place during Christmas time in 1975, hundreds of Santa Clauses gave away goods from Copenhagen's supermarkets and were collectively arrested singing Christmas carols, they carried a big crucified chicken with them on their way to prison. These great city-theater spectacles transform the whole of Copenhagen into a real Temporary Autonomous Zone for hours at a time.

I myself live in a former culture squat, ZAAL 100, in Amsterdam. It's now regulated, combining a living group, small alternative offices, a vegetarian restaurant, stages for music, theater, multi-media, etc. When I first started participatinge in activities there there was no stage for poetry and the walls were empty. I declared the walls of Zaal 100 to be "Gallery 100, an Autonomous zone for the arts." This means that anybody can exhibit here "I make no curatorial choices. Nothing is insured, so the artists take a certain risk, but when a work is sold they don't have to pay any gallery percentages. For the poetry-stage I have the same attitude.

I also have a studio in Ruigoord, where I'm involved in setting up the yearly sculpture route, and assisting with the poetry events organized by Hans Plomp and the Amsterdam Balloon Company shows. Besides those activities I also run the Nomadic Museum, inviting friends to exhibit on important free cultural spaces. In Baarle, a former squatted military complex, the ambassadress of Mongolia opened the Nomadic Museum exhibition while the local Dutch authorities showed no interest at all.

Free cultural spaces are also playgrounds and laboratories for alternative forms of organization. Researchers in Amsterdam undertook an inventory of the different ways squats functioned and their different organizational structures. One of the major points of distinction was the difference between the ones that organized a bar, versus the techies and the artists. The ones who sold beer often seemed most financially autonomous, because they generated money enough to pay for repairs, etc. The study showed that there are many ways to be organized. Every place had its specific infrastructure, and all of them were valuable models for future development.

Seeking help, a group of Belgian artists/poets and activists from the village of Doel near Antwerp recently arrived at Ruigoord. Doel, as had almost happened at Ruigoord, was about to be erased to make way for harbor expansion. Since the harbor is unlikely to be built and the village is empty these activists see the possibility of transforming it into a free cultural space. To assist them, the Amsterdam Balloon Company cooperated with them in raising an *Axis Mundi* in Doel, with Ruigoord opening a consulate in Doel and Doel doing the same in Ruigoord. A few weeks later, the Ruigoord Consulate was evicted by the Belgian police. We have yet to decide how we will respond. At the very least, a letter will be forwarded to the Belgian authorities from the citizens of Christiania and Ruigoord. While at this moment the village is a graffiti museum, not so long ago, the Doel activists organized a Do It Yourself Festival the name indicates the idea: Do it Yourself. If you want to help shape a Permanent Autonomous Zone, go to Doel!

Cultural freehavens like Christiania (Denmark), Thy-leijren (Denmark), Ruigoord (Netherlands), Doel (Belgium), UFA-Fabrik (Germany), Catarredor (Portugal) and countless other culture squats and communes in Western Europe are mini-societies where festivals play a central role. No Permanent Autonomous Zones without Temporary Autonomous Zones within their boundaries! In Catarredor there is a hotel where you can sleep for one euro a night, there's a bar, there are weekly concerts, etc. It's a mini-society of people that explores living together in a different way. They eat together in changing groups, etc. Mini-societies are not simply laboratories for social relations, playgrounds for alternative architects, artists and farmers, in important ways their ecological and environmental concepts give shape to, or are the real foundation for, trans-industrial landscaping and future city development ...

The stress of institutionalization can bring about cooperation. If Christiania, Thy-leijren, UFA-Fabrik, Doel, Ruigoord and Boom join forces, we can make stronger statements about aspects of freedom, ecology and culture in general. This year [2011] Christiania celebrates its 40th anniversary. Ruigoord and Doel and possibly Boom will establish embassies in Christiania, and vice versa. In 2012, Ruigoord will celebrate its 40th. A trans-national conference on free cultural spaces all over the world will be a main aspect of the celebration activities. A physical network complementing a virtual one is the aim: a network leading to collective investment in tours involving artists, musicians, writers, performers, ecological farmers and representatives of tribes from all over the world. Oral traditions will gain importance, and with them the exchange of ideas ...

In recent years the Amsterdam Balloon Company has placed three *Axis Mundi* in, respectively, Ruigoord, Christiania and Doel, building up a trans-national network through cultural journeys to alternative cultural free-places and festivals. The aim of this network is to work together on different levels in the future. Since our city-tribes are pushing for recognition, it is important to find ways to contact other tribal communities in the Americas, Asia, Africa and Australia.

An *Axis Mundi*, or "World Axis," symbolizes the center of the world. Through history it has been the notion projected on a sacred mountain, a column of smoke, a tree, totem pole or an imaginary line to the polar star around which the earth was believed to spin. Upholding the heavenly dome, depicted as world pillars or trees of life, they form centers for peoples living in microcosmic environments. An Axis Mundi establishes, for example, the four cardinal directions, and for many cultures it connects all the visible and invisible spheres. Seen as rising from the navel of the earth, an Axis Mundi serves as an umbilical cord for people like the Mongolian shamans.

Psychonauts claim space for the spirit. In 2008, the ABC was invited to an inter-tribal gathering in Christiania. During this "Two Urban

Tribes" Meeting, a manifesto was written that began with the following lines: "Ruigoord and Christiania, are both urban tribes of people who are different, slightly aberrant, conforming not to what the world dictates, but to their inner voice, their spirit. Tonight we conform our spirits by shifting the Axis of our world to this location, where the magical tree *Yggdrasil* will be erected."

The manifesto ends with the lines: "Urban Tribes have a much wider importance than simply representing a nice way of living, an escape for a happy few. We show the world that there are alternative ways of living, working and being together. The world needs experimental zones where alternative models of inter-human relationships, government, decision making and social structure can be developed. They don't need to succeed, but they must allow us to learn new processes and possibilities. Let's celebrate life, let's make this planet sing! We declare Christiania to be the center of our world."

Excerpted from "The Emerging Network of Temporary Autonomous Zones (TAZ)" by Aja Waalwijk

81

Denma

82

Christiania: How They Do It and for How Long

Jordan Zinovich

CHRISTIANIA'S POLITICAL AND ECONOMIC STRUCTURE

A self-governing, self-sustaining community where the individual takes care of the collective.
Jacob Ludvigsen, 1971

From its inception, Christiania committed itself to developing a self-governing society based on active participatory democracy and dedicated to the goals of individual freedom and self-fulfillment. All of Freetown's residents are entitled to participate in the democratic process on an equal footing. Within the community's boundaries an overall consensus-based structure coordinates a federation of 15 autonomous geographic areas by means of an interlinking matrix of regular meetings.

Area Meetings
Each of the 15 areas the Loppe building, Fredens Ark, Praerien,

Tinghuset, Psyak, Maelkevejen, Fabriksområdet, Løvehuset, Mølkebøtten, Nordområdet, Den Blå Karamel, Bjørnekloen, Syddyssen, Midtdyssen, and Norddyssen holds its Area Meeting once a month. The areas vary dramatically in size and population, with the largest housing more than 80 Christianites and the smallest only 9. The Area Meeting discusses area concerns, including but not limited to: building maintenance, communal work days, applications for vacant dwellings, payments of utility fees and rents, personal interactions and grievances, and more general affairs of concern to Christiania as a whole. Everyone attending the meeting is entitled to a vote.

Each area elects a Treasurer who manages the area accounts, collects area fees and rents and then transfers them to Christiania's Common Purse, presents the area's plans and requests for funds to the Common Meeting, and acts as a kind of area representative.

The House Meeting

The House Meetings are specific to Christiania's large communal dwellings. They cover issues of concern to that community group, and any disagreement that can't be resolved is referred to the appropriate Area Meeting.

The Common Meeting

Unless non-Christianites are specifically invited to attend, The Common Meeting is open only to residents of Christiania.

As a kind of parliament, The Common Meeting deals with issues of concern to all Christianites every permanent resident of Freetown is entitled to attend and has an equal vote and the right to be heard. In consultation with the areas, The Common Meeting develops and adopts the annual budget of the Common Purse, negotiates with the Danish Government, manages conflicts with the police, and decides how to implement the various consensus decisions that emerge from the collective debates. It also keeps the Freetown community informed regarding all the important issues in play at the time of each meeting.

As a kind of collective judicial body, serving as an arbitrator of last resort, The Common Meeting resolves all disputes, instances of violence, and issues that can't be resolved at any of the other meetings. Common Meeting decisions are reached by absolute consensus, and are accepted by the community as the final word.

The Treasurers' Meeting

Once a month all 15 Treasurers meet with Christiania's Economy Group to develop the area economic plans and to discuss maintenance and housing strategy. The Economy Group provides up-to-the-minute financial information and coordinates feedback from The Common Meeting.

The Economy Meeting

The Economy Group administers Christiania's Common Purse and manages all collective common institutions and activities, including: the children's institutions, general renovation, electricity and water supply, building maintenance, community infrastructure, postal services, the information office, the health clinic, etc. The Economy Meeting takes place once a month and is open to all Christianites. Its agenda covers institutional accounts, payments from and licensing of community businesses, and applications for project and activity funding. It also maintains a running discussion of current problems, work group activities, and interactions with the nearby Christianshavn neighborhood council.

The Business Meeting

The Economy Group sponsors The Business Meeting once a month at a different business site, with the schedule rotating in turn among the businesses. The Business Meeting offers the businesses an opportunity to discuss common problems, to negotiate their payments to the Common Purse, to settle on rights of use, and to vet and endorse new businesses.

The Associates' Meeting

The Associates' Meeting is the forum central to running each of Christiania's collectively organized businesses. A particular business's Associates' Meeting is normally held once a week and concerns issues specific to that business.

The Building Meeting

The Building Meeting is held once a month and is Christiania's Technical Administration. Representatives from all 15 areas attend, as do all the people involved in running the Building Office and building-related institutions, with representative members from at least 7 areas required to form a basic voting quorum. The Building Meeting prioritizes building projects and tasks and determines the use of Building Office funds. The Building Office is funded from Christiania's Common Purse.

The Common Purse

The Common Purse was one of the first institutional instruments Christiania adopted. As the structure of the collectivity's

common economy evolved, The Common Purse developed from a cigar box filled with donations to a multi-million kroner financial management strategy. Christiania pays the same municipal rates and taxes paid by other citizens of Copenhagen. It also finances its own renovation projects, all electricity and water consumption, the maintenance of its children's institutions, a postal service, the Building Office, and the Machine Hall (which maintains the collective's mechanical equipment).

The Common Purse is funded by residential rents, a communal "subscription," meter-regulated consumption rates, payments from businesses, and a common internal VAT.

Distribution of Common Purse funds is decided at an Annual Budgetary Common Meeting. Because all decisions are consensus based, the budget meeting frequently lasts several sessions before an acceptable balance of disbursement is determined.

If funds are low, The Common Purse resorts to a carefully determined list of priorities: all taxes and external expenses are paid first, with internal institutions, projects, and area coffers dividing the remaining balance according to a predetermined distribution plan. This strategy has afforded Christianites the weird distinction of having politicians and municipal and state authorities proclaim them "model citizens" who pay all consumption rates and taxes in full and on time.

For many years The Common Purse has also maintained a separate savings account earmarked to cover unforeseen expenses and catastrophes. In 2004, Christiania's Common Purse budget amounted to approximately 18 million Danish Kroner.

A CHRISTIANIA TIMELINE

1969/70

Residents of Christianshavn, a neighborhood in eastern Copenhagen, breach a fence at the corner of Princessegade and Refshalevej, invading an abandoned 85-acre naval base to construct a playground for their children.

1971

When the Copenhagen Police demolish a flourishing nearby squat, the squatters occupy the former naval base, naming it Freetown and broadcasting a call for settlers throughout Denmark's active Squatters' Movement. *Hovedbladet* (Head Magazine) exhorts Copenhagen to "Emigrate with bus number 8." Hundreds of settlers from as far away as The New Society's Jutland camp at Thy respond.

Christiania is born.

Police try to evict the squatters, but there are too many and the issue ends up in the Danish Parliament.

1972

The Christianites negotiate with the Ministry of Defense and are officially designated a "social experiment." As part of the agreement, the government opens a competition calling for ideas for future use of the site. The "social experiment" will continue until a plan for future use is settled on.

1973

A new right-leaning Danish government declares that Christiania must go. Christiania's theater troupe, *Solvognen* (Chariot of the Sun), responds by crashing Copenhagen's June 1973 NATO conference with a Happening they call *Five Days for Peace*. They so successfully disrupt the conference that Christiania becomes a central player in the Danish Peace Movement. (Nils Vest's film *Five Days for Peace*, 1973, documents the events. [English-language version, 2007])

Within Christiania an overarching political structure is emerging. By consensus, different areas of the base organize into autonomous units, with The Common Meeting of all autonomous units serving as the highest authority for all residents. A base-wide "Garbage Team" institutes fundamental recycling programs, and various performance venues focus community activities.

1974

Government-directed police harassment resumes [documented in Nils Vest's film Lov & Orden i Christiania, 1 (Law & Order in Christiania, 1)]. The Christianites forge the electoral pact "Valgborgs Favn" and win a seat on the municipal council for Women's List candidate Tine Schmedes. At Christmas, Chariot of the Sun's Christmas Army invades Copenhagen's department stores, distributing free gifts to the masses. Images of Danish police officers bludgeoning Santa Claus hit the international media.

1975

Contention over Christiania breaks out between the City of Copenhagen and the Government of Denmark, with the Danish Parliament declaring that Freetown will be cleared of squatters by 1 April 1976. Chariot of the Sun responds with "Elverhøj," a theater piece parodying the government. With 40 sold-out performances, Elverhøj becomes the most successful Danish theater event of the year.

Inside Freetown, communal baths and the first children's center appear, recycling and composting programs advance, and communal shops and work shops come into

being. A first Annual Christmas Dinner for Copenhagen's poor is instituted. (In 2008, the event served thousands of people.)

1976

Christiania brings a "breach of promise" action against the Danish Government, insisting that no eviction can be legal until the terms of the 1972 agreement with the Ministry of Defense are implemented. The community is ably defended by prominent left-wing lawyer Carl Madsen. When a general call for support is broadcast, thousands of ordinary Danish citizens respond, mobilizing as the rainbow army. April 1 comes and goes and Christiania remains.

1977

Christiania loses its case but appeals to the Supreme Court. A gargantuan work party cleans and repairs Freetown's infrastructure. The "Love and Chaos" exhibition opens at the Royal Danish Academy of Fine Art, and Our Music appears, a CD featuring music and poetry by Christianites.

1978

Denmark's Supreme Court rejects Christiania's case. In the municipal elections Christiania again wins a seat on the council. Its new representative rails publicly against property speculators and bulldozer slum clearances, and Parliament proposes a local area plan that will lead to "normalization."

By 1978, hashish and heroin have permeated Denmark's social fabric. Since its inception, Christiania has supported hash as its visionary vehicle of choice. Dealers on Pusher Street sell hash publicly and contribute to Christiania's Common Purse, assisting in the maintenance and improvement of community facilities.

Beginning in the late '70s, the Danish police instigate a clandestine operation to overwhelm Freetown. Junkies and other hard drug users are not prosecuted if they agree move to Christiania. Christianites house the users and provide them with medical treatment, but the influx of hard drugs alarms them. To expel the heroin dealers, they cooperate with the police in an action to clear the community of hard drugs. The police betray Christiania's trust by ignoring the heroin and attacking the Pusher Street hash market instead.

1979/80
Christiania terminates its alliance with the police and institutes a "blockade against junk." Hard drug users are forced to accept rehab or leave the community. Dealers are bodily ejected. Chariot of the Sun stages the musical "White Castle," which traces the heroin economy's connection to the arms industry.

1981
The Danish Government employs Møller and Grønborg, a consulting firm, to work out a plan for future use. The consultants recommend that Christiania be allowed to develop as an experimental city maintaining a large degree of autonomy. The community is left to evolve in peace.

When, later in 1981, Sweden's conservative government smears Christiania as the narcotics capital of Europe and the root of all evil, Christianites respond with a "Love Sweden" action, flooding the streets of Stockholm, Göteborg, and Malmö with parades, cabarets, and art exhibitions.

1986
Christiania publishes "*Voilà*," a report demonstrating how, given tax relief for its businesses, Freetown is capable of maintaining its common infrastructure and institutions.

1987
The Danish Government appoints an intermediary management group and puts forth a plan for "legalizing" Christiania. The Ministry of Defense has all the chimneys and roofs renovated.

1989
The instrumental nature of the government's "legalization" and "normalization" rhetoric becomes

89

clear. Overturning the group license under which they had previously operated, "legalization" imposes individual licenses on Freetown's bars and performance venues. "Normalization" divides Christiania into "rural" and "urban" areas. The rural areas will be cleared of dwellings. The urban area may continue its social experiment.

Inside Christiania, hash dealers at the main gate are becoming aggressive. In a fit of fury, Christiania's women wall up the main gate and draw a yellow line across Pusher Street, permanently restricting the limits of the hash market.

1990

The Ministry of Defense appoints a Christiania Secretariat, which publishes its "Aims and Means of Legalizing the Christiania Area." Recognizing the threat in the partition strategy, Christianites reply with 90 objections to the government proposal. Nils Vest releases the film *Christiania You Have My Heart.*

1991

As part of its 20th Anniversary Celebrations, Christiania replies to the Ministry of Defense plan by publishing a visionary alternative Green Plan. The Green Plan proposes an ecologically sustainable urbanism with a super-efficient infrastructure in which water and usable trash are recycled, organic waste is composted, energy derives from renewable sources, and energy-efficient dwellings include houseboats on the moat and rammed earth and turf structures. As a first step, Christiania's maintenance team renovates Freetown's original water system, reducing waste and cost within the community. (The resident population has risen to 700, more than 200 of them children.)

1992

The Ministry of Defense increases the rent. When the Copenhagen Council refuses to pay full housing benefits/subsidies to Freetown's new businesses, Christiania publishes its collective budget, documents the financing of all its "public" institutions, and installs utilities-consumption meters on all businesses. The Council releases the benefits.

Responding to active outreach by Christiania, international tourists begin visiting the community. In September, in an attempt to clear Freetown of hash, the Copenhagen Police institutes a special 70-officer Christiania Patrol, which keeps the community under round-the-clock surveillance. Violent police tactics traumatize the Christianites, particularly the children.

1993

Documented by the media and overseen by lawyers, widespread dialogue concerning the excessive violence opens between Christiania, the Christianshavn neighborhood, Amnesty International, the Parliamentary Justice Commission, the Christiania Secretariat, and the Copenhagen Police. The Research Institute of the Counties and Municipalities undertakes a study of Christiania, concluding that the community is exemplary and that Denmark and the world can learn from its strategies and experience. Nevertheless, the Christiania Patrol continues.

1994

In anticipation of an upcoming UN Copenhagen Social Summit, the ministers of Defense and Justice declare that Christiania will be shut down if the hash market is not dealt with. Christianites respond by advocating an enlightened policy that differentiates between hard and soft drugs. Amnesty International and the Danish Nurses Association point to video documentation of illegal police violence. When Parliament reenacts its previous drug policy, Christiania conducts the world's first "hash strike." For five days, dealers and their customers and supporters file petitions and hold massive smoke-ins and demonstrations throughout

Copenhagen. After the world press and the Minister of Justice visit Freetown to "observe" the phenomenon, the Christiania Patrol is disbanded. Christiania takes part in the UN Conference and welcomes visiting international activists.

1995

To accommodate its increasing population of children Christiania builds the *Rosinhuset* (Raisin House), its fourth major children's institution. The Ministry of Defense declares Christianites "model citizens" when it comes to payment for public utilities. With the establishment of www.christiania. org, Freetown becomes a virtual village.

1996

Christiania celebrates its 25th Anniversary by agreeing on a development plan that includes elements of both the Ministry of Defense's 1989 plan and the Green Plan.

1997

Christiania institutes its own currency, the Løn, which is valued at 50 Danish Kroner and is legal tender for all transactions inside Freetown's boundaries. The community also initiates Denmark's most broadly-based ongoing discussion of the "problems" related to hashish and marijuana [documented in

Law & Order in Christiania, 2]. (In 2001, the discussions conclude with unconditional endorsement for a revised drug policy by representatives of the police, the judiciary, the medical community, the academy, the agricultural lobby, and the arts community.)

2000

A new generation of activist businesses has taken root. Christiania Bikes is world famous, and the ALIS Skateboard Company has built and maintains Wonderland, Northern Europe's largest indoor skateboarding facility. Christiania Radio is active, and the Loppen Cultural Center is recognized as an important regional musical venue by the Ministry of Culture. Bob Dylan performs two sold-out concerts in Christiania's Den Grå Hal venue.

2001

As Christiania celebrates its 30th Anniversary, Denmark elects a right-wing government which aims at a total normalization of Freetown. The new government's redefinition of "normalization" insists on individual ownership of all Christiania property and the construction of 300 new dwellings, thus destroying the communal land base that sustains Freetown's collectivity. At the 30th Anniversary Party, Chariot of the Sun resurrects music and songs from Elverhøj. Guests, friends, and supporters from all over the world gather for a week of festivities.

2003

Copenhagen's Society for the Beautification of the Capital recognizes Christiania's long and tireless effort to create and develop alternative accommodations. Denmark's Grassroots Foundation bestows its Jubilee Prize on the Christiania Cultural Society.

In an attempt to satisfy the conditions of the 1989 agreement, the government arranges a competition calling for ideas for the future use of Christiania's land base. (No "architect of merit" enters, and the competition is deemed a failure.) In response to the obvious attack, the Christianites publish *Christiania at Work: From Vision to Reality*, and Nils Vest releases *Lov & Orden i Christiania, 2* (Law & Order in Christiania, 2), which documents the new threat of closure. The original main gate is reopened and Christiania declares an Open House. Nearly 100,000 Danes attend. The government retaliates by sending a police force to reoccupy Freetown.

2004

According to a Gallup Poll, 75% of Copenhagen's citizens want Christiania preserved. In an effort to ensure Freetown's survival, the hash dealers remove their booths from Pusher Street. The City of

Copenhagen appoints a former Freetown resident as its Special Christiania Consultant. Ignoring the gestures of solidarity, the National government transfers responsibility for Christiania from the Ministry of Defense to the Ministry of Finance.

With support from its neighbors, Christiania establishes an "embassy" in Christianshavn. A team of lawyers and activists proposes the creation of a foundation to secure Freetown's autonomy and preserve its collective rights of use and development. A petition signed by more than 100,000 Danes urges that Christiania continue as a social experiment in self-government. The Royal Danish Academy of Fine Arts agrees. But the Danish government passes a law abolishing the collective, treating its 900 members as individuals. Christiania's newest adversary becomes a bureaucratic commission from the Palaces and Properties Agency.

2005
After Christianites stage a series of protests, the police begin to patrol Freetown 4 to 6 times daily. Each patrol consists of between 6 and 20 officers dressed for combat and sometimes accompanied by dogs. (In 2006, the number on an outdoor board recording the patrols exceeds 1000.)

2006
The government directs that Christiania become a "mixed alternative community and residential area" and proposes that condominiums be built to house 400 new residents. Christiania rejects the directive, countering with a community-driven proposal that is awarded the Initiative Award of the Society for the Beautification of Copenhagen. Its sustainability goals and democratic process receive endorsement from the municipality of Copenhagen and the Agenda 21 Society.

2007
Incorporating material from the Christiania plan, a negotiating group assembled by Copenhagen's mayor proposes a deal. A few newer structures will be razed to restore the Bastion ramparts to their original 17th century condition. The government will then sell the rest of Christiania at below market rate to the philanthropic investor/developer Realdania, which will lease the properties at far-below-market rates to Christiania's residents via a housing foundation on whose board Christianites will have the majority vote. The new Freetown will be managed by two "sister" nonprofits, with one controlling commercial, cultural, and social institutions, and the other managing 24,000 square meters of new construction that Realdania will finance and design as an

experimental "laboratory" for green architecture and engineering. Christianites balk at the loss of their collective land base.

2008

The Palaces and Properties Agency loses patience and petitions the Danish High Court for permission to evict Christiania. When police remove an "illegal structure," the Christianites riot. Using the common law right to "property by adverse possession," Christiania petitions the Danish High Court to regain control over its affairs.

2009

Denmark's Eastern High Court affirms that the government can clear Christiana.

Despite all the legal distractions, members of Chariot of the Sun manage to organize the *Climate Bottom Meeting: Windows of Hope* as an alternative to the 2009 Copenhagen Climate Summit (COP15). (See: climatebottom.dk/en)

In 2011 the Christianites managed to purchase Christiania from the Danish government and were able to keep their land base intact.

For a clear assessment of Christiania's current political situation, read Charles Hayes "Can Christiania Survive? A Countercultural Enclave in Denmark Fights for its Life," in *Reason Magazine*, March 2009; online at reason.com/archives

Compiled by Jordan Zinovich from the *Christiania Guide*, *The Copenhagen Post* online, *IceNews*, reason.com, and Wikipedia, and with input from conversations with Chritianites Britta Lillasøe, Nils Vest, and Frants Pandal. Prepared for *Radical Urbanism 2009*, at The Center for Place, Culture & Politics, CUNY Graduate Center, 10 December 2009; with final update.

Reproposed fortifications in Christiania

Christiania Art and Culture

Britta Lillesøe,
Christiania Cultural Association

"Live life artistically!" These are the words of one of Christiania's many painters. And those words speak for the Freetown. Because Christiania is an artist town. Not only for 'real artists'—artists in the common understanding—but for people expressing themselves artistically in everyday life—in small and big things—and in ordinary things. If you see a hole in the asphalt on the road, maybe next day it will be filled with marble mosaic pieces or glazed tiles from another of our artists. And one of our scrap artists, who from recycled and scrap materials—iron, bicycle tires—makes the most beautiful chairs, sofas and tables. Furniture which are functional and at the same time artistic in shape. They are real sculptures, exposed for public use around in the Freetown, in many squares and places. Beauty is just as important as function.

Do you have to ask the municipality if you can exhibit your creative abilities? No, here it is the close environment that decides. Culture binds us together. And with almost 800 grown-ups and 200 children we have a lot of different combinations. From here grow both artists and life-artists. In Christiania, if you have a good idea, then most of the time it is not the money which governs, but the strength of the idea and the spirit. It is a place where young people can make theatre, play music, paint, do workshops—or maybe organise an event— and they only have to pay for the heating and electricity. They can do that in several of the beautiful common rooms and areas of the Freetown.

Christiania is nearly the last bastion of culture. Here we always have—quite naturally—managed to blend so-called resource-weak and resource-strong inhabitants. Something which rarely happens in other places. It is therefore a very contradictory place. But the positive meeting of contradictions creates flowering and growth. This positive meeting can support artistic everyday life, the basis for many different expressions. We have a natural environment with many spaces where people can meet and exchange ideas. And it is in this way that new projects are born. You can also describe Christiania as one big cultural workshop, which helps to fill the cultural void of contemporary Denmark.

Yes, the Freetown has a very rich cultural life with a lot of associations, clubs, music venues, theatres, galleries, meeting places, a cinema, several sound studios, a radio and television station, many different art workshops, blacksmiths, carpenters, music and dance groups, indoor and outdoor skate ramps, night church and much much more. A lot of working artists live in Christiania, more than 50 painters, sculptors and similar, actors, singers, DJs, dancers, choreographers, theatre and film directors, light and sound artists, installation artists, designers, scenographers, architects, photographers, poets, writers, playwrights, composers and a lot of active musicians and bands who contribute to an overwhelming and colorful music scene. We are at the same time artists and organizers.

The Freetown is becoming a mix of Paris' Montmartre in the last part of the 19th century and a village in Bali—with a little drop of the golden age and the Skagen painters.

Christiania is a living work of art and an artistic place to live. A BIOTOP in the middle of the big city. A unity between humans, animals, plants, houses—life being lived. This artwork can be worked on further. But from the artworks soul itself.

Bolsjefabrikken: Autonomous Culture in Copenhagen

Tina Steiger

In recent years one of Copenhagen's most vibrant places for the production of underground and alternative culture has been a series of houses each known as Bolsjefabrikken—the Candy Factory.

When Jagtvej 69 was evicted, the protests mobilized a lot of the city's creative forces and people came together in various constellations, ultimately forming the nucleus of the first Candy Factory
"Sarah," Activist

It all began when a group of artists, activists and craftsmen in 2008 used the premise of an abandoned candy factory to set up workshops, studios and host parties. When they were kicked out, they sought out another empty building in the neighborhood - put on nice clothes, drafted a proposal and asked the owner to use the premises. Since then the collective has been housed at the nearby Lærkevej, and later the municipally owned facilities at Ragnhildgade.

Although not squatted, this series of autonomous and self-managed culture houses has many similarities with occupied social centers found across Europe. The aesthetics of the buildings and their interior spaces, the horizontal and participatory organizational structure, and the non-commercial ideology and DIY production of culture bear a striking resemblance to the activities and productions emanating from squatted projects.

AESTHETICS

The wooden fence along the garden is plastered with posters, and the house appears as an explosion of color amidst the red brick apartment

98

buildings of the surrounding Nordvest neighborhood on the northern periphery Copenhagen's inner city. Brightly colored graffiti cover the walls and a hand painted sign gives a list of instructions:

Respect your neighbors, they live here.
No noise after 22.00
Graffiti only on our own buildings
Working-process: Begin, stop & clean up!
Always clean up twice as much you've been messing up.
Save electricity
Take part in the community
Remember to kiss hug and acknowledge each other.

Inside the yard, a striped door reads "Free Shop + Info Point" while hammering noises emanate from within a workshop. A bold graffiti mural across the main façade of the building reads "Bolsjefabrikken," and the windows of the top floor seem to be boarded up from within.

A heap of bicycles lean against each other, cargo bikes filled with scrap wood, psychedelic colored flower beds and curved benches are arranged in front of the house. From above, a metal ventilation pipe bends down from the roof, blowing smoke into the yard below.

Once inside the main building, the scent of stale cigarettes, beer and lingering vegetarian food prevails. The walls are covered in tags and stickers, and the floors are worn and dirty. A dining room leads to a self-built kitchen, equipped to serve up to 60 people during the people's kitchen on Friday nights.

Like many squats, everything is built according to functionalist, transparent and do-it-yourself attitudes - both the interior and the furniture are makeshift, raw, without unnecessary accessories.

ORGANIZATION

Its not like the house is political, but many find ideas of anarchy attractive.
"Martin", activist

The activities within Bolsjefabrikken are organized by principles of direct democracy, cooperation, solidarity and mutual aid, something the activists have termed the 'Do-It-Together' philosophy. It's a form of DIY culture and direct action, which places emphasis on mutual aid and collectivity.

During the general assembly, all decisions are made which affect the entire house at Lærkevej, here at least one member from each workshop group attends to discuss upcoming events, pays into the collective utility fund, and is able to discuss general problems.

The decision-making structure is non-hierarchical, and everyone attending the assemblies is expected to invest patience and time into deliberations in order to reach consensus and the best possible outcome for the collective. Discussions are organized by means of agenda setting, a facilitator and hand motions allow for everyone to voice their opinion, while a note-taker ensures that resolutions from the meetings are recorded.

Like many squats, Bolsjefabrikken also experiments with alternative economies and forms of exchange by recycling and re-using objects made available in the city. This is mostly done by dumpster diving food, harvesting building materials from construction sites, and refurbishing bike parts, machines or other technical equipment. The Free Store allows anyone to take what they need, and bring what they no longer have use for. Production at Bolsjefabikken is not driven by competition, but rather by working together, and up-cycling materials that would otherwise be thrown away.

CULTURE

All three of the Bolsjefabrikken centers have had a vibrant production of non-commercial culture, spanning a wide spectrum from music and media, theater, performance and visual arts, to workshops for sewing, screenprinting, woodworking and bicycles. It has contributed significantly to the alternative and socially critical cultural scene in Copenhagen, while functioning as a node in an international network of leftist activists.

Embedded in the local neighborhood, while remaining autonomously organized, Bolsjefabrikken at Lærkevej provided space for a range of socially critical collectives and initiatives to emerge. For example, KAOS TV, a group of media activists who were always on the spot for documenting pirate parties and demonstrations, were based in the top floor. The open bike workshop "Røde Hammer" not only freely provided tools, spare parts and advice to the public, but also organized an annual bicycle festival exhibiting their penchant for tall bikes. The serigraphy workshop became known for their detailed and unique handmade posters announcing concerts, events and parties taking place at Bolsjefabrikken

The "M.O.R.F.A.R" (Grandad) collective with its mobile sound system sparked spontaneous street parties throughout the city, and the wood workshop with its connection to the architectural intervention collective "Bureau Detours" built benches, swings and other installations in public space. "Biblioteket" (the Library) offered space for relaxation and a board game club, while the basement bar "John" reverberated with heavy bass during parties. On the second floor, the cinema "Kvidrekassen"—furnished with recycled cinema chairs—showed provocative documentaries as well as political and quirky films. The list continues, to include sewing workshops, ateliers, a photography darkroom, garden, people's kitchen, recording studio and common rooms in which countless events, meetings, concerts, and support parties have taken place.

The Galleri Stald, the former stable of the premises, was transformed into Copenhagen's first free supermarket during the "Taste the Waste" exhibition. Bolsjefabrikken activists wearing supermarket aprons bustled among the neatly arranged produce baskets filled with apples, bananas, potatoes, carrots and other foods. Signs advertised "100% Rabat" (100% discount) and a cashier bagged the groceries of exhibition visitors turned grocery shoppers. It was a supermarket redistributing food that would otherwise be thrown away. The exhibition boldly raised awareness about the abundant food waste in Danish society, while actively engaging people to use it.

In 2009, Bolsjefabrikken became a vital organizing space for almost 2,000 alter-globalization activists who came to Copenhagen for the COP15 Climate Summit. When the Occupy Wall Street movement ignited demonstrations worldwide as a reaction to the global economic crisis, Bolsjefabrikken activists were vital in providing skills, materials and experience to support the movement for the Copenhagen Occupy Camp,

In the summer of 2012, Distortion Festival, an annual five-day party tsunami which originated from illegal street parties became increasingly commercialized and mainstream, attracting over 100,000 people by the summer of 2012. Bolsjefabrikken offered an alternative. Since 2011, they have hosted the parallel "Dxtortion Festival" with cheap beer, free concerts and after-parties, as an alternative to the increasingly expensive and commercially sponsored Distortion Festival.

Time and again, Bolsjefabrikken has contributed to solidarity demonstrations, protests and actions supported by the broader autonomous movement with their playful, festive and yet critical appeal. They have been able to temporarily inhabit buildings, by pragmatically approaching the owners and even the municipality, to create spaces of autonomy. In some ways, the collectives active in Bolsjefabrikken present a sweetened, more cooperative generation of the Copenhagen squatter movement and autonomous scene.

Denmark

This article is based on interviews and research conducted during my master thesis, completed with the UNICA Euromaster in Urban Studies. For more information about Bolsjefabrikken visit their website at www. bolsjefabrikken.com.

On the Youth House Protests and the Situation in Copenhagen

Mikkel Bolt Rasmussen

During the last year Copenhagen has been the scene for hundred of demonstration as well as riots following the raiding of the Youth House that took place on March 1 2007 when Danish police forces stormed the house at Jagtvej 69. The raiding was conducted in a very brutal and spectacular manner, with helicopters in the streets around the youth house.

BARRICADED STREETS

Within the next few hours after the police action, young people started building barricades by pushing dumpsters into the street and as the police tried to remove them they were meet with stones. At around five o'clock that day thousands of protesters went into the streets fighting broke out between the police and protesters who set cars on fire trying to take over the streets of Nørrebro, the neighbourhood where the Youth House was situated. In the next days more and more people including young kids of Arab descendent hit the streets and joined the demonstrations that spread to Christianshavn where the hippy free city Christiania is located. Cars were burned and barricades kept being set up faster than the police could remove them. Peaceful demonstrations as well as violent clashes with the police and the thrashing of a high school took place. It was not just the usual political activists that were out in the streets, thousands of young people joined the protests out of frustrations with the direction that Danish society has been heeding for the last decade. The Danish police had to get help from the Swedish police in order to handle the problem and policemen from all over the country were sent to Copenhagen.
　　Throughout the entire process the police did not hold back in their

use of force: they broke up demonstrations by firing large amounts of illegal, deadly teargas into them, they arrested hundreds of people with or without relation to the events, they searched a number of addresses without search warrant, and they repeatedly beat up protesters. This however did not prevent thousands of youngsters from showing their discontent in the streets. Politicians and so-called 'experts' on social affairs were busy, of course, distancing themselves from what was going on; dismissing the protests as the work of juvenile troublemakers and refusing to consider the question as a political problem.

But, as the continuous protests demonstrated, these explanations were completely wrong. Although there has been a decrease in activities lately, people are still protesting and there are still demonstrations at least once a week every Thursday. If somebody thought that the battle for a new youth house would quickly die out. or that the youth house only mattered to a few hundred of activists, they were wrong. The protest movement is so confident that it publicly announced in advance to the media that it would squat a specific house October 13th, 2007.[1] And although the police tried hard to prevent it, several hundred protesters out of a demonstration comprising more than 8,000 people actually managed to get past the police and into the house. This incident and others like it. all testify to the fact that there has occurred a kind of generalization of the struggle in Copenhagen: More and more people support the fight for a new youth house and for the right to live another life, different from the one supplied by the ruling order of work, family and ever new commodities.

RACISM AND NEO-LIBERALISM IN DENMARK

The widespread support for the fight for a new youth house has to do with the so-called "normalization campaign" that has been sweeping across the country for the last seven years. Ever since the elections in 2001. where the liberal candidate Anders Fogh Rasmussen formed a government backed by the extreme right wing party, The People's Party, the political system in Denmark has developed a peculiar mixture of democracy, racism and chauvinism. A kind of national democratic authenticity totalitarianism primarily expressed as a cultivation of authenticity and hatred towards foreigners.[2] Having won the election in 2001, Fogh Rasmussen launched the so-called 'battle of culture' aimed at the left and Muslims alike. We have seen a steadily growing repression of various groups that somehow do not fit the dominant vision of Danish identity. The eviction at the youth house and the following events have, along with the Mohammed drawings, been the most visible signs of this campaign against alternative life forms. Excessive use of violence and criminalization of formerly accepted expressions and actions have been the order of the day. This local development is of course linked to a global process which, although currently termed "the war on terror", actually constitutes an extensive neoliberal counterrevolution expanding the power of a closely defined capitalist power.

The campaign against foreigners may seem strange, as Denmark is one of the least mixed countries in the Western world. Denmark has had very limited immigration as the country, even before 2001. had very severe immigration laws. But because politics has been reduced to authenticity in Denmark, the idea of a multicultural society has become a threat. The challenge of globalization has been met with entrenchment. The Muhammad cartoons epitomized the cultural crusade against Muslim migrants. The cartoons were not at all about free speech, they were yet another attempt by the right wing newspaper *Jyllands Posten* to demonize Muslims. The mishandling of the affair by the Danish prime minister was symbolic of the attitude towards foreigners that are perceived as unwilling to 'integrate' into Danish society.

Cultural heterogeneity and cosmopolitan sensibility is not an option for the minority government as it depends on the support of the explicitly racist *Dansk Folkeparti* (Danish People's Party). *Dansk Folkeparti* gained thirteen seats in the Parliament in 1998 after a campaign based exclusively on the hatred of foreigners. This situation forced not only the other right wing parties, but also the Social Democratic government, to react. The Social Democrats choose to enter the fight for racist votes and tightened the immigration rules several times after June 1998. Already at that time it became common for politicians to throw suspicion at foreigners using a very brutal language. Several Danish newspapers helped pave the way for this development by publishing 'exposures' of migrants' 'misuse' of the Danish social security system.

With the "State of War" proclaimed by the American President [Bush] after September 11th [2001], where the question of a global equality between rich and poor countries was transformed into a war against terror, racism was finally legitimized in Denmark. Fogh Rasmussen's right wing party won the election and took over the government supported by *Dansk Folkeparti* that got 12 percent of the votes. Unlike in France, where it was possible to isolate *Front National*, *Dansk Folkeparti* participated in the composition of the new right-wing government's program. Of crucial importance in this program were new restrictions in immigration making it very difficult to gain asylum in Denmark. But the launch of the defence of the Occident against Muslim immigration was just one component of the new government's politics. Another one consisted in siding with George W. Bush and his war on terror. The Danish government was there right next to Bush and Blair, invading Afghanistan and then Iraq. Danish troops have taken part in operations in both countries. According to the Danish prime minister, being against a Danish participation in the invasion of Iraq was the same as being Saddam Hussein's ally. Whenever someone during this bloody occupation of Iraq has tried to question the Danish participation in the operation, they were told that they were playing the terrorists' game.

The xenophobic campaign against Muslim immigrants was accompanied by an attack on seemingly everything left wing in Denmark. According to the government and *Dansk Folkeparti* the country is in need of a cleansing of old left wing and 1968 ideas that threaten to destroy the Danish community in favour of a multicultural society. To an

unprecedented extent the government has tried to put pressure on a number of public institutions like state television and universities wanting them to distance themselves from what the government perceives to be dangerous 68ist currents. Former employees from the state television have reported drastic increase in attempts to influence programming, and the university system is currently going through a changeover where corporate ideas are replacing classical notions of *Bildung* and autonomy. Funding for schools and hospitals are being reduced. In this situation, where the government is involved in a thoroughgoing attempt to make hegemonic a particular Danish neo-conservatism, both the Youth House and Christiania have been thorns in the side of the right wing parties that constitute the government. In their own ways the two places have been able to create alternative communities with values different from the ones the government is promoting.

FIGHTING BACK

In a way it might seem strange that it took so long before a reaction manifested itself in Denmark. But even though the Fogh Rasmussen government since 2001 has promoted a Danish national democracy expressed as racism along with complete support for the US-led 'war on terror', hatred towards the intelligentsia the left, political correctness and of course Islam, it took the raiding of the youth house to prompt action in the streets. The big demonstrations in May 2006, where more than 100,000 people protested against the government's welfare cuts, were easily channelled into the existing political system's traditional logic of exchange and thereby neutralized; at that time it proved impossible to introduce something new and it was easy for the Social Democratic party to falsely stage the protests as merely a wish for a new government, rather than a wish for a break with the current and entire political establishment which caused this situation in the first place. But the demonstrations in 2006 do testify to a growing discontent among large sections of the Danish population who had until then remained passive. So far it has remained difficult to connect the different protests, protesting welfare cuts and the fight for a new youth house, and so far no one has really got involved in each other's battles, added anti-racism and resistance to the war with critique of the government's neo-liberal policy.

That is one of the problems right now: there is no coherent resistance. The protests in favour of the youth house are thus far completely disconnected from what is going on in the workshops around the country. Thus there is a deep abyss between the street and the

shop floor. The militancy of the street has not been able to expand itself into militancy other places. The fight for a new youth house is not yet connected to a wider resistance encompassing rejection of the process of normalization and the racist national democracy, which the neoliberal forces are trying to create in Denmark. And the protests against the raiding of the Youth House are thus not understood as the result of long-term counter organizing that finally began to bear fruit, but are seen as more a question of being enough for a critical mass of people. This is without a doubt one of the tasks that lie in front of us: to formulate a coherent critique in which the individual objects of critique are not separate but joined together in a radical critique of the capitalist system and its money and state form. Confronted with the repressive movements of the Danish state that seeks to represent all critique as terrorism, is it necessary to politicize the protests even further and give them a powerful voice in the present consensual political atmosphere.

The situation demands careful consideration. Becoming militant necessitates a discussion of goals and means and requires the development of a new language and new strategies combining critique, creativity and illegal actions. Many insist that non-violent actions are the only right ones. But in this situation, I think, it would be inopportune to rule out the use of violence in the form of property destruction (banks and corporate headquarters) or squatting. Indeed violence in this situation is to be understood as a premonition of the far greater conflict that will inevitably occur if we do not succeed in blocking militarized neoliberal capitalism and its attempt to hold on to wealth and power by means of control, market expansions, a provocatory public sphere, "white health" and extreme tourism. After the protests last summer in Germany in connection with the G-8 summit. we witnessed the movement being divided into two fractions: a violent and a non-violent one. It is necessary to reject this division. The street battles in Copenhagen in March 2007 show that for the state there is really no difference between violent and non-violent protestors. The passers-by were arrested along with the more unruly elements, indiscriminately.

This is the important lesson for the local scene of what took place in the streets in Copenhagen last year. In this way the state tries to destroy not only the effectiveness of the protests on the street, but also the protestors' credibility in the media. The state knows very well that another world is possible and that the threat is real. Therefore the state tries to isolate the mere rebellious elements by using official institutions like unions and parties or different left wing groups connected to the political system. At the same time the state tries to reduce resistance as illegitimate non-political babble: "this is just the actions of irresponsible youngsters who have not been properly raised by their parents."[3] If this is not enough, the state creates a state of emergency setting up so-called visitation zones where people can be stopped and searched at random by the police without being suspected of any criminal activity, making everyday life difficult for ordinary people. If it is not possible to identify and control the unruly elements, whole neighborhoods are closed down.

This took place in Nørrebro and Christianshavn in March 2007, and it is happening again right now in other neighborhoods in Copenhagen. If it is not possible to catch the fish, the water is polluted. That is why groups within the Youth House movement launched the slogan, "we are all militants" In an attempt to reject the deamonization of the protests it is not possible to divide us into a black and a blue block. The protests are an expression of a general will to resistance and a common wish to do things that run counter to the interests of the state and are subversive with regard to capitalist valorization. It is necessary to move beyond the usual and recurrent attempts to distance oneself from militant resistance. That the established working class organizations and left wing parties participate in such a move is not a surprise. It just illustrates that they are closely linked to neoliberal restructuring that, according to David Harvey. has been taking place since Chile 1973.[5] It is not from them that we should expect any solution. They have no interest in seeking alternatives to the present order of things.

The automatic rejection of violence and militant resistance in favour of a non-violent critique risks consolidating the status quo and effectuates a falsification in so far as it is not possible to envisage a revolutionary movement that refrains from the use of violence in the battle against capitalism and the state. Denunciation of violence is opportunistic. It is either an attempt to gain acceptance in a consensual political public sphere where all radical expressions are derailed or recuperated, or it is a sign of a wrong and misguided understanding of the necessity of critiquing the ruling representations about violence and terror.

Naturally, every effort must be made to ensure that militancy does not reduce itself to the individualism of rebellion or end life. It is never the individual that is militant, it is the collective that uses militant measures in a political battle. Even if individual revolt, in certain situations, may present itself as morally effective it is always politically inexpedient and necessarily results in various mental short circuits where the fighting isolated individual sees himself as chosen and regards others as objects of mobilization. As if the mission was to force people into doing something. The task is never to organize others but to organize oneself with others. When individual militancy strives to rouse others by the use of violence through exemplary actions, it risks being caught up in a suicidal mirror trap in which power becomes nothing more than a homology to power.[6] Thus, the point is not to glorify violence—it is not certain that violence is a key ingredient in the foundation of a new society. But it is clearly stupid to imagine politics without violence. There is always a need to strike back in defence of the new.

NOTES

1 Cf. http://www.aktiong13.dk/

2 Cf. Mikkel Bolt Rasmussen: "Counterrevolutionary Times in Denmark", Mute, no. 24, 2002.

3 For an analysis of this kind of de-politicization, see Jacques Rancière, Disagreement: Politics and Philosophy, trans. Julie Rose (Minneapolis & London: University of Minnesota Press, 1998) and

idem: Hatred of Democracy, trans. Steve Corcoran (London & New York: Verso, 2006).

4 Cf. http://vierallemilitante. wikispaces.com/

5 David Harvey: A Brief History of Neoliberalism (Oxford: Oxford University Press, 2005).

6 That's of course one of the 'lessons' from 1970's terrorism. Cf. Oskar Negt: "Sozialistische Politik und Terrorismus", in

Heinrich Böll, Freimut Duve & Klaus Staeck (ed.): Briefe zur Verteidigung der Republik (Hamburg: Reinbek, 1977).

Reprinted from "On the Youth House Protests and the Situation in Copenhagen," by Mikkel Bolt Rasmussen, Journal of Aesthetics & Protest, no. 6, 2008, p. 222-226. Guest Edited by Team Colors Collective.

A mural by American artist Shepard Fairey at the former site of the Youth House (*Ungdomshuset*). The project lead to a contentious debate about the recuperation of political aesthetics and the instrumentalization of art in urban development.

113

United Kingdom

114

Partisan Notes Towards a History of UK Squatting (1980 to the Present)

x-Chris
56a Infoshop, London

OUR HISTORY: BUT WHO ARE WE?

The unorthodox bible of UK squat history is *Squatting: The Real Story* (1980). Since then no new detailed publication on the complex and ever changing histories of squatting and squat cultures in the UK has been produced. Published at the dawn of a whole new wave of squatting and new but often hybrid squatting cultures, it seems now vital that the more recent people's history of UK squatting demands to be written.

As squatting was never a criminal offence in the UK (until very recently), thousands of people have been squatters, each adding their own flavour to the ever-shifting discontents of squatting histories. This was mostly in the inner cities—Bristol, Birmingham, Brighton, Manchester, with London unsurprisingly as the squat capital of the UK, at least by number. A lot of those histories remain visible because the squatting movement produced a large body of flyers, newsletters, photos, and videos as well as a vast oral history that comes from the lived experience of those who were part of these scenes. A lot of this material is archived at places with long and strong connections to the squat scenes (e.g., 56a Infoshop, or Advisory Service for Squatters). Such material bears witness to the continuity of squatting as a political act, and its attendant processes and projects of how to collectively organize those acts. It also strongly shows how organising traditions have maintained themselves politically in UK squatting (local squat groups, legal groups, practical advice sessions and so on), and also how UK squatting culture and subculture re-invents itself continually around need and desire—squatted women's refuges, crèches [for childcare], bookshops, protest camps, art spaces, social centres, convergence centres, and so on.

But there are also thousands of people who squatted with little or no connection to the larger and more consciously political squatting scenes whose stories remain invisible. Those histories are just as urgent, and represent a class and ethnic composition of a much more marginalized group of squatters. Their invisible history often only surfaces at the point of contact between them and legal advice offered by more actively organized squatters groups. Or it just doesn't surface at all.

WE ARE HERE: BUT WHY?

The political landscape and ideology of the UK state has changed beyond recognition since the 1970s. Squatting then reflected the long wave of economic and political struggle that maintained itself from the late '60s to the early '90s. Squatting as a political strategy and as a means of survival was part and parcel of a wider housing struggle around council housing, fair rents, decent housing and also questions of cooperative and communal living. Organized family squatting and attempts to work with the local state (mostly mediated through local Labour party councils) sat cheek by jowl with attacks by a more radical edge on that local state, criticizing its social democratic function and pacification of class struggle. Good examples of the antagonisms and agonies around these differences can be read in the 1973-74 minutes of the All London Squatters Meetings (online) and in Allison Fell's novel *Every Move You Make* (1984). The documentary *Lefties: Property is Theft* about the squatters of Villa Road in Brixton in the 1970s (online) extends the differences further, as feminist, primal scream squatters battle entrenched male Trotskyist squatters for hegemonic victory. Although somewhat comic to view now, it's important to say that squatting also maintains itself as a site for experiment and the testing of freedoms, this being at its most important when the collective nature of squatting and squat culture is emphasized. The Gay Liberation Front squat at 78 Railton Road in Brixton in the mid-'70s could stand as a high point of how squatting can attempt to prefigure entirely new and radical social relations and unapologetically so.

By the mid-'80s it felt like the Left had dumped squatting as both a political project and as a practical solution to aspects of the housing crisis. This could be partly explained by the far Left parties' electoral successes in local cities. Upon taking power, these parties became virulently anti-squatting in supposed political defence of working class

117

council tenants (their electorate). But more so, the ever-narrowing political outlook in the UK, especially in the realm of housing, fed the disinterest in squatting as a radical strategy. Council housing as social housing was under attack as were the Labour councils who ran the areas with the most of it. Political struggles became more defensive, more pragmatic and much less radical or utopian. Organized squatting groups were more or less maintained and endlessly re-created by anarchists. Different modes include militant squat defence reflecting inspiration from Dutch and German autonomist movements (see Stamford Hill Estate resistance, 1988). Or, maintaining the idea of community as a basis for building mass squatting locally, the unwritten history of SNOW (Squatters Network of Walworth) from 1983 to 1988 stands as a great example of dogged local community work. Their TASCS (Tenants and Squatters Campaign of Southwark), working with council tenants demanding 'Homes for all', is also illustrative of this mode.

By the 1990s, squatting felt like it had become much more subcultural, and disconnected from the waning levels of class struggles around labour, welfare and housing, although it was never entirely severed. Squatting came to reflect protest culture (anti-roads, defense of rave culture, issues of globalization and what is nebulously called 'anti-capitalism' from 1999 onwards). Desires for personal freedom combined with a politics more likely to speak about environmental issues, or attacks by the state on the squatting lifestyle, or global struggles and solidarity with the Zapatistas, or Narmada dam in India (two examples). Squat politics slowly moved away from organizing with non-squatters from a shared position of struggle. Exceptions to this rule exist, such as the ARCH squat in Hackney in 1996 was established by long-term squat activists for refugees living in London with all the learning that comes from such practical acts of solidarity.

A state-sponsored moral panic around rave parties resulted in the strongly-contested Criminal Justice Act of 1994. As participants in one of the first popular subcultures that widened out questions of how we live and how we would like to live, thousands of young people experienced both the squatting of private property, the collective nature of this occupation, and its cultural experiments. Although this was probably less significant than the legacy of punk from the 1970s, with its politics and culture of autonomy, many people were affected politically by what they experienced and understood from rave, and took these understandings forward in their personal lives. Self-reflection on squatting culture itself was created at 1999's *Cultures Of Resistance* and 2000's *Cultures of Persistence* squatted exhibitions in London. In the early 2000s 'social

The Advisory Service for Squatters (ASS) Squatting Handbook

center' squats, modeled on the Italian '*centri sociali*' model of community-based centres, attempted to convene grounds for less subcultural places of political sharing and work around the material emergencies of daily life—precarious work, high rents, migration etc.

With the 'financial crisis' in 2007, and the slow but increasing austerity of the UK that pushed many into total survival mode, the politics and activisms of squatting has returned to its place in a wider housing and labour struggles. In 2012 the squatting of residential buildings was finally made a criminal offence. Squat groups and squatted centres have made explicit the connections of squatting to the wider housing crisis, and attempted both protest and local networked organizing around housing struggles.

Numerous squats (as free schools) also accompanied a mass of struggles around education in 2010–11. Squats have also been active against the continual gentrification of the UK's inner cities in ways that are antagonistic and not accommodating to gentrification processes. Culturally the rise of the 'art squat', particularly in London, has been a more difficult moment however in that dynamic reinsertion of squatting into more mainstream everyday struggles. Yet other dynamic self-promotions of squatting have been crucially sharp and focused on defending its history and endurance. *Squattastic* meetings held irregularly pulled in a loose association of many squatters and social centres around political desires for collectivity and resistance in response to the ban on residential squatting. From the same orbit, the *Made Possible By Squatting* exhibition in 2013 was conceived as a celebration of the myriad ways in which life today has been materially influenced by the last 50 years of UK squatting.

Another full circle can be seen in the 2014 empty council homes protest squat on the decanted Carpenters Estate in East London made by a collaboration of Focus E15 Mothers (former hostel residents threatened with being moved out of London), the Revolutionary Communist Group, Feminist Fightback, and activist squatters.

REFERENCES

56a Infoshop: http://56a.org.
uk/

Advisory Service For Squatters:
http://www.squatter.org.uk/

Squatting: The Real Story, Nick
Wates, Editor (1980).

The Local State, Cynthia
Cockburn (1977)

UK Squatting Archive: http://
www.wussu.com/squatting/
index.htm

Every Move You Make, Alison
Fell (novel; 1984)

Lefties: Property Is Theft, BBC
TV documentary series, 2007:
https://www.youtube.com/
watch?v=Erp2utEgZp4

Squattastic: http://squattastic.
blogspot.co.uk/

Made Possible By Squatting:
http://www.madepossiblebys-
quatting.co.uk/

Carpenters Estate Squat, 2014:
http://www.theguardian.com/
commentisfree/2014/oct/05/
focus-e15-mums-fight-for-right-
to-home

121

"Our Enemy is Dreamless Sleep!" On the Cultic Creation of an Autonomous Network

Kasper Opstrup

In 1973, the performance group COUM Transmission moved into squatted premises in Hackney, East London. With a lot of people passing through the premises over the years, this squat has since become infamous in subcultural lore as the centre for countless experiments with new forms of living. In many ways, it was a cultural equivalent to the social centres known from the more explicitly political parts of the movement. The only marker of this past today is a black door in a row of terraced houses on to which a so-called 'Psychick Cross' is still studdded. Otherwise, it is just another residential building in a part of London that has become rapidly gentrified.

Located at 50 Beck Road, it has been home to not only the aforementioned performance group but also the band they grew into, Throbbing Gristle (TG), their record label, Industrial Records, as well as, later on, thee Temple of Psychick Youth (TOPY). First TG and then TOPY would be in the middle of an international network first and foremost held together by mail as well as touring. The Beck Road squat served as a key 'Access Point' until activities around TOPY started to fade in the early 1990s.

The idea behind TOPY is to be found somewhere in between of a new social movement, a Psychick TV (PTV) fan club, an art collective and a cult. They wanted to create an informal network of people who would prove their commitment to the group by doing an unusual thing which, more often than not, took form as performing ritual and/or sex magic. As

122

they wrote in their 'bible', Thee Grey Book, "We are not seeking followers, we are seeking collaborators, Individuals for a visionary Psychick Alliance". As such, TOPY consisted of a loose networks of individuals from ex-members of Throbbing Gristle to ex-members of its occult forerunner The Process Church of the Final Judgment to fans of industrial culture who got in touch after finding the address in the liner notes of albums such as PTV's Force the Hand of Chance (1982). In their own words, they were 'cultural engineers' who, heavily inspired by William Burroughs' and Brion Gysin's ideas about a 'third mind', wanted to intervene into the cultural mainstream and change its flow with 'occultural' ideas, a term they coined to describe their particular meeting of art, activism and esotericism.

Leaving the techno-pagan aspects of TOPY aside, I want to call special attention to the way they self-organized. From day one they sought organizational autonomy. They wanted to self-organise and build their own networks through which they could disseminate information and philosophy through newsletters, 'zines and albums. In hindsight, it is obviously in direct continuation of certain tendencies from the underground of the 1960s that aimed for world domination by building a counter-culture as, for example, the Scottish Beat writer Alexander Trocchi's *Project Sigma* or William Burroughs' dreams of founding an *Academy 23*.

The more enthusiastic individuals that got in touch with TOPY were told it was an open, self-generating and non-hierarchical network

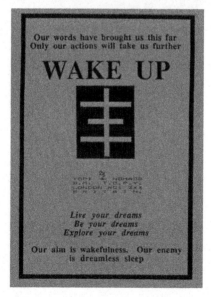

and were invited to open up their own Access Points—subgroups administering sigils, questions and suggestions for the region or zone as well as distributing information, newsletters and various kinds of tapes, videos, etc. The Access Points were overseen by what became the TOPY Stations, main headquarters that administered a whole country or territory. At its peak, there were three stations: UK, USA and Europe.

50 Beck Road became the London TOPY Station and later the TOPY STATION UK. Several initiates lived and worked there after 1988 when the inner circle around P-Orridge relocated to Brighton which became home to the TOPY GLOBAL STATION. In Brighton, the Temple soon occupied five houses and became part of that city's acid house and early rave scene. The move was part of a search for a 'Big House'—a long term aim to create a TOPY tribal research centre—that went on until 1991 when the Brighton houses were raided by Scotland Yard in a 'satanic panic.'

Besides meeting up weekly to socialize and do rituals, the members of the London TOPY Station produced 'zines, books, videos and tapes centred around their interests and research which they distributed in the TOPY network. They also reached out towards the local community and arranged events, concerts, performance art evenings, workshops,

social outings to stone-circles, etc. After 1991, TOPY activities declined rapidly and many members drifted on to initiatives on the broader 1990s squatting scenes, populated with semi-fictional groups and identities such as the Association of Autonomous Astronauts (AAA) and Luther Blissett and/or the growing Tactical Media-scene.

At its peak in the late 1980s, TOPY, according to P-Orridge, had around 10,000 individuals sigilising and/or connected worldwide with Access Points in England, Scotland, Holland, West Germany, U. S. A., Canada, Italy, Australia and Scandinavia. As Eden 229 points out, the Temple had a massive turnover, though, with many people being involved for short periods of time and then leaving again. At his estimate, it was never more than c. 200 people sigilising and being productive at the same time. Beyond them, there were maybe 10,000 people buying the records, reading the books and being interested in the ideas and beyond them a wider group of family and friends who had a vague idea.

TOPY needed in ideology for those involved, levels to achieve, secrets to reveal, an inner and an outer order, symbols and uniforms, regalia, internal writings and so on. In order to make it appear as a serious, focused, militant network, TOPY started out with a logo and a strong visual look inspired by the Process Church of the Final Judgment—notoriously known as the 'Mindbenders from Mayfair' in the 1960s—who had an identifiable visual image: they wore tailor-made black uniforms and was often accompanied by German Shepherds.

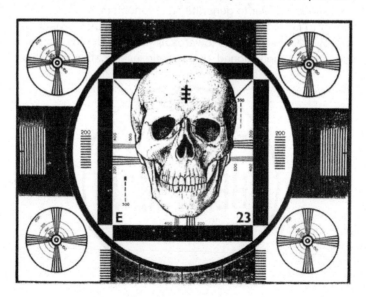

Besides a shaved head with a ponytail, parts of the early TOPY uniform were a grey priest shirt, grey military-style trousers, combat boots, a Psychick Cross—a vertical line with three horizontals, the central line shorter than the other two and all the lines in the proportion 2/3—as well as a number 23 insignia. This uniform was roughly adhered to in the period from 1981 to 1985-6 when the Temple entered its second, so-called 'hyperdelic' phase.

It had become clear to the inner circle that in order to continue to evolve, TOPY had to become the template for a way of life by combining a system of living with spiritual and mental exploration: "Transformation can only occur if the Individual is prepared to sacrifice all they have, including a previous personality, and place in a status quo. Smashing old loops and habitual patterns is essential". In order to maintain the network and the costs of post and printing, TOPY Benefits and TOPY Merchandise were initiated which made TOPY more visible in the street culture and drew in more people who in turn began more Access Points. At the end of the 1980s, quite a few TOPY individuals had become nomadic and travelled about the Access Point network exchanging labor and other skills for shelter.

As such, TOPY was the inheritor of a century's worth of occult and countercultural 'science', and then some, a crustpunk laboratory where radical and, in many cases, previously forgotten ideas were synthesized into a way of life. TOPY tried to break personal habits and preconceptions in order to generate an autonomous space for the practitioner to individualize their identity and create their own chosen narrative. By being suspicious towards all forms of dogma, the Temple was interested in "non-aligned, undogmatic investigation into what

exactly is going on. Minus the bullshit of organized religion, the rhetoric of party politics, or the promises of 'occultism' that only serve to pervert that understanding and thus strengthen the foundations of Control". It tried to trigger people's own imagination by existing in the form of a question.

With its decentralised network, the structure of TOPY is reminiscent of 19th century anarchism even though it is more indebted to Stirner than to Tolstoy or Bakunin, due to a focus on individualism and imagination instead of, respectively, love or revolutionary force. The aim was to establish communities of free spirits where the exchange of (dis)information between the various individuals in the network played the binding role in the social structure that dogmatic hierarchies often play in more orthodox religions.

The most common criticism of the sort of individualist anarchism that fueled TOPY from a Left perspective is that revolution becomes a question of lifestyle instead of class struggle. Individualism easily creates hierarchies, thus excluding all individuals who are not living their life animated by strong passions; the one's who are fully awakened become an elect few, the *übermenschen* of human evolution. It stresses how techniques of cultural engineering are equally important for right as for left libertarians: both want a Nietzschean transformation of humanity where the individual 'becomes who he is' and makes a work of art out of himself. TOPY's quest for ecstatic experience was also a search for the psychedelic superman.

Germa

128

We Don't Need No Landlords ... Squatting in Germany from 1970 to the Present

Azomozox

Squatting in Germany, as well as struggles against private property have a long tradition. In 1872, as a result of a dreadful housing shortage, 21 encampments of shacks and huts arose without permission in Berlin. The largest of these was the Freistaat Barackia on Kottbusser Tor (district Kreuzberg) with around 160 families. At the end of the year 1872, all 21 shantytowns had been evicted, in some cases with great resistance. After the eviction of six encampments and one shoemaker in the Blumenstraße, who could not pay his rent anymore, the famous "Riots of Blumenstraße" occurred, with street battles lasting for days, where people used flowerpots, stones and barricades against the approaching police.

One hundred years later, at the beginning of the 1970s, a new squatting period emerged in the wake of the worldwide 1968 movements: The various squatting movements that spread in West Germany were concentrated mostly in larger cities like West Berlin, Hamburg, Köln (Cologne), Frankfurt, Hannover, and München (Munich), and, during 1989-90, the time of the unification of two Germanys, in Potsdam, Leipzig, Dresden, Rostock and East Berlin. In Potsdam after 1989 we experienced more then 40 squats, in Hamburg over 50, and in Berlin (East and West) over 630 since the beginning of the '70s. All together that total was surely more than 1,000 squats, and more than 100 squatted *wagenplatz* or "wagon places" for living in house trailers.

The composition of the squatters varies greatly and expresses a broad diversity within the frame of anti-authoritarian, emancipatory ideas and politics, and reflects the influence of and interrelation with other social, cultural and political movements. Amongst the squatters we find people of different class backgrounds and political tendencies (anarchist, anti-authoritarian, anti-imperialist, autonomous, anti-fascist, environmentalist) as well as people of color, migrants, inter- and transnationalists, refugees, creative artists, workers and more, but also, autonomist wimmin and dykes, radical queer and trans people, gays and drag queens and kings.

The first wave started from the early '70s, when a large movement which created independent and autonomist youth centers around the country with up to 200 occupied or self-determined places. A large squatting scene developed in Frankfurt am Main for cheap housing and against speculation and demolition of buildings. Probably the first squat in West Germany took place in Köln in Roßstraße 16. The greatest movement against housing-speculation, rent increase and gentrification then was in Frankfurt am Main, with around 20 squats from 1970-1974, including squats by immigrants and women only. The movement gained widespread support, mobilized thousands of people, and organized large demonstrations with more than 10,000 people. But the movement slowly declined, and by the end of 1974 the last squat was evicted. The squatting movement was accompanied by large organized rent strikes from Italian, Kurdish and Turkish, Greek, Spanish and Yugoslavian migrant workers who were suffering in Frankfurt under lousy living conditions and were no longer willing to pay horrendous rents. But the movement gradually abated due to state repression as nearly all of the trials for non-payment of rent were lost.

A harsh state repression took place in Hamburg, when one squat in Ekhofstraße 39, only six weeks old, was evicted on May 23rd 1973 by hundreds of police, including special units armed with machine guns. Seventy people were chained inside the house, and later 33 ofthem were charged under anti-terrorist laws for support of a criminal organization. The house was demolished, and some squatters were sentenced from several weeks and months up to one year in prison.

The second big wave of the squatting movement started at the beginning of the '80s when different political, social and subcultural movements, including punks, *autonomen*, lesbians, ecology movement, anti-nuclear and anti-roads struggles (in Frankfurt am Main) emerged, interacted and exploded as a a new movement. This had its own subculture, alternative economy, collectives, cooperatives and organized structures of resistance expressing the hunger (desire) for a "different life."

During this period around 400 houses were squatted in more than 74 cities throughout West Germany, with the highest number of squats (around 200) in West Berlin. In West Berlin, where about 5,000

131

people lived in the squats, a large movement grew, with demonstrations of 15,000 to 20,000 people and widespread support from university professors, artists, some union chapters, parishes, writers and public figures. But the West Berlin senate and state prosecutors used several different laws against them—using and promoting violence, resisting arrest, inciting a riot, and the anti-terrorist law against forming a criminal organization—to crack down on the squatting movement. From December of 1980 to October of 1982, 7,809 preliminary proceedings were carried out, 1,409 arrests made, and 172 arrest warrants issued leading to numerous prison sentences, 18 without parole. At the peak of the movement, on September 22nd, 1981 during protests against the evictions of eight squats, squatter Klaus-Jürgen Rattey was chased by the police in front of a public bus. It was the first death inside the movement.

With squatters divided into several factions over issues including the question of negotiations, the movement slowly declined. The state played the factions against each other. Finally 100 squats were legalized, and by 1984 the last eviction took place and the movement ended.

A major conflict took place in the Hafenstrasse of the St. Pauli district of Hamburg in 1987, with some 100 people living in several houses. Squatted in 1981, the Hafenstrase was on the verge of eviction, as all contracts were canceled and the police prepared to move in. But the squatters had built up solidarity within St. Pauli. Tension grew as the inhabitants put up barbed wire on the roof, metal barriers inside their houses, mobilized their supporters through pirate Radio Hafenstraße, and declared to defend their homes. Several thousand police gathered nearby, awaited the order of eviction. In the end a contract was signed, and the city refrained from the eviction. Today the Hafenstraße, which in the '80s was a symbol of autonomous anti-imperialist strength and a reference point of militant struggle, is a legalized housing cooperative.

The third wave of squats coincided with the fall of the Berlin Wall and the unification process of the two German states in 1989-90. This time the squatting wave extended mostly in the former East German state, the DDR, with strongholds in Leipzig, Potsdam, Dresden, Rostock and Weimar. The gradual collapse of the East German state led to an uncertain legal situation, a kind of vacuum, which presented for all willing to squat, the perfect preconditions to appropriate en masse the many vacant houses. In East Berlin, 130 houses were occupied until the magistrate of East Berlin issued a decree not to tolerate any more occupations.

While the majority of squats were willing to negotiate contracts, preliminary talks with municipal authorities were canceled in October

1990. One month later, the 11 squats in Mainzerstraße 2-11 were evicted. Some 200 squatters and many hundreds more supporters resisted for two days, building barricades, digging holes in the streets with Caterpillars, throwing stones and molotov cocktails, and using slingshots and flare guns against the police. Some 3,000 police officers from all over Germany had to use water cannons, tanks, teargas, sharp munitions, helicopters and special combat units, causing injuries and 417 arrests.

Although the 11 squats were lost, the fierce resistance as well as the critical media coverage of the first big operation of West German police in East Berlin after unification, resulted in two outcomes: the Berlin Senate coalition ended after the Alternative Liste quit over the eviction decision, and roundtables between squatters, politicians and mediators were institutionalized and led to the legalization of most squats in former East Berlin.

Today in 2015, squatting is more difficult. Most squats get evicted much sooner. Only a few squats without any contracts and no payment of rent have survived. The Rote Flora in Hamburg has, since the occupation in 1989, neither legal status nor contract. Also the Refugeee Strike House in an occupied school in Ohlauerstraße 12 in Berlin has survived since December 2012.

Although squatting seems more difficult in general, squatting is still ongoing, and in some cases has resulted in contracts. In 2009, the predominantly artist squatted houses of the Gängeviertel in Hamburg received a contract, also the Autonome Zentrum in Köln (2010). Then, probably the oldest squatters in Germany, the "grannies" of Stille Straße 10 in Berlin Pankow, a group of 300 pensioners aged 67 to 96, squatted their senior center in 2012. After some three months and widespread support, they signed a long term contract.

SQUATTING IN EAST GERMANY

Although it is not very well known, from the late '60s until the collapse of the DDR in 1989, squatters occupied thousands of flats and houses in East Germany, predominantly in Leipzig, Berlin, Jena, Halle, and Rostock. Squatting in the East had quite a different character than in West Germany and the occupations in the DDR responded to different necessities: on the one hand, to create and protect free spaces for a different way of life, but on the other, for the very basic need for shelter. Both necessities required secrecy.

Prior to the fall of the Wall in East Germany, shortage of housing was most often the primary motivation for squatting. Even though rents

133

were affordable, the total number of available flats made available by the DDR government was inadequate for the population. Due to the fact that demolition was expensive, many houses closed by the construction supervision agency stood empty for years. This picture of abandonment characterized many cities in the DDR. Estimates of the number of abandoned apartments in East Germany range between 250,000 and 400,000. Even though reliable numbers of squatted flats do not exist, we do know that in 1979, for the city of East Berlin, 1,200 occupied apartments were listed by authorities. Eight years later, in 1987, the number grew to 1,270 for the Prenzlauer Berg district alone. From that number one can deduce that several thousands squatted flats existed in East Berlin in the late 1980s. At the same time Rostock had around 700 squatted apartments.

Beyond the need for a flat, squatters hid their activities for political reasons. Artists and collectives also appropriated buildings to establish alternative and communal lifestyles. While this accounted for a smaller portion of the total squats, these activities were more visible since these groups used occupied spaces for exhibitions, concerts (from rock to punk), events, and even anti-authoritarian children's nurseries. Notably, one of the first occupations at Kleine Marktstrasse 3 in Halle in 1967 was used to host a book club.

In several different squats, an anti-authoritarian group of 15 to 30 people met. After being infiltrated by a police informant, two members of the group were arrested in 1973 and convicted of subversive activity, which led to the group's destruction.

For many East Germans, this new wave of squatting in the re-united Germany was nothing new, but rather a continuation of life as they had known it in the DDR. The new squatting movement that occurred when the Berlin Wall came down preserved several known squats that had functioned as important communal and political spaces in East Germany including Brausestarsse 20, Neudorfgasse 16 and Dufourstrasse 34 in Leipzig, Wollenweberstrasse 50 in Rostock, Quergasse 12 and Zwätzengasse 7 in Jena, and Rykestarsse 27, Mühsamstrasse 63, Dunckerstarsse 21, Lychener Strasse 61 and Fehrbelliner Strasse 5 in East Berlin.

Autonomy!

Ashley Dawson

Before the book, a place and time: Berlin, summer 1990, or actually, the
road to Berlin. I'd spent the last two days on the move, hitchhiking without
sleep to get from Amsterdam to Berlin. I was delirious, having spent
hours talking to a Dutch businessman who spewed a stream of racist bile
about Muslims taking over his country and an even longer time with an
Italian truck driver who insisted that he was carrying a large consignment
of weapons for the Sicilian mafia. Beggars can't be choosers. Night
blurred into day and back again. Now I was on the final leg of the journey,
crammed into a dilapidated Opel with a disheveled elevator salesman and
his advertising gear. The highway ran like an artery of light through what I
knew was the pitch-black East German countryside. Groggy with sleep,
I struggled to keep up a conversation with the driver. The surreal sense of
being deep under water I felt coming over me was brought up short when
we pulled into a grimy gas station glued to the dark margin of the highway.
As I got out to stretch I saw the East German soldiers, their machine guns
pointing at the ground, standing around smoking cigarettes.
    The next day, after crashing on the floor of friends of friends in
West Berlin, I made my way across the city to Checkpoint Charlie. As
I approached the crossing on the elevated metro line, I saw the graffiti-
covered remnants of the wall and, equally oppressive, the huge gash
running through the center of the city, an ominous blank space carved out
for hundreds of feet on either side of the wall to ensure maximum visibility
of escapees. At Checkpoint Charlie, the wall was no longer intact, but
the guard tower from which East German security once watched over
and at times killed their compatriots, was still there. I walked through
the crossing, feeling as if history was turning upside down on my way to
Mainzer Strasse.
    During the Cold War, Berlin was the only city in which young West
German men could escape mandatory military service. Supported by
the Allies as a symbol of resistance to communism, the city ironically
became a haven for West German dissidents and a forcing house for the
diverse social movements that came to be known as the autonomen:
antiwar, antiracist, feminist, environmentalist and many other strands of
the German extra-parliamentary Left who retained strong links with the
traditions of direct, participatory democracy pioneered by the New Left

during the late 1960s and by subsequent radical tendencies such as
the Greens. The autonomen were concentrated in the relatively poor,
heavily Turkish neighborhood of Kreuzberg, which, during the Cold War,
was located in the far eastern section of West Berlin. After the wall
was torn down in November, 1989, the autonomen moved east into
neighborhoods where huge numbers of late nineteenth century apartment
buildings had been left vacant by the East German government whose
plans to demolish them and build hideous tower blocks in their place
had been scuttled by the collapse of communism. Now, West Germans
and East Germans, as well as radicals from Italy, Japan, Peru, and other
points around the world, joined to occupy over a hundred buildings in the
neighborhood just across the River Spree from Kreuzberg.

Mainzer Strasse was special, though. Most squats were isolated,
or existed in clumps of two or three houses. On Mainzer Strasse, an
entire block of twelve abandoned tenement buildings had been occupied.
There was an autonomen movie theater; several info-shops distributing
radical zines, books, and films; separate gay and lesbian houses; and
autonomen cafés and bars, each with decoration more imaginative than
the next—my favorite was the wedding themed bar in the lesbian house,
with a gigantic white wedding bed that seated at least twenty people.
The reputation of Mainzer Strasse had travelled all the way to the United
States; friends told me that I had to go to on a pilgrimage to the place
while I was in Germany to polish my language skills before taking the
mandatory exams in grad school.

After walking through seemingly endless streets filled with once
elegant but now ramshackle five-story apartment buildings, I finally turned
into Mainzer Strasse. After walking past several houses that seemed
completely uninhabited, I stopped in front of one with a bright purple
façade where two young guys were sitting in the sun playing chess.
Biting the bullet, I blurted out an awkward hello in German and then
explained in English that I was in Berlin for the summer and wondered if
they had a place for me to stay. Neither seemed particularly nonplussed
by what seemed to me a ridiculously bold and invasive request. Oliver
turned with an amused look on his face to Mischa and said that he
thought they probably had room. Mischa replied that yes they probably
did, but they'd have to ask the house council if I could stay. I sat around
watching them play chess and smoke hand-rolled cigarettes with exotic
Dutch tobacco. They seemed quite personable and we talked about
where I was from and what I wanted to do during the summer.

This information came in handy a couple of hours later when they
put my case to the house council. Even though I was in Berlin to polish

my German, I didn't understand much of the business conducted at
the council, which took place in a volatile mix of West German, East
German, and international autonomen argot. The mixture of people
from both parts of the country—so soon after the dismantling of the
wall—was impressive, as was the pretty even mix of men and women in
the squat. I felt distinctly uneasy, though, when discussion turned to my
application to be a member of the house and I felt people's eyes on me.
Oliver whispered to me that things were going relatively well, although
there was quite a lot of suspicion of an unknown outsider like me since
the "*Osi*'s" had grown up subjected to the pervasive spy network of the
hated *Stasi*, the East German secret police, and the "*Wesi*'s" had been
battling the authorities' anti-squatter moves for much of the last decade.
Perhaps equally worrying, I was an "*Ami*," a citizen of the universally
hated imperialist power across the Atlantic. But though I felt nervous,
I also felt elated: this was my first experience of radical participatory
democracy in a commune.

My application for membership approved by consensus by the
house council, it was time for me to learn the ropes in the commune.
Mischa took me to see my room, which faced onto the backyard of the
building, beyond which lay a cemetery studded with beautiful cypress
trees. My room was on the first floor of the building, and consequently
abutted onto an imposing steel security door that clamped down with
a huge wheel across the stairway leading up from the ground floor café to
the rest of the house. The whole affair seemed rather like something one
might encounter on a submarine or in a space station. There was a buzzer
system that allowed people to get in after curfew each night. Mischa
explained to me that just recently a group of neo-Nazis had broken into a
nearby house and savagely beaten some autonomen living there. neo-
Nazis who'd squatted a house in a nearby neighborhood also apparently
liked to blast down our street in their jeep, firing flare guns into the houses.
Mischa told me that sentries were posted with walkie-talkies at either end
of Mainzer Strasse, and that the autonomen were worried that they'd be
attacked by a mob of either neo-Nazis or police sometime soon.

Needless to say, I had trouble going to sleep. Although I eventually
dropped off, I woke in horror in the middle of the night to a deafening
clanging on the steel security door. After nearly pissing myself with fear,
I eventually realized that the clanging wasn't the noise of someone trying
to dismantle the door but rather of someone patiently trying to wake the
evening sentry up and get into the house. But this was cold comfort—
perhaps it was a neo-Nazi trap! Eventually someone else woke up and
came down the stairs cursing in colorful German. It turned out that the

person whose turn it was to keep the buzzer in their room had closed it out on the landing and gone to sleep, leaving a partygoer to wake half the house in order to get in.

The next morning, while I was eating breakfast, Oliver asked me if I'd like to come to a protest against the neo-Nazis. This seemed like a good idea after the terrible night I'd had! When I agreed, Oliver asked me if I had a motorcycle helmet with me. Sure, didn't he see the motorcycle in my backpack yesterday? Okay, no problem, but bring your passport with you in case you're arrested, he said—you don't want to get stuck in an East German jail with no identification.

As autonomen gathered for the march, I saw that Oliver hadn't just been trying to wind up the new *Ami* housemate. Dressed almost exclusively in black, the autonomen around me really were gearing themselves up with helmets and other homemade riot gear. The march nevertheless set off towards the neo-Nazi squats with a remarkably carnivalesque air. When we got to the street occupied by the fascists, though, we found that a convoy of East German police trucks was blocking the way. This, Oliver told me, was typical. Since the wall came down, neo-Nazi movements had sprung up across Germany. Judges sentenced perpetrators of increasingly-frequent attacks on immigrants

to short jail terms or light fines, while the Social Democrats had joined with conservatives to deport tens of thousands of Roma and help rewrite the country's constitution to seal the borders to political refugees. The autonomen, growing out of an anti-imperialist movement and very much aware of their links with the German Left in the 1930s, sought to protect Roma and other immigrants from the marauding neo-Nazis, but, unlike the neo-Nazis, they were violently repressed by the police on both sides of the old border. For the autonomen, the East German volkspolizei or people's police lined up in front of them were supporting the fascists by defending their squat.

While most of the autonomen marched past hurling only jeers, a group clad in helmets and leather jackets waded into the cops with the pipes and trash can lids they'd brought along for the occasion. This most militant segment of the black bloc seemed a pretty even match for the relatively lightly armed East German police. Soon, though, the melee heated up as Molotov cocktails went flying and police trucks caught on fire. In the United States, of course, the police would have just shot the "terrorists," but instead, the thin green line of East German police held fire and held firm, the neo-Nazi squats remained safe, and the march moved on. I was shocked by the violence, but appreciated the willingness of the autonomen to put their bodies on the line to challenge the Nazis. After being attacked a number of times by skinheads during the course of the summer, I came to understand the autonomen's militant attitude a bit more.

We marched on towards a complex of housing blocks where Vietnamese immigrant workers had been living in terror for months, unable to get back to their country and repeatedly attacked by the neo-Nazis. Along the way to these tower blocks, the marchers stopped briefly to torch a truck filled with cigarettes from a recently arrived Western corporate cigarette company. After a buoyant march through the dreary concrete jungle of outer East Berlin, an autonomen delegation peeled off to meet with representatives of the Vietnamese workers and to express solidarity with their struggle against racism in the new Germany. As the balmy summer afternoon wore down, the autonomen dispersed, with clumps of black-clad men and women waving flags of the former German Democratic Republic, the bottom golden stripe ripped out to leave only black and red stripes over the embossed hammer, compass, and grain insignia of worker, farmer, and intellectual unity.

Now we go to Tacheles, Oliver told me. Located in the once predominantly Jewish neighborhood of Berlin Mitte, and subsequently used by the Nazis to house French prisoners of war, Tacheles was a hulking derelict former department store that had been occupied by autonomen a scant three months after the wall came down. Tacheles had blossomed into a community arts center, and now boasted scores of artists' workshops, exhibition spaces, a bar, and a movie theater. The building itself was a labyrinthine gaping wound. Once the entrance to the Friedrichstadt Passage, a shopping complex akin to the covered shops written about by Walter Benjamin, Tacheles featured historically important early steel architecture, but had been partially demolished by penniless communist functionaries after World War II and was slated for final demolition in spring of 1990. The autonomen blocked this demolition and created a vibrant space for experiments in communal living and aesthetics.

When we arrived at Tacheles, the sun was just beginning to set. The entire back wall of the building had been removed, leaving its rooms exposed like a giant honeycomb. This particular evening an Irish performance artist had spread canvas from floor to ceiling in each room. Inside each room she had stationed a slide projector; each projector was in turn wired to a central computer control. She had created a gigantic version of one of Nam June Paik's video installations. The net effect was a mesmerizing collage of coruscating images, sometimes flashing in completely disconnected rhythms, sometimes composing themselves into a single sixstory canvas, all in time to music played by a jazz band in the massive courtyard behind Tacheles. Oliver gestured to me, and we began

climbing up the scaffolding attached to the outside of the building, the giant images flashing in front of our faces as we climbed. When we got half way up, we turned around, twined our legs round the scaffolding, and sat watching the sun go down over a free Berlin.

When I returned to grad school at the end of that summer, I found myself studying with quite a few colorful professors, but Sylvère Lotringer was one of the more memorable. He was teaching a class on mutant French theory: Bataille, Artaud, Deleuze and Guattari during their polymorphous perversity phase. At the time he was helping a member of the Black Panthers who'd just been released from jail put together a collection justifying the party line. When Lotringer heard that I had been living with the autonomen in Berlin and that I spoke Italian, he immediately gave me a dogeared copy of his journal *Semiotext(e)* from the late 1970s. The theme of the journal: Autonomia.

Autonomia, which has recently been reissued in the *Semiotext(e) Foreign Agents* series, contains the collective efforts of intellectuals active in radical Italian organizations such as *Lotta Continua* [Continuous Struggle] and *Potere Operiao* [Workers' Power] to gain a theoretical grip on events during the country's *anni di piombo* or "years of lead," when the nation was convulsed by a startling variety of extraparliamentary radical movements. In the mid 1970s, the Italian Communist Party (PCI), repudiating Soviet dogmatism, had forged a "historic compromise" with the country's long-serving, endemically corrupt Christian Democrats. It thus fell to the PCI to discipline increasingly restive workers during the first major economic downturn of the postwar period. Workers began organizing autonomously of the Communist-controlled labor unions, engaging in spontaneous actions to shorten the work week, to overturn management control in workplaces, and to demand higher wages, all by organizing in workplace councils.

Even more alarmingly for authorities, social struggles began to move out of the factory, with *autoriduzione* (autoreduction) movements coping with the rising cost of living by collectively determining a reduced price to pay for public services, transportation, housing, electricity, and groceries. In addition, sectors of the population invisible to traditional Marxist theory began to assert themselves. Groups like *Rivolta Femminile* challenged the patriarchal values that pervaded Italian society in general, but also the workers' movement and the PCI. Feminists introduced new styles of organizing in small groups with horizontal links rather than the top-down vanguard style of many traditional vanguard groups, and pioneered fresh discursive and decision-making strategies based on open general assemblies and consensus. In tandem, youth movements began to assert their right to the autonomous self-governance of education. A vibrant, playful counterculture quickly developed in Italy's major cities that struggled to build *centri sociali* (autonomous social centers) where young people could escape the oppressive confines of the patriarchal family and carve out a vision of community outside the alienating confines of the mass consumerist society of the spectacle.

The articles collected in *Autonomia* track and attempt to theorize these polymorphous Italian social struggles. Writers such as Mario Tronti, Sergio Bologna, and, of course, Toni Negri articulate the tenets of operaismo (workerism), the theoretical approach to conceptualizing autonomous worker activism developed in Italy during the struggles of the late 1960s and 1970s. The operaismo analysts drew in their work on a long tradition of radical theory, the most prominent branch of which led back to France's *Socialism or Barbarism Group*, where Cornelius Castoriadis had first articulated notions of workers' autonomy. In turn, Socialism or Barbarism had been influenced by the investigations of wildcat strikes in American auto plants carried out by the Johnson Forest Tendency, a dissident Trotskyist group founded by Trinidadian polymath C.L.R. James and Russian exile Raya Dunayevskaya. Writing in

Germany

journals such as *Quaderni Rossi*, Negri and his colleagues challenged the hierarchical tenets of Marxist-Leninist theory, focusing instead on the "spontaneous" forms of shop floor organizing evolving in sites such as FIAT's giant car factory on the outskirts of Turin. Operaismo theorists also revamped classical Marxist theories of value by arguing that in modern societies wealth was produced increasingly through "immaterial" or "social" labor—the collective work of social reproduction carried on outside the wage relation by women, students, the unemployed, etc. Although it remained grounded in theories of class struggle, operaismo expanded the definition of the working class to include many of the social movements that were transforming the political landscape of Italy during the 1970s. Italian Autonomia had a dramatic impact in Germany, helping to catalyze the movement in which I participated in Mainzer Strasse.

Looking back at Autonomia from my current vantage point—which coincides with the twentieth anniversary of the fall of the Berlin wall and the tenth anniversary of the Battle of Seattle—I'm struck by the germinative character of these theoretical labors. Not that they lack flaws: as its name suggests, operaismo retained an emphasis on production that ineluctably marginalized many of the issues around which social movements such as feminism and the youth counterculture mobilized. In addition, the theorists of Autonomia remained relatively silent on the unfolding new international division of labor. This perhaps helps to explain the blindness in Toni Negri's subsequent attempt to theorize Empire as a decentered, all-pervasive force that leaves accounts of nation-state-centered imperialism in the dustbin of history. The Iraq War put an end to such modish, *pomo* accounts of power. Nevertheless, in their attempts to theorize new forms of grassroots organizing and to develop fresh theories of the production of value in contemporary capitalism, the work of the Autonomia theorists was prescient and remains valuable.

For all its faults, Autonomia has provided one of the most expansive theoretical frameworks for understanding the spontaneous, horizontal politico-social forms that I experienced among Berlin's autonomen and that have since become a crucial feature of the global justice movement. While other theorists such as Manuel Castells also tracked the development of grassroots struggles in urban locations around the world, few have reinvigorated historical materialism and provided the framework for conceptualizing fresh efforts at organizing from below to the extent of Autonomia. Indeed, we might think of Autonomia as one of the most useful articulations of historical struggles that bind together such disparate phenomena as the autonomen in Germany and other parts of northern Europe, the efforts of the Brazilian Workers' Party to establish participatory budgeting, the independent township groups of the Mass Democratic Movement that brought down apartheid in South Africa, and the struggle of the Zapatistas against neoliberalism and for autonomous indigenous governance in the Lacandon jungle in southern Mexico.

The Mainzer Strasse commune I lived in no longer exists. Three months after my return to the United States, the Social Democratic government of Berlin sent in more than three thousand police, including SWAT teams, and smashed the autonomen resistance. But while the Battle of Mainzer Strasse was lost, the struggle against the forms of dispossession and alienation imposed by neoliberal capitalism lives on. All power to the communes!

REFERENCES

Autonomia: PostPolitical Politics, edited by Sylvère Lotringer and Christian Marazzi (Semiotext(e), 1980; MIT Press, 2007)

Reprinted from the Nov 27th, 2009 edition of The Advocate graduate student newspaper of City University of New York; posted at gcadvocate.com/ 2009/11/autonomy/; reprinted with permission. Also printed in House Magic #3, 2011.

Stutti

Sarah Lewison

Stutti was the informal name for "Hotel Stuttgarter Hof," an erstwhile
Berlin hotel that was squatted by artists from spring until late December
1988. Located at Anhalter Straße 9, our neighbors included the Gestapo
headquarters (Topographie of Terror), the Martin Gropius Bau Museum
and the shuttered Anhalter Bahnhof. Stutti's entrance and facade were
pockmarked by shells from the war but otherwise in good condition. The
entry hall was heavily damaged however, and acacias grew from a pile
of rubble, through a hole in the first floor where Abraxa, a Spanish artist
from Darmstadt, crafted a treehouse apartment for herself. Coming from
the United States, Berlin offered me material evidence of a war I had
previously taken only to exist on faith. Not only the buildings wore scars;
one frequently encountered older men in the streets with missing limbs
and other injuries.

At Hotel Stutti we found promotional materials for the facilities in the
dining room; ephemera that led one to imagine it's heyday. Was it closed
abruptly, or slowly suffocated by the division of Berlin? Two building
wings were set in an EL-shape. A four-story structure with 60 rooms ran
perpendicular to the street. Everyone had 3 or more rooms; the collective
Kommittee Präsens the entire fourth floor. In the rear was a solid high-
ceilinged main house with offices, meeting rooms, dining and banquet
facilities that we used for studio and gallery space. There was a lovely
courtyard garden where we ate in summer and fall beneath luxuriant trees
and vines.

About twenty people, mostly artists, squatted the building. Spaces
were organized for living, studio and exhibition space. I can't remember
a real kitchen. We wired the entire building for electricity, and squirreled
a telephone line from under the sidewalk- by digging through from
the basement. Our one telephone was hidden in a pile of feathers in an
ersatz grave, in an installation.

One of the exhilarating aspects of living in a raw building was the
freedom to make holes in the walls, breaking through tiny boxes to
remake one's space, all spaces, along the way exposing new views and
the strata of construction from another era.

I built a darkroom on the third floor, hauling water down the hallway
from the bathroom. This is where these photos were printed. Each month,

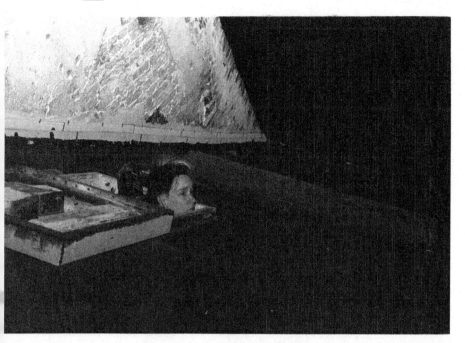

152

we pulled together exhibitions of installation art and paintings, along with live acts by bands and performance artists. We charged one mark at the entrance and the party would go until dawn, usually netting about 1000 marks. The next day would begin with an opulent breakfast and heated discussion about how to divide the proceeds between art supplies, construction materials, food, and hashish. Each Sunday, we would pull a sledge to the Flömarkt, where we would pick up colorful and elegant clothing from the vendors' discards, sometimes tossing back our own dirty clothes from the week before. There was so much of use that people were just throwing away.

Stutti was next door to the famed KuKuCK (*Kunst- und Kultur-Centrum Kreuzberg*), a gigantic squat and cultural space that hosted punk music and experimental theater through the early 80s. Someone once showed me photographs of KuKuCK along with a normalization proposal they had prepared with the subsidy and blessings of the city. The idea was nonetheless rejected, the building razed. Less organized, we maintained open spaces for art practice as long as we were able and people came by to shoot films, perform in and use our studio spaces. Facing closure, we publicly protested at the nearby Martin Gropius Bau museum by chaining ourselves to the balcony railings amidst a DADA retrospective.

156

A newspaper article about the protest led to visits by supporters and a curator who wanted to ship some of the art to another city. In a show of solidarity, people decided against breaking up the "collection."

A year or so later some former Stutti'ers joined with East Berlin artists to start Tacheles, again as a public exhibition space, but with a bar, kitchen, and more separation between living and work. I returned briefly, squatting a new house on Kleine Hamburger Straße with people from Stutti, the Synlabor collective, and Ramm Theater. We wrote a flyer for East Berliners that described how the transition to capitalism would threaten their housing security, and posted it the hallways of old buildings. I left on the day East Berliners were lined up at banks to exchange their Ostmarks for Deutschmarks.

Psy-CH-Art Hotel Stuttgarter Hof
am
Anhalter Bahnhof

Auf ca. 1000 qm² bilden seit Juli 88
20 Künstler aktuelle Gegenwartskunst.
Besuchen Sie uns!
1,- DM Eintritt tgl. 14⁰⁰–18⁰⁰
Anhalterstr. 9 1 Berlin 61

AM 11.11.88 ab 23 Uhr
Maskenball mit den abgebrannten Zün-
diches u.a.

Sciencefiktionromen vom 13.5.88

Auf dem Raumschiff Erde nichts los?

Geschichte: im Jahre 2000
DieRückfrontDesMondesIstBewohnbar
hergerichtet.DieErstenSchiffeStarten
MenschenGefielWerbung:LebenAuchSie
einigeZeitAufDemMond.DochMondsantrit
Schreck-10JahreGefangenschaft&&Bei
2,3MilliardenBesuchernFindetX-Mal
HolocaustStatt.2.Mauerbaufeiertag!!
DieMenschheitüberlebt!!Denn2,3Millia
lebenLängerVonDenRessourcenals10Mill

im Jahre 2010
WohlstandFürAlleAuserwählten(VZ?)
+ 6 Meter Humus
Nun gibt esKreativtechniker a la
Computersimulation & Arbeiter,die
Computer 1 zu C2 schicken,der C3das
ProduktHerstellenLäßt.

zurück ins 3. Reich
es starben 6Millionen,erster
Großversuch?
Gegenwart
CDX-dieHoheMoral & die Arche
China liefert Trägerraketen für
Ost & West!!!
DieTechnikIstSoWeit&SoFrei,istEinem
noch wohl dabei...
Neuzeit-Raumzeit-Echtzeit-
Wirklichkeit
HM!!

Regenbogen Fabrik: the Rainbow Factory

Alan W. Moore

March 2011: Everyone is gathered in the center of the courtyard, around Andy, a smiling older man wrapped in what looks like a red Sandinista neckerchief. We are waiting for the tour arranged for the SqEK meeting in Berlin to begin. Carla MacDougall is translating. Children are playing in the yard, mothers coming and going. There is some changing of the guard there, as one period of time in the *kita* (childrens' place) is ending and another beginning.

Andy was born in Kreuzberg. The Regenbogen Fabrik has been around since 1981. He intends to give us something like a history of the Kreuzberg squatting scene and what is left today. In the 1960s and '70s, Kreuzberg was an urban renewal area. There were plans for a highway, a "clear cut urban renewal" to tear down existing housing. In the 1970s this housing was beaten down and mostly abandoned. Speculators were hovering around, and they wanted Kreuzberg to be torn down. Many of the tenants were organizing, and there were a number of rent strikes.

The Kotbusser Tor area was torn down and redeveloped. The buildings in Kreuzberg had only a few remaining tenants. Most took money to move out. U.S. soldiers stationed in Berlin practiced urban warfare tactics in the rundown mostly abandoned area. (Andy showed us photographs of this.) In the late 1970s, around 1979, people began to renovate houses in protest against the government policy of abandonment. Until December 12, 1980 it wasn't really a movement *per se*. A squat here and there. But on that day police prevented a building from being squatted and there was a riot. It lasted three days, and marked the start of a movement.

There was a background of corruption in the municipal government. There was a housing shortage in Berlin, and many of the buildings in Kreuzberg were standing empty. After three days of riots the police said they would no longer evict people. Eighteen houses were squatted that month. By March 120. And by May of 1981, 160 to 170 houses had been squatted.

The movement, as it grew, came to have mixed motivations. It was against the housing policies of the city, for collective living and working, with political intention, etc. For some people it was about getting an apartment. At the Regenbogen Fabrik you have workshops so people could work collectively. For others political issues were most important, for people in the larger left alternative scene, the peace movement, anti-war, etc.

This is the Rainbow Factory. The back house was also squatted. Some people from the 1981 action still live there. (He shows pictures around the group of the rundown ruined group of shacks it was in 1981.) The ground was totally contaminated, so it all had to be dug out and removed. The first squatters were single mothers and people involved in labor union movements and the radical left scene. Most were drawing social welfare money. Those who were here to study in Berlin stopped their studies and picked them up again ten years later.

What were the motives of those first squatters? It was difficult to find an apartment with only one child. Some wanted to raise their children collectively. Some wanted to work collectively. This is how they envisioned their living situation. The original idea was to have a neighborhood center.

Now he will talk about how it used to be. This factory was built in 1878. In Kreuzberg, buildings then often had a factory behind them. This land is close to the canal. This was a steam-powered sawmill. The chimney remains. The squatters see it as a monument to that period, and saw themselves as contributing to the preservation of these historic buildings. Then the place became a chemical factory and made paint. It closed in 1978. The ground was contaminated.

The first thing they did when they squatted the place was to hold a neighborhood party. Just recently, they held the 30th anniversary of this party. There was more citizen participation then than there is now. Now the area is more commercial. Now they like more to do a street party.

The people who squatted here were open to negotiation. They worked with the neighborhood center and politicians. In the early 1980s scene that was a big issue. The bicycle workshop was a successful negotiating point. People could help themselves to build and repair their bicycles. This was a popular idea in Kreuzberg. A lot of the bicycle workshops became shops, but this one is still as it was, collectively organized. You think of Berlin now as a bicycle city. Then it wasn't, but in Kreuzberg it was because the Berlin Wall interrupted car traffic in this district.

The cinema or *kino* was originally a space for parties. There was a fire probably set by neo-Nazis, and it had to be fixed up again.

161

A question: What about the negotiations? How quickly was the squat legalized? It was squatted in 1981, and in 1984, the agreement came. The Alternative List (AL) got many votes in Kreuzberg. AL's first political position was the buildings commissioner. A man named Orlovsky was politicized because the Kreuzberg Center built near the Kotbusser Tor cut off his business from the street. The house was owned by a private investor until 1990. In 1991 they decided to resquat it. Now the district of Kreuzberg owns it.

The squatters were supposed to pay rent, but they didn't. Now the 25 and 30 year contracts are expiring, just as they are in Amsterdam. The city is setting onerous conditions for a new contract. An extended soil removal [for the contamination] was required, very expensive. The group refused.

[We move to the cinema, a large long clean room, with a bar along one side. It is painted a dark color, with raised banks of couchs, big upholstered sofas going up towards the projection room.]

The principle of the squats was to do what people wanted to do, what was fun for them. So here people organized to show films that they wanted to see. There were many cinemas in squats. Also in the east, many squats had cinemas in them. The kino group are all volunteers. They also welcome initiatives from the outside, particularly political initiatives. They can show 16mm, 35mm and they have a beamer for digital content.

The hostel and the cafe (formerly a VoKu) on the street are the two money-making projects of the Regenbogen Fabrik.

published in House Magic #3,
2011

163

A Stay at the Rote Insel

Alan W. Moore

March 2011: Finding the Rote Insel in Schöneberg from Tegel airport at night proved a little tricky. Two bus drivers gave me wrong steers, so I ended up heading to Mitte, to the huge City Hostel. Even in the morning I succeeded in making every wrong turn—on the last, out of the Metro, I passed a new "bio-cafe" and co-working space, and then a lot of anarchist graffiti on the railway overpass, defiant billboards, discolored with age from the rusty trestles, some still deformed with slugs from the war. Finally I find the Rote Insel—hard to miss it with its 5-story high murals. M___, my host is awaiting me on the street—I called from a nearby *locutorio*—and he lets me into the big double apartment building. It's a real warren of units, tidy but rundown in German *deshabille*. The guest room is really big, with mattresses for a dozen people in a loft above a room full of couches. With a poster of masked street fighters at Leon Cavallo CSOA on the wall, the place feels like an anti-capitalist wartime home. Over coffee, M___ laments that the movement is in decline. Yorckstraße in the past had some 90 squats, and now almost none remain. With anemic squat defense, the squats have been picked off one by one. The Kreuzberg squatters deplore the "*Schwaben*," tourists with big sunglasses. They are eager to photograph the remnants of oppoculture, but their attention is denaturing it, turning it into spectacle.

There are a few guests already staying there, a guy from Istanbul and two from Euskadi, Basque country. The big room must be vacated that night at 6pm for the assembly, 24 people in all, who make up the house. I will present my project, and ask for permission to photograph the walls of the house. Tomorrow night the rest of the SQEK crew of researchers arrives—Miguel and Elly from Spain, Lynn from Vermont, Thomas and Margot from Paris, and Edward from London. Others are staying in hotels...

On the night of the Rote Insel *VoKü* (Volks Küchen, People's Kitchen), several members of the Rote Insel told us the story of their house. The twin buildings were squatted in 1981. At that time, in West Berlin, there were 180 squats. Some were in Schöneberg (the district was called the "Rote Insel" for the radical workers living there), but most

were in Kreuzberg. These were occupied by young people and students. This house had many different people in what were really two separate buildings. In 1984, this was the last squatted house to make contact with the owner. The government made a program then to support squats with money, up to 85%. The city became the owner of our house, and we had nine months to get a contract with a construction company to make the improvements. We went from 1984–87 on one-year contracts. We needed that long a time to get a reconstruction contract. We were 20 young people with lots of problems, so it took a long time. The government then was putting a lot of money into calming the movement. We had two architects, an electrician, a carpenter, and a person to make the paperwork—and 20 people making their own house. For some time, they all lived in half of the building; 25 people had only one small kitchen. There were many discussions about the work, and sharing the load. Our first contract went until 1997. The current contract expires in 2017. The city gave many houses away to private companies because they didn't want to pay the costs of administration. Berlin was a city state inside the GDR (communist East Germany), and they had lots of money to distribute. "With this money they could bring down the movement." [I wonder how the Hafenstrasse squatters got legalized in Hamburg?] Also happened in Freiburg and Frankfurt. [Freiburg where the new mode of co-op collective home-buying is coming from.] To get a contract we had to have an official association. We joined with a youth center nearby which helped us in order to get this contract. The youth center also began in an occupation. They still have a project of car repair from those days.

The Rote Insel is self-managed. The assembly meets every two weeks. The rules of the house are no violence. Problems are resolved by talking. If you live here you must do something for the house. It's not fixed—everyone determines what he or she is going to do. It is made by social pressure and reputation. Some do more, some less, some nothing. We have in the past evicted people. At the end of the 1980s, we had some problems with heroin addiction. The playground next to us was a hot spot for drug dealing. Now Tacheles is still a place where you can get any drug you want. There are rumors that in the 1980s the prices for heroin were the lowest ever. Some suspect that this was in order to crush the movements. We made a policy that addicts had to go out. We are self-managed, so we make the rules. We don't ever have legal problems. Everyone who has lived here has accepted it. It's always a question of how you keep the rules of the house. No opiates. Anyone we see with small beady eyes—[gestures "out"].

The bar is a private club. People here are guests, friends, so no official rules apply. It is a private club, but it is publicized through the *Stressfaktor* [calendar for left subculture and politics]. We have a bicycle workshop. Kids can come and do their own repairs. The publicity on this is informal. Our collective can't support the workshop as an open public project. Our silkscreen workshop is "a little bit sleepy" because people don't work on it. It depends on private interest: who is here, and what they offer to do. The bar collective can be approached to do parties or concerts. We make pizza there on Fridays. There is also a rehearsal room where bands play for the cost of electricity. [Members speak German, English and Spanish.] We have people here who have no working papers and can't pay rent. But they must stay in contact, and open up their problems to the house. During the '80s a *Besetzenrat* [squatters' council] existed, but with the era of contracts the organization was broken. Now there is a *syndikat*, or association, to help houses to get legal help, but not to move into private ownership. A GmbH (limited liability company) buys 49% of the shares in a house. [M___ shows a chart.] It is a decentralized structure of money that cannot be broken if one house goes down. So there will never be an owner who can sell it.

M___ outlined a bit the movement of squatting in Berlin. For two or three years there has been an attempt to evict the Köpi [Köpinicker Straße 137]. The "*wir bleiben alle*" [We all stay] campaign was strong for a couple of years, then it was dropped. The structure here is inclined to be dependent on personalities. The first wave of squatting was in the 1980s. The second wave was in the '90s, from 1989-92, in the districts of Prenzlauer Berg and Mitte. In 1992 the riotous eviction of the Mainzer Straße squats took place. At that time, sexism was the issue dividing the movement, especially when a leading political man was accused of rape. Now the divide is over the Israel-Palestine issue, which emerged in the mid-1990s in the "antifa" [anti-fascist] movement as the "anti-Deutsch" position. [This anti-nationalism has been called by some "ethno-masochist," and involves unconditional support for Israel.] Now the only consensus is to stand against evictions and repression. A musical tour circuit works through private contacts. They are not really working with political parties. There is also a division over the vegan question.

The most lively movement now is probably Media Spree—there again is a personality up front. This concerns gentrification in Kreuzberg and Friedrichshain, as the riverside land on the Spree has been sold off. That movement has itself split, with one side going with the Green party and the left, and the other holding to an Autonomist position and disturbing the process.

published in House Magic #3, 2011

Gender and Squatting in Germany since 1968

Azomozox

The new wimmin, lesbian and gay movement of 1968 worldwide had a great impact on the emerging squatting movements in West Germany from the beginning of the '70s and initiated important debates over gender, sexism, trans- and homophobia, heteronormativity, inter-sexuality and anti-patriarchal struggles.

Alongside the slogan "the personal is political", which emerged from the 1968 movement, wimmin and lesbians have pointed out patriarchal power structures within the society – related to the structure of families, sexuality, and the "given roles" of men and women. The oppression of women is analyzed and defined: violence against women, control of their choice to give birth, commercialization of the female body in ads and media, hetero-sexist and male-dominated pornography, genomic and reproductive technologies, exploitation of their labor in the workforce such as unpaid domestic work or less wages in their "real" work life. But it has also to be mentioned that the slogan "the personal is political" has been criticized by women of color (and not only them) as a white universal feminist perspective which does not take into consideration the privileges and benefits contributing to the reproduction of power structures in contrast to the realities of migrant women and women of color.

The "private" living spaces of mixed squats became some of the various new battlefields, scenes of the renegotiation of gender relations. In particular the fields of reproductive work, the understanding of and behavior within roles, and everyday sexism in all of its many facets, love relationships, sexualized violence, and the right and the power of definition came to determine and frame debates and conflicts within the squats.

But the diverse feminist gay and lesbian movements led also to the development of an independent, autonomous organization of wimmin, lesbian, gay, queer and trans people within the squatters' environment and other social movements. Apart from mixed structures and places,

168

they squatted their own houses, created their own social centres, bookstores, publishers, newspapers, radio and video groups etc., organized spaces for wimmin and lesbian, queer and trans people only. The first feminist and lesbian occupation of a flat in West Germany took place in 1973 in the Freiherr vom Stein Straße 18 in Frankfurt am Main. From the first big squatting wave in 1980/81, until 2015, around 20 houses in West Berlin and Berlin have been squatted by women, lesbian, gay, queer and trans people. Among others: The *Hexenhaus* "Houses of Witches" at Liegnitzerstraße 5 was the first on January 5th 1981, with a feminist women's health centre. It was followed by the "Marianne Devils" at Mariannenstraße 97, the Naunynstraße 58, the Womencafe at Jagowstraße 12, the Kottbusser Straße 8 - the only occupation by migrant women - the Danckelmannstraße 15 with the FFBIZ (Women, Investigation, Information and Education Centre), the sex-worker squat (with the self-organized group Hydra) at Potsdamer Straße 139 or the woman centre chocolate factory at Mariannenstraße 6.

More squats followed in the '80s, among them the first woman *wagenplatz*[1] next to Georg von Rauch Haus in 1984, and during the second wave of squatting in 1989-90, especially in East Berlin. Some have been evicted after a short time, including: the Mariannenstraße 9-10 (after one day in 1989), Erkel (1990), Dieffenbachstraße 33 (1990), the women-house at Mainzer Str. 3 or the *Tuntenhaus*[2] (House of Drag) at Mainzer Str. 4, but some places still exist: the wimmin-lesbian-trans-house in Brunnenstraße 7, the queer-anarcha-feminist houseproject in Liebigstraße 34, the women's backyard house in Grünbergerstraße 73 or the queer *wagenplatz* Schwarzer Kanal. In December 2012 another such house existed: the women's only space in the occupied Refugee Strike House at Ohlauerstraße 5.

SEXISM WITHIN THE SQUATTING MOVEMENT

Sexism and sexualized violence against woman is an ongoing phenomenon in mixed squatted spaces in Berlin and other cities. Issues of domination and sexism became important for many squatters to work on. A report by the group "women and squatting" during a nationwide meeting in Münster, West Germany, in 1981 pointed out: "Structural patriarchal violence has many faces and comes along sometimes more subtle, sometimes more massive in various manners and shapes." (*Frauencafe Moabit* 1982: 38-39).

At that meeting women reported their treatment by men, noting that they were not taken seriously, that there was a lack of respect towards autonomous women's spaces, that they were confronted with mistrust, a lack of understanding, rejection, insults, that they were sworn at and called names ("men-hater", "uptight tense feminists"). Such verbal attacks led to a crossing of boundaries, sexualized violence and even rape against women. For these and other reasons it seemed, unsurprisingly, that the women of the *Hexenhaus* did not want to live with men. "Nobody wanted to do that voluntarily, that would have been at least one step backwards", explained one of the witches.

Several occupations of lesbian, gay, drag queens, queer and transsexual houses in Berlin can be understood as emerging from the deconstructionist and queer-feminist discourses that, since the 1990s, began to question categories of sex, and to break open the regularity of given bipolarities of sex. These projects have made the growing criticism of heteronormativity within the squatting scene more visible. The new queer politics arose from a critique of lesbian and gay identity politics, as well as bisexual and trans-gender questioning of dichotomous and fixed identity concepts.

Queer and feminist theoretical discourse is marked by an intersectional approach in which other components of domination and existing power structures contribute to a broader concept. People of color and other precarious people criticize the invisible normal of whiteness and middle-class positions, and demand greater attention to the complex character of identities. Critical whiteness, post-colonialism, feminism, anti-semitism, anti-ziganism [racism towards Romani people] or anarchism are just some of the political concepts and movements that have been contributing to this new understanding of the complexity of power relations.

The first Tuntenhaus was occupied in 1981 in West Berlin in Bülowstraße 55 and evicted two years later. It was well connected with the gay scene, and monthly meetings of the Berlin gay groups happened there. The second Tuntenhaus, where 30 gays were living, was very visible, glamorous and enigmatic. It was squatted in May 1990 in Mainzerstraße 4 in East Berlin, but soon after evicted after three days of fierce resistance. The Tuntenhaus distanced itself from the mainstream and institutionalized gay movement and came into conflict with them. During the annual Gay Pride demonstration in 1990, some of the radical drag queens of the Tuntenhaus were thrown from the stage while reading a solidarity statement with relatives of imprisoned RAF[3] members. On the other hand they were well integrated in the left gay scene and very active in the squatting movement. The Tuntenhaus was best known for their Tuntenshows in their backyard. In the Mainzerstraße, where in

170

total 11 houses were occupied and some 200 people were living, they became a public symbol of the whole street. "The Tuntenhaus, the tuntentower, the haunted house of the street, was far and away the most beautiful, pretty, most kitschy, trashy, and garish house and the biggest stumbling block for all the neighbors." The third Tuntenhaus, located in Kastanienallee 86, was installed after the eviction of the second one and has been legalized. Some of the inhabitants have participated in political projects like the *Schwule Antifa* (Gay Antifa), the *Querulanten*, and the newspaper *Tuntentinte*. They have participated in debates about homophobia, sexism and macho behavior, and joined and organized mobilisations for the *Rattenwagen* (rat track), the Transgenial CSD (Gay Pride), the *Stöckeltreffen* (meetings of drags with stiletto heels), the *Tunten Terror Tour*, or the *Homolandwoche* (annual week-long meetings of radical gays at different places in Germany). They celebrate their famous *Tunten Festival* in their backyard every year, with people in drag, shows, singing, and German pop music.

The queer *Wagenplatz* Schwarzer Kanal was first squatted in 1989 as a "mixed project" and had to move two times due to gentrification measures in the district Berlin Mitte, the centre of Berlin.

The Schwarze Kanal plays an important role in the squatting and wagon place movement as well as in the autonomist queer and trans scene. They organize the Queer and Rebel Days as well as the annual Entzaubert DIY radical queer film festival, and take part in broader mobilisations like the Queer Barrios at the Anti-G8 Summit Camp in Heiligendamm (2007), the autonomous *Queerruption Festival* (2003), and are active in the *"wir bleiben alle"* (we stay all) campaign.

NOTES

1 Literally translated "wagon place," a *Wagenplatz*, is, a location where house trailers for living are located, usually squatted

2 The *Tuntenhaus* (House of Drag) is a community of gays, queers, drag queens and per-verts, after their own definition. See tuntenhaus.squat.net.

3 RAF (*Rote Armee Fraktion/* Red Army Fraction) was an urban guerrilla group from 1970 to 1998.

Gängeviertel, Hamburg

Nina Fraeser

1

In late August 2009, a gathering in the remains of the historically working class Gängeviertel in Hamburg turned into a crowded, colorful party. One by one, the vacant and forgotten houses were opened up to reveal exhibitions of all kinds in an action orchestrated by a small and secret group called 'the family.' The visitors, ranging from families to journalists, artists and party people, did not notice that this happy spectacle marked the official day when 12 buildings in the city centre of Hamburg got squatted. 'The family' had held regular meetings. They had prepared banners for a demonstration in case of police repression, and a refuge inside one of the buildings ready to resist eviction. Civil paramedics were present as well as lawyers connected to a media centre, and activists reaching out to local politicians inviting them to the Gängeviertel. Margit Mayer called this first weekend-long event a form of 'squatting with performance character'. Monday morning came and went. Against the expectations of everyone involved, the police had not come to evict, and local newspapers, even conservative ones, reported positively about the artist-squat.

The Gängeviertel was awakened from the oblivion it had fallen into following decades of disinvestment. The formerly rebellious workers quarter became a new home to the radical ideas of free spaces, anti-gentrification, autonomy and the right to the city movement. The historic area's look and feel contrasts with the polished central shopping and business areas surrounding it, located as it is between the Springer publishing house and the former Unilever headquarters, the Emporio high rise of glass and steel.

The last remaining sector of harbour workers' housing, production and struggle was endangered by the sale to Hansevast, a Dutch investor, in the early 2000s, but the occupation on August 22 2009 changed everything. Since then, more than 200 people have joined the Gängeviertel association and half of them consider the quarter their everyday living space. Today it is as much a working and living place, as it is a cultural venue, experimental zone, political centre, party location and tourist attraction.

2

The Gängeviertel emerged out of a conversation about rising rents and living costs, gentrification, the shortcomings of interim-use policies, the exploitation of cultural production and social work, and a critical assessment of Hamburg's politics of neoliberal urban competitiveness and welcoming of the so-called 'creative class'. On the Monday after the festival the activists understood very well that the main reasons they were not evicted as usual were the overall positive media response and widespread public support, which stood in direct relation to their artistic appeal. Simply put, their appearance differed strongly from previous attempts to squat. The same day the Gängeviertel held a press conference applying their tactical mixture of improvisation, professionalism and humour, in which they announced: Dear city of Hamburg, we are helping you to reach your goals facilitating a creative city of talent – here we are, with a cultural programme and a space; we are many and multiplying.

Gängeviertel courtyard

This initiated a second critical phase in the life of the Gängeviertel. It was collectively decided to focus on cultural programming, organizing events and exhibitions while taking a rather cooperative stance towards authorities. The group invited politicians for conversations and also regretfully moved out of two central buildings after the city came into conflict with the owner, Hansevast, for tolerating the occupation. The tactics of emphasizing the architectural heritage and applying artistic playfulness to the process resulted in broad support from local elites and media. The outcome of a constant internal struggle among the diverse group of squatters, their strength was a wide variety of actions stemming from the experience of artists, architecture and media professionals, radical autonomous activists and others. All this together put pressure on the city's political elite to accept its responsibility not only for this unique piece of built history but also to deal with the demands and questions raised by the occupation.

3

The simplifying process of mass media coverage made the Gängeviertel known as the artist-squat throughout Germany and beyond. Despite the much more contradictory and colorful reality, and the differences among those engaged in the Gängeviertel, the group was fully aware of the power of the creative and cultural concept as it related to the neoliberal urban strategy of the creative city, which was prominent on the local political agenda in Hamburg. By assuming an artistic image instead of that of radical political activity they survived not only the first 48 hours but also the second critical phase which lasted until some kind of legalization of the occupation was achieved. The group even tactically avoided the term 'squat' in their communications with the press and politicians. In December 2009, the impossible happened and the city signed a reverse transaction with Hansevast, in fact buying back the Gängeviertel from the private developer and announcing the willingness to develop a future for the quarter together with the Gängeviertel association.

4

From the very beginning the Gängeviertel consciously traded on its cultural and creative capital with the local government. Thus there is a fear amongst some activists and critical observers that it will develop in the future into just another clean and neat artistic urban space. In a complex process of institutionalization and negotiation with the public authorities, the buildings in the Gängeviertel are currently undergoing renovations carried out by the city's housing development agency

174

(SAGA). Thus, the process is closely tied to the Gängeviertel's working group on development, backed up by the weekly general assembly, based on a use and development scheme the activists presented to the city in mid-2010. The future of the Gängeviertel is unclear however, particularly as regards how much autonomy will be left for the inhabitants and those otherwise involved. There is a concern about the commercial pressure of the rents after the renovation. An underlying question is also how to keep people involved in such a communal space while at the same time having long-term rental contracts, which will force many to make a living outside of the Gängeviertel.

So far most of those engaged see their activities as a collective effort, but people are prepared for the moment when this turns into exploitation. It seems likely that the Gängeviertel will still offer an exciting cultural and important social programme while having to pay rents and taxes and the collective effort will turn into voluntaryism. Until now, institutionalization is understood as a performative condition constantly trying to resist co-optation, but the Gängeviertel remains an 'endangered space of possibility' – a *Möglichkeitsraum* Based on my personal experience in the Gängeviertel, I would say that as a result of

A Press conference at Gängeviertel

the processes of institutionalization, renovation and co-optation there is
a tendency for radical political activists to leave the quarter seeking other
more autonomous spaces. At the same time, it remains a point of entrance
to social movement activity and political engagement due to its openness.

5

Until now the Gängeviertel's 'look and feel' differs from its surroundings
and prevents many from entering its courtyards, especially those visitors
who feel more comfortable in the the consumption-based public spaces
making up much of the rest of central Hamburg. It is important to mention
here that the Gängeviertel is not just made out of the occupied buildings
but draws essential qualities from the courtyards within as well. They
remind us of the multiplicities of what "public space" could be. These
spaces of entrance to the Gängeviertel are counter-public spaces,
transmitting the feeling of entering a semi-private place, challenging
the dichotomy of public-private. Such places of encounter, of living in
difference, where usage and engagement can overrule questions of
ownership, are experiments towards a spatial practice of commoning.

6

Those dynamics create internal tensions which I want to address briefly.
As argued above, it is largely due to creative and artistic appeal, and
the tactical reference to neoliberal 'creative city' politics that the radical
action of squatting has been tolerated and legalized instead of violently
repressed, making space for the ongoing cultural, social and political
activities in the Gängeviertel. Moreover, there is a constant negotiation
between the autonomy of the space and its willingness to institutionalize
and cooperate with the city authorities. Taking this into consideration, I
see a tension between the two poles of autonomy and institutionalization
on the one hand, and artistic and political activism on the other. These
can be imagined in the shape of a cross, in one dimension the two
poles autonomy from the state versus total institutionalization; and in
the other dimension radical collective political activism versus individual
artistic realization. Somewhere in the centre between those tensions lie
spaces of what I have called 'creative autonomy', spaces such as the
Gängeviertel. Creativity itself is a contested concept. It is a contemporary
struggle to give meaning back to it, or as Peter Marcuse states, to turn
it into a conceptual opposition to commerce and use it as critique of
capitalist productivity. Different forms of 'flexible institutionalisation' as
Miguel Angel Martínez calls it, have entered the discourse of autonomous
movements. Under neoliberal capitalism it seems, the aim of radical

political autonomy as the (only) subversive tactic is called into question. It may be that through institutionalisation and an emphasis on creative and artistic appeals, spaces for radical and critical cultural, political and social activities can last in the city centre.

FINAL

For five years now, the Gängeviertel has embraced its changing state. Rather than reviewing social movements in terms of their 'successes', or giving another account of how a neoliberal urban regime co-opts, commodifies and exploits radical activities, its example calls for a different perspective. Describing the case of the Gängeviertel shows how the contradictions of current capitalism can be hacked for the benefit of social movements and spaces of collective inventiveness. Within such spaces of creative autonomy as the Gängeviertel in Hamburg we need to focus more on social reproduction as a battleground creating accessible spaces 'beyond contemporary forms of domination' as Stavors Stavrides calls it, from which we can move collectively towards a radical imagination. However, it cannot be forgotten that it is a fantasy of antithesis which keeps alive projects refusing to be projects, attractions refusing to commercialize their spectacle, creativity refusing to be trapped in the borders of productivity and profitability.

Space is a doubt: I have constantly to mark it, to designate it. It's never mine, never given to me, I have to conquer it.
Georges Perec

REFERENCES

This text is inspired by my experiences at the Gängeviertel and also the thoughts and questions in the collective's publication Mehr als ein Viertel published for their fourth anniversary in 2013.

Miguel Angel-Martínez (2014) How Do Squatters Deal with the State? Legalization and Anomalous Institutionalization in Madrid. International Journal of Urban and Regional Research, 38(2), pp.646–674.

Peter Marcuse (2012, video) The Right to the Creative City.

HUB Westminster. At: http://vimeo.com/29290392

Margit Mayer (2012, German) Hausbesetzungen als politische Aktionsform seit den 1970er-Jahren. In: M. Nußbaumer & W. M. Schwarz, eds. Besetzt! Kampf um Freiräume seit den 70ern. Wien: Czernin Verlag GmbH und Wien Museum.

Georges Perec (1997) Species of Spaces and Other Pieces, London: Penguin Books.

Stavros Stavrides (forthcoming 2015) Re-inventing Common Space. Towards a Politics of Urban Commoning, London: Zed Books.

Activism and Camping in Documenta 10, 11 and 13

Julia Ramírez Blanco

Documenta's great art exhibitions, taking place in the city of Kassel every five years, were one of the first in Europe to include the presence of contemporary activist groups. Over time, the relationships between artistic institutions and radical movements have taken different forms and iterations. This article examines this tradition of encounter through different editions: Documenta 10, with *Kein Mensch Ist Illegal*, Documenta 11 with *Park Fiction* and the *PublixTheaterCaravan*, and Documenta 13 with *dOccupy*.

One of the first times in which activism was included in a major exhibition took place in 1997. During Documenta 10, curated by Catherine David, "some three or four dozen political activists, media activists, photographers, film directors and artists"[1] published a manifesto entitled *Kein Mensch Ist Illegal* (No one is illegal).[2] Cultural activist Kamen Nedev speaks of the total novelty at that time of seeing an activist event inside an artistic venue.[3] The manifesto would be the starting point for a coalition of autonomous anti-racist groups defending freedom of movement for all people. From this group emerged the No Border network which in 2001 started to install its so-called No Border Camps "as near as possible"[4] to national frontiers.[5]

In 2002, Documenta 11, curated by Okwui Enwezor, was dubbed the "postcolonial Documenta". Together with many political works commenting on the problems of national borders, there was also an installation that talked about Park Fiction, a collective planning process against gentrification in the neighborhood of St. Pauli in Hamburg. Entitled "Multiplicity and Park Fiction", this work by activist-artists Christoph Schäfer and Margit Czenki was a thematically organized archive comprising photographs, maps, letters and drawings. A flowchart painted on the wall, represented the relationships between the different neighborhood agents taking part in the process. This representation in Documenta is now seen as a crucial step in an activist victory that effectively used an accumulation of cultural capital.

However, also in Documenta 11, there was conflict with another autonomous group linked to antiracist struggles. That summer, the No Border coalition, together with a group of Roma people (aka gypsies) at risk of being deported, organized an event called *Platform 6* in front of the Friedericianum Museum. This experience was not featured in the exhibition program. On August 1, 2002, the Publix Theater Caravan, a caravan of performing and media activists[6] who formed part of No Border, parked their vehicle in the square in front of the museum. Once there, the idea was to convert the space into what they called a "NoBorderZone", carrying out radio broadcasts, interviewing visitors and staging performative actions.[7] After several hours of these activities, the security services of the event appeared on site. In his text "Liar's Poker", Brian Holmes describes some reactions from within the art world:

> *Okwui Enwezor, artistic director of Documenta, phoned New York. The curator Ute Meta Bauer and other collaborators and artists supported and intervened. Thomas Hirschhorn and other artists and workers at the event passionately debated the hierarchies of Documenta and the security systems. In brief, an intense night.[8]*

In spite of the support of the artistic team, the activists would be forced to show their documentation to the security staff and would later be evicted. In front of the building of the Documenta in 2002, real repression opposed the supposed freedom and autonomy of the art space.

Five years later, Documenta 13 seemed better prepared when a group of people attempted to stay in the space outside the museum. In 2012, taking the name dOCCUPY, a group of artists connected to the Occupy movement but differentiated from it, decided to camp next to the Fridericianum Museum building. Instead of evicting the activists, there was now a welcome on the part of the curatorial team. The curator herself took a stand, supporting Occupy and linking it to the glorious tradition of Documenta and the mythologized figure of Joseph Beuys.

She said, "It appears to me to be in the spirit of the moment and in the spirit of Joseph Beuys who marked Documenta and its history significantly, embodying another idea of collective decision making and political responsibility through direct democracy."[9] The reference to Beuys was something conscious on the part of the dOCCUPY movement itself, which took as a slogan the artist's famous phrase, "Everyone is an artist."[10]

In these moments, the occupation of the Documenta space could be read as part of a larger story where, as we have seen, the encounter between the quinquennial event and the protest camps took on different meanings. In the light of the precedents, what happened in 2012 can be seen as an iconographic reiteration of the question of the activist camp in front of the Friedericianum. It is as if in a re-enactment, the situation has been corrected, changing its outcome to one that is more politically correct. This change can be framed in an ongoing evolution of the relationships between art and radical politics, where accounts of autonomous movements now seem to be integrated into the official artistic discourse. What this actually means for social movements, however, is an important question open to discussion.

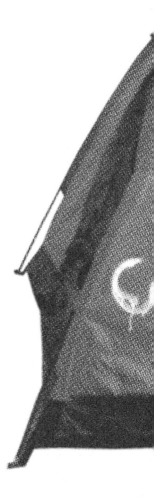

NOTES

1 Florian Schneider, "Hackeando la frontera" [Hacking the Border], in Paloma Blanco, Jesús Carrillo, Jordi Claramonte and Marcelo Expósito (eds.), Modos de Hacer. Arte Crítico, Esfera Pública y Acción Directa [Ways of Operating: Critical art, public sphere and direct action] (Salamanca: Ediciones Universidad de Salamanca, 2001), 208.

2 Kein Mensch Ist Illegal, http://www5.kmii-koeln.de/; Deportation Class Project, http://www.noborder.org/archive/www.deportation-class.com/.

3 Personal conversation, January 20, 2014.

4 "Direct Action. No Borders, No Nation", in Notes from Nowhere (ed), We Are Everywhere (London/New York: Verso, 2003), 429.

5 During the summer of 2001, a whole series of settlements was set up simultaneously in places such as the Polish border, the Strait of Gibraltar, Tijuana, and Frankfurt airport. The camps were not only protest spaces but were also configured as communitarian experiments. The one at Strasburg was the biggest example of this kind of enclave. See Gerald Raunig, Art and Revolution. Transversal Activism in the Long Twentieth Century (Los Angeles: Semiotexte, 2007), 245-265.

6 The Publix Theater Caravan is a project started in 2001 by members of the activist theater group Volxtheater Favoriten, which was founded in 1994 [in a squat in Vienna – ed.]. The Publix Theater Caravan was conceived as a nomadic caravan which forms part of the No Border network, where activists practice performative actions and media interventions. See Raunig, Art and Revolution, 245-265.

7 See "Publix Theater Caravan Moves on to the Documenta 11 in Kassel", No Border Network, accessed March 2, 2014, http://www.noborder.org/strasbourg/display/item_fresh.php%3Fid=138&lang=en.html.

8 Brian Holmes, "Liar's Poker", in Unleashing the Collective Phantoms: Essays in Reverse Imagineering (Autonomedia, 2008), 87.

9 See "dOCUMENTA (13) Artistic Director welcomes the 'occupy' movement", accessed March 3, 2014, http://d13.documenta.de/#/press/news-archive/press-single-view/?tx_ttnews%5Btt_news%5D=159&cHash=e26d0c1a6f7c d3f67904003cbb2aeb33.

10 Aislinn White and Amy Walsh, "Occupy dOCUMENTA: The state of dOCCUPY", 2011, August 14, 2012, accessed March 2, 2014, http://www.inthetent.org/research/?p=496.

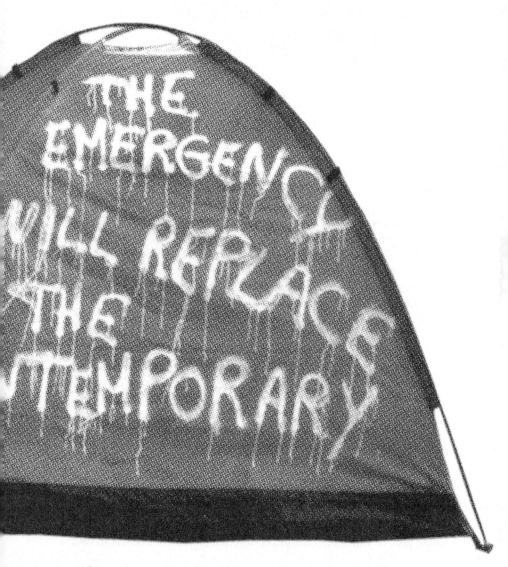

The City for All! The Appropriation of Space and the Communication of Protest

Tobias Morawski Translation by Jeannette Petrik

CURRENT URBAN MOVEMENTS OF PROTEST

Currently, the political agendas of many western metropolises feature topics such as the increase of rental prices, housing shortages, displacement of people with low income, increasing privatisation of the public space and calls from the general public to participate in urban planning. Social movements around the world are organising and connecting against the implications of neo-liberal urban politics—for a "right to the city" for all. An important part of their demand is the creation of affordable housing in a social city. All urban residents should, supposedly, be able to decide how urban life is shaped independently from their origin or social status.

... USING THE EXAMPLE OF BERLIN

The "*Mediaspree Versenken*" ("Sinking the Mediaspree") campaign initiated a broad social debate against the privatization of the riverside by the Spree. Within a few years protests increasingly formed against increases in rental prices and the wave of accompanying evictions. Calls for broader social co-determination became increasingly louder—e.g., against the planned development of the former airport Tempelhof, and the extension of highway A100 through the city Center of Berlin.

URBAN APPROPRIATION

Social movements intervene in the struggle for power and partake in the urban sphere with symbolic and concrete actions. Their aim is to create spaces by means of appropriation, making meaning, collectivization, and making them accessible and open for participation independent from a capitalist market economy (rent, entrance fees, etc.) which therefore allows for equitable social cooperation.

Current debates around the topic of gentrification often create the impression that unwritten laws following the logic of the free market economy have directed urban development, and that these mechanisms are hard to counteract. It's not only the history of squatting in Berlin which shows that there are and have been possibilities to interfere. I'd like to use the history of squatting and urban art in Berlin as examples in order to give insight into current urban protest movements and, thereby, present applied strategies for the appropriation of spaces.

SQUATTING IN BERLIN

In the early 1980s, the squatting movement was a determining subject in the urban politics of Berlin. The city's squatting movement was triggered by a growing lack of housing. While whole streets were vacated of tenants and left to decay, tens of thousands looking for housing remained

without a home. InstandbesetzerInnen created an awareness of this
serious deficit by moving into those ruins and making them livable again.
Thus, squatting was widely accepted and became a popular medium
for civil disobedience. The squats of the 1980s prevented large-scale
destruction of old buildings, and the planned construction of a highway
through the Kreuzberg district. Squatting actions created cultural and
social spaces in the city which have been protected against neoliberal
uses in the long term.

After the fall of the Berlin Wall, a second big squatting wave came
over Berlin in the early 1990s which affected predominantly the city's
cultural development. Today, there are hundreds of housing and cultural
projects all accross the city which have their origins in squatting. They
can abstain from the housing market and its speculations due to property
contracts negotiated from positions of strength. Their existence as
social spaces in the Center of the city is secure, unlike privately owned
properties.

Due to the "Berliner Linie", a decree which allowed for the eviction
of newly squatted properties within 24 hours, and a lack of empty
buildings squatting has seemed less and less possible, especially in
central areas.

REVIVAL OF SQUATTING AS A FORM OF ACTION

Even so, with the rise of numerous urban protest movements since
2012, a growing number of houses and squares have been occupied.
Senior citizens occupied their meeting place in the Wedding district to
secure its existence. Inhabitants squatted a square around the U-Bahn
station Kottbusser Tor and built a hut as a place for meetings and protest
against rising rents and displacement called "Kotti&Co". Refugees set
up camp on Oranienplatz in protest against their bad living conditions
on the margins of German society, and squatted a former school in
Kreuzberg in December 2012 ("Refugee Strike"). A self-organised space
with community gardens, camp site and open-air gallery for graffitti grew
up on one of the last undeveloped properties by the River Spree in
Kreuzberg, the "Cuvry-Brache".

SQUATTING AS A STRATEGY FOR COMMUNICATION

Most current forms of squatting have shifted their focus away from the
concrete occupation of space. Like a permanent demonstration, squats
today predominantly work as a means to communicate protest and

represent the socially excluded or displaced.

The hut of the initiative *Kotti&Co* at Kottbusser Tor is frequently used as a meeting space by tenants of the surrounding high-rises to organise against the rises in rent and displacements from their district. It is built from wooden pallets after the example of a Turkish *gecekondu*, a building constructed overnight. Since the occupation of the square and the setting up of the protest camp in early 2012, neighbors and tenants have demanded the lowering of rents, limits on rents, communalising of social housing, and a stop to forced relocations. They aim to stay until all of their demands are met. The initiative uses the means of physical appropriation of space. Through the squatted square and the *gecekondu*, a place for communication, exchange and networking between neighbors is created. The initiative regularly organizes noise demonstrations through neighboring areas.

REFUGEE STRIKE—FOR BASIC PARTICIPATION

The refugee protest camp at Oranienplatz in Kreuzberg evolved as an organ for refugees who speak up for freedom of movement and

acceptance of their basic needs. The camp was set up in October 2012 after a 600-kilometer-long protest march of refugees from Würzburg to Berlin. Their action initiated an unprecedented wave of protests by refugees and illegalized migrants in Germany.

The refugees counteracted their "invisibility", lack of economic means and refused rights to participation in social daily routines with offensive strategies of communication. They make themselves noticed through occupations at central places, with demonstrations and hunger strikes in the vicinity of Centers of political power around the Brandenburger Tor.

To avoid having to spend the winter outside, some of the refugees squatted an empty school at the Ohlauer Straße in Kreuzberg at the end of the year. Both the building and the protest camp became drop-in Centers and accommodation for more than 100 refugees and illegalized migrants. These points were used to organise their spectacular protest actions. Shortly after their arrival in Berlin, the refugees organized one of the biggest demonstrations by asylum seekers in Germany, and gained media attention with squatting actions.

FREE PARTIES

The techno culture Berlin serves as an example to underline the importance of temporary squats for the realm of cultural production. The situation after the fall of the Berlin wall—large numbers of empty spaces, the political vacuum of power and unsolved property issues—facilitated more than a second wave of urban squatting. Simultaneously, illegal parties in factory buildings paved way for today's clubbing and party culture.

Squatting enables the avoidance of bureaucratic and economic issues. Often official licenses, legislative terms and rental prices stand in the way of creating temporary open spaces of encounter that can withdraw from economic forces, state control and existing social conventions. Part of the techno movement still practices the concept of free parties, meaning self-authorised, freely accessible and therefore parties and cultural events uncontrolled by government. A large part of the city's techno scene also distanced itself from its initial ideals, however, and chose to commercialize.

Since the turn of the millennium, sound systems have conquered parks, empty spaces, derelict land and other public space. Central urban spaces are transformed into dance floors, whereas formerly raves were held in factory buildings. As empty space and derelict land increasingly

disappear from the city Center, more and more organizers of open air festivals have turned to public parks like the Hasenheide in Neukölln as event venues.

DESIGN OF THE PUBLIC SPACE: URBAN ART

In the process of design and appropriation of the public realm, both political and artistic movements intervene while supporting and interacting with each other. Art and design in the public realm always involves a political dimension. It is inseparably connected with questions of what the public sphere should and could be, as well as whose interests are heard and considered.

The Berlin Wall presented the city with a unique situation for the development of graffiti culture. In West Berlin, police mostly tolerated painting the Wall. It therefore developed into one of the world's biggest open-air galleries.

In West Berlin, the squatting movement shaped the urban landscape since the early 1980s. With graffiti slogans commenting on housing struggles and violent conflicts with police, squatters appropriated whole walls and facades as creative spaces. In the east of the city, slogan graffiti was used to criticise the state of the DDR popularly and anonymously. Security agencies rigorously tried but mostly failed to suppress the public graffiti culture.

As in many other cities of Europe and Latin America, the so-called style writing developed as a youth culture. This is the writing of names or words as images, and has become popular through depictions in documentary films and movies about U.S. graffiti culture, e.g. Wild Style, Style Wars and Beat Street. Since the early 1980s, it has effectively changed the appearance of most cities of the world.

Like squatters and free party organizers, spray can graffiti writers took advantage of the situation after the fall of the Berlin Wall in 1989, the legal vacuum and the many empty walls in eastern districts to paint uncontrolled on a large scale. This sudden exceptional opportunity for appropriating of space helped the city of Berlin to gain an image as the "graffiti capital of Europe". An increasing number of artists used the open public space to experiment with new techniques. Soon, "street art", the more illustrative branch of graffiti, became a highly visible mass phenomenon.

Since the mid-to-late 2000s an increasing amount of large-scale graffiti has a political content that often points to urban political protests. Slogans such as "Love Art—Hate Cops", "Fuck off Mediaspree" or "Please Live" refer back to the wall drawings from the era of squatting.

The increasing popularity of self-empowered design in public space is by now also used by the advertising and urban marketing industry. A facade drawing of Blu on the formerly squatted Cuvry-Brache by the Spree, which shows a chained person wearing a formal suit, has become one of the best known and most reproduced graffitis of Berlin in spite of, or maybe due to, its socially critical content. Even the urban marketing platform "be berlin" used the image for advertising on its homepage. After property owners had the Cuvry-Brache evicted in order to build luxury flats on the property, the artists covered the large-scale drawings with black paint. His art was not supposed to become a set for urban revaluation and displacement.

CONCLUSIONS

The city, public space and its design always express, and are the result of, social debates and tensions. It is a scene of struggles. Expressions of protest in urban political conflicts are processes of communication within the public sphere. The staging of protest in the form of

demonstrations, or artistic interventions such as graffiti, or depictions of space through maps, demonstrate presence in the urban space. The city Center of Berlin is a daily scene of lively public debates.

On the one hand, appropriation and preservation is central to creating the basic premises for an equal debate, that is, equal access to space and its use. On the other hand, the appropriation of public space is always a symbolic act. Choices of the means of communication, such as imagery and symbolism give hints about the status of access or exclusion from public spaces. Therefore, to question means of communication is to consider access to or exclusivity of means of communication, and possibilities for participation.

Means of communication which can be used by the majority of inhabitants of urban spaces, e.g. non-commercial billboards, or freely usable house walls bring into being well-balanced possibilities to participate in public debates. Berlin's walls clearly show that its residents have a large need for communication and discussion. Space, artistic creation, communication and politics are interdependent. Space is needed to facilitate communication, creation is needed to make communication heard, and on a political level, to debate conditions which allow for spatial encounters.

Actions of appropriation such as the squatting of buildings or squares, blockades of planned constructions or evictions, demonstrations about rental prices, neighborhood gardens, graffiti culture and uproars by illegalised migrants are expressions and strategies of urban protest movements advocating grassroots urban developments. The city belongs to all.

REFERENCES

www.graffitiarchiv.org − Graffiti archive in Berlin

www.reclaimyourcity.net − Online archive of Urban Art & the communication of protest in the public space

Italy

194

195

Centri Sociali (Social Centers) in Italy

Eliseo Fucolti

Centro Sociale Occupato Autogestito means Self-managed Squatted Social Center. In a few words ...

Self-managed Squatted Social Centers are spaces, generally but not necessarily urban, occupied by a heterogeneous collective of people, acting independently of any external political supervision, who use it to meet their own needs and to give space to creative projects outside commercial and speculative business. Social Centers have a radical left political orientation, and many of them are related to post-autonomist or anarchist practices. Self-management involves self-organization in the repudiation of racism, fascism, sexism, social hierarchies and all forms of oppression.

The name "Social Center" expresses the attempt to produce an open, liberated, alternative space in opposition to private, closed, and guarded commercial spaces. Squatting is the fundamental action that gives abandoned areas back to people. Squatted buildings include abandoned schools, churches, factories, theaters, military fortresses, and farms. Squatting opens a confrontation with authorities that can lead to eviction, tolerance or legalization (recently some Social Centers in Genoa were legalized by the municipal council).

There is not a single way to organize self-managed activities, and the debates among the various Social Centers is always open. Generally, Social Centers are organized through regular weekly meetings. But running large buildings where dozens of collectives work is rather different than carrying out activities in small premises. In Milan, the Social Center Leoncavallo is located in 10,000 m² of a former printing factory. In Rome, Forte Prenestino occupies a former military fortress extended over approximately 100,000 m²! Nevertheless, many Social Centers manage small spaces between 300 and 500 m².

Currently, the list of activities proposed by Social Centers is huge, and they are offered with a continuity not covered in the commercial circuit. All kinds of socio-cultural activities are offered: study courses in music, photography, dancing, yoga and martial arts, movies, concerts, rehearsal and recording rooms, art exhibitions, restaurants and wine bars, libraries, legal advice, theatre, dancing hall and gyms, hacklabs and bookshops, etc.

Money for activities is collected through voluntary contributions made by people attending them or through fund raising organized with special events, in a few cases some cooperatives were set up.

LEGAL FRAMEWORK

In Italy, the occupation of a property of others (even if dilapidated) is an illegal act ruled by the article 633 of the penal code: invasion of land or buildings (*invasione di terreni o immobili*). Squatters are also charged with theft of energy (gas or electricity). Since 1985, more than 500 Social Centers operated all across Italy, many were evicted but many others are still run by various collectives.

MUSIC

Social Centers have supported and encouraged musical creativity. Many bands that are linked to Social Centers have became popular, for

example: 99posse, Africa Unite, Alma Megretta, Assalti Frontali, Banda Bassotti, Bisca, Bloody Riot, Brutopop, Casino Royal, Franti, Kina, One Love Hi Pawa, Piombo A Tempo, Radici nel cemento, Sangue Misto, Subsonica, Sud Sound System, Ustmamò.

SOME COMMENTS

Bureaucracy and political parties do not like organizations that they cannot control, unless they are aristocratic clubs. Those are fine, even when they commit horrendous illegal activities such as gambling or betting.
Dario Fo

Even today, in Milan, the municipality has large quantities of empty and available spaces, but it always prefers to let them deteriorate and crumble, rather than make them available to someone who is not part of their political gang.
Dario Fo and Franca Rame

Though it may be hard to tell at first, the social centers aren't ghettos, they are windows—not only into another way to live, disengaged from the state, but also into a new politics of engagement
Naomi Klein

Leoncavallo, thank you.
Gabriele Salvatores

I had the opportunity [to gain] *a better understanding of young people involved in social centers and in anarchist circles. I found them brave, proactive, dialectical, and demanding attention. I think they are the only ones who can uncover and make clear to other young people the attempt to act against them, against freedom and the earth.*
Luigi Veronelli

In social centers I meet people with whom I can talk about subjects that interest me, and then I always end up playing.
Manu Chao

CHRONOLOGY

Beginning the 1970s, in Italy radical left movements in Italy have squatted abandoned buildings to set up social activities. Since Then squatting has been part of a large social movement opposing the reactionary policies carried by the Christian Democracy party. The Social Centers in the 1970s were mainly limited to Milan, and in a few,cases Bologna or Rome. Since the mid-1980s, however, the experience of Social Centers has, in a series of phases, spread all over Italy.

MAIN PLACES AND EXAMPLES BY PERIOD/PHASE

1975–1984
First generation of squatting linked to the movement of the 1970s and the Autonomia movement:
Milan (Leoncavallo, Fabbrikone, Fornace)

1985–1989
Second generation punks, anarchists, post-autonomists:
Bologna (l'Isola), Catania (Experia), Florence (Indiano), Genoa (Officina), Jesi (TNT), Milan (Cox18), Neaples (Eta Beta), Padova (Pedro), Palermo (Montevergini), Pisa (Macchia Nera), Rome (Forte Prenestino), Turin (El Paso)

1990–1999
Third generation following the movement of students in universities at the beginning of year 1990:
Cosenza (Gramna), Falconara Marittima (Kontatto), Livorno (Godzilla), Milan (la Pergola), Neaples (Officina99), Rome (Corto Circuito, ex Snia, Viscosa)

2000–
Fourth generation linked to alterglobalization movement and new wave of squatting for housing:
Bologna (Bartleby), Genoa (Pinelli), Milan (Casa Loca, Vittoria), Reggio Calabria (Angela Cartella), Rome (Acrobax, Ateneo, ESC, Metropoliz)

Not Only Liberated Spaces: Italian Social Centres as Social Movement and Protest Actors

Gianni Piazza

Social Centres in Italy are not only "liberated spaces", empty and unused large buildings occupied by groups of radical left activists to self-manage political, social and countercultural activities. They are also social movement and protest actors, whose repertoire of actions includes other unconventional forms beyond squatting, such as civil disobedience, symbolic protests, pickets, road and railway blockades, raids in institutional offices and unauthorized demonstrations, sometimes ending in clashes with police. They are urban protest actors because, by being spatially localized in city centres or in peripheral/working class districts, they can be involved in denouncing the scarcity of space for sociability outside of commercial circuits, and campaigning against market-oriented renewal and urban property speculation. Their reach of action is often not only local, but also regional, national and global: local struggles (for social spaces and services, for housing, against urban renewal, etc.), always set in global framework, and related to extra-local ones (for migrants' rights, no militarization, no war, alter-globalization, etc.). In fact, since the beginning of the new millennium, Italian Social Centres' activists have contributed significantly to the alter-global and No War movements. More recently, they have participated as important actors in current social movements: the student and university movements in defence of public education (the Anomalous Wave); protection of the "commons"; and in the movement against the privatization of water and the Locally Unwanted Land Uses movements (*No Tav in Val di Susa* and *No Messina Bridge*

Take Over The City

Our struggle involves everyone
Who doesn't want to be a slave any more
Who's conscious of their strength
Who's not afraid of the bosses any more
Who wants to change the world in which we live
    into the world that we want
Who knows that the time to fight is NOW
    that there's no time to wait

If we don't have a house we take one
In our communities we fight against rent
We defend ourselves from evictions
We want justice for the people
And to be free to live a communal life

Together, we, the working class, are rising
We know that the barracks we live in
    are a weapon used by the bosses
From the estates to the shanty towns
From the factories to the schools
There's only one struggle

We've turned the bosses' schools
    into Red Bases
Bourgeois culture can't touch us any more
There's a revolt in the prisons too
Soon they'll be empty
To make room for the bosses

Refrain

    A red wind is blowing
    Over the factories and estates
    It unites everyone of us
    Who've decided to fight
    For revolution
    For freedom
Let's take over the city

(A Lotta Continua song)

against large public works, *No Dal Molin* and *No Muos* against U.S. military bases in Veneto and in Sicily, etc.). Social Center activists contribute to transform these movements from local (NIMBY—Not In My Back Yard) to global (NOPE—Not On the Planet Earth). Another key example is the anti-austerity movements against national and European Union governments. There is no significant radical left movement in Italy without the fundamental activism of Social Centres.

Teatro Valle, Rome

Teatro Valle

The occupation of Teatro Valle, the oldest still functioning theatre in the city of Rome, dating back to 1727, happened on June 14th, 2011. This event followed a series of fortunate and related circumstances which designed, from the very start, the theatre's vocation as a meeting point for common practices.

On one hand, structural budget cuts and rumors of privatization—which give an alarming picture of the situation of culture in Italy—were the focus for a more mature and extended phase of the fight for workers of the immaterial. At the same time, the referendum against the privatization of public services related to water, held just one day before, highlighted the role of the public sector in defending citizens' rights.

The rest is history: the temporary occupation was a striking success. The echo was huge, and the theatre filled with people all day and all night long. Important artists offered free shows, culture personalities gave public endorsements in support of the protest which turned from temporary into permanent.

Teatro Valle Occupato won the Ubu Special Award for 2011 from the Italian Academy for Theatre. More prizes would be awarded throughout 2011 and 2012, among them the EuroMed. In 2014, Teatro Valle Occupato was awarded the European Cultural Foundation Princess Margriet Award.

For three years Teatro Valle Occupato has been an established reality in town, both as an artistic landmark with a vocation for the contemporary, and as a political laboratory where the theory of the commons is elaborated through the practice of collective self-government.

Teatro Valle functioned as a host theatre. Writing, acting and stagecraft workshops filled out the artistic program. *Crisi* by Fausto Paravidino (director and author of *Exit* and *Texas*), and *Cavie* by Cristian Ceresoli (author of the acclaimed *La Merda*, winner of the 2012 Edinburgh Fringe Festival), were followed by the new workshop *Rabbia*, for research in new dramaturgy. *Nave Scuola* ("Training Ship", whose name recalls the sailing background of the first stage technicians) has

202

been training new professionals, who can learn stagecraft by practicing on the spot in one of the few stages which still works with manual machinery.

But artistic programming was just one side to the vocation of Teatro Valle Occupato. A few months on from that incredible summer, the occupiers and the larger assembly involved in the experience decided to launch an experiment: creating an institution of commons. The slogan "Like water, like air, let's take culture back" became more and more concrete. The idea is that some things are not commodities but belong to the community—natural resources, human creations, material and immaterial things, ideas and places. The occupiers, helped by jurist Ugo Mattei, wrote the future foundation's statutes (Teatro Valle Commons Foundation), and published the drafts under discussion on the website, to gather further feedback from the associated citizens. Meanwhile, through a citizenship share offer, funds were raised to establish the capital of the foundation. More than 5,000 founders contributed over 130,000 Euros.

Out of the various and complex political practices undertaken by the activists, the *Constituent of the Commons*[1] was born, in April of 2013. Promoted by Professor Ugo Mattei and a group of jurists and scholars who intended to revive the results of a commission chaired by Professor Stefano Rodotà in 2007, the *Constituent* defined the commons as a third entity between private and public property, with the final objective of revising a part of the Italian civil code.

The *Constituent of the Commons* emerged in several self-governed and occupied spaces across Italy, and at Teatro Valle where the law-drafting sessions took place. It was an innovative experience based on the belief that the system of law is alive and can be changed and reviewed through bottom-up processes.

On September 16th, 2013 the occupants signed the final draft of the statutes in front of the notary public and established the Teatro Valle Commons Foundation. Since that moment, the attitude of Italian institutions towards this unusual occupation, which brings horizontal participation to the threshold of the corridors of power (Teatro Valle lies just two blocks away from the Italian Senate and the Government offices), became openly aggressive.

In February 2014, the Prefect of Rome denied the legality of the Foundation when application was made. The denial didn't concern the contents of the statutes or the self-government model, but rather the simple fact that the official street address of the Foundation was an occupied space, and the Foundation has no title to it. The day before

204

the arrival of the letter of denial, the Prefect disclosed during a press conference that the situation of Teatro Valle could not be solved with a public order, but "needed a political solution", which the Mayor of Rome inappropriately called a "final solution" during a TV interview.

On July 15th, 2014, an international call to protect Teatro Valle Foundation from eviction was launched. Among the many signatories were David Harvey, Slavoj Zizek, Étienne Balibar, Michael Hardt, Costas Douzinas, Fabrizio Tamburini, Stefano Rodotà, Salvatore Settis, Christian Laval and Pierre Dardot. On July 31st 2014, the municipality of Rome urged the occupants to leave the premises. After a press conference the occupants succeeded in gaining ten more days, which then became a permanent assembly where the citizens participated and contributed to the decision to stay or leave the theatre. The choice was conflictual and very difficult. The heterogeneity of the assembly made the decision process a real challenge. The choice to allow the work of renovation to proceed prevailed. Now Teatro Valle Foundation, as an informal institution, confronts and monitors public institutions on matters which involve choices on Teatro Valle as common ground and, ultimately, the relationship between decision-making processes, participation, and self-government.

Presently, the collective of occupants meet more than once a week at different friendly spaces. They continue to discuss and debate about culture and politics, and continue to struggle. The game is open. One of the fields in which the Foundation is playing is the *institutional* field: are the public cultural institutions ready to engage in a real, innovative, revolutionary bottom-up process? Can the impressive three years of experience be considered significant enough to formulate a completely new way of governing a public cultural space? Stay tuned, because it has to be continued ...

NOTES

1 Here the word "constituent" means "while constituting", or "in the process of constituting", so the Costituente dei beni Comuni, or "Constituent of the Commons", is both the assembly and the process where this new construction regarding the commons takes place.

Telestreet: Pirate Proxivision

Patrick Nagle

Telestreet is the name for the collective of short-range television stations in Italy that take advantage of gaps in signal coverage to broadcast their own content. Telestreet stations make use of TV receiving technology's capacity to transmit signal. Franco Berardi (a.k.a. Bifo), a founding member of Italy's first pirate station OrfeoTV, notes that because Telestreet employs consumer-grade technology for broadcasting, its range is limited to a small area; thus, Telestreet is not so much tele-vision as it is proxi-vision.

There is a historical precedent for pirate broadcasting in Italy set by Radio Alice, a pirate radio station started in Bologna in 1976 broadcasted from an old tank transmitter. The station was politically affiliated with Autonomism, known in Italian as *Operaismo* (literally "workerism"), a distinctive subset of Marxism that focuses its analytical efforts on the functioning of the workplace and the importance of immaterial labor to capitalist economies. The station eventually closed in 1979, but not before inspiring countless other pirate radio stations throughout Italy, some of which still operate.

Yet Radio Alice and Telestreet share more than an independent ethos: Franco Berrardi, who founded OrfeoTV, is an autonomist thinker who played a role in Radio Alice. Telestreet is thus part of a rich tradition of pirate broadcasting and autonomist politics in Italy. But to understand Telestreet, we cannot merely locate it in a historical tradition; we also need to contextualize it within its moment—Italy at the turn of the 21st century.

Italian TV has two main networks: one is state owned, the other is a private station started by former prime minister Silvio Berlusconi. According to the *Economist*, Berlusconi, while in office, had retained effective control of 90% of all national television broadcasting. He also owned a print publishing house and a myriad of other enterprises. We can therefore read Telestreet as a reaction against Berlusconi's domination of the media. Yet while the emergence of Telestreet is infused

Stills from the video documentary <u>Telestreet: The Italian Media Jacking Movement</u>, including interviews with activists from TeleAut and SpegnilaTV and media theorist Franco "Bifo" Berardi.

with past and present Italian leftist politics, the medium is by no means the exclusive domain of the radical left.

Broadcasted content, which varies by station, is often a mix of popular entertainment; segments by local video journalists and documentarians; amateur ventures into video art, film, and even traditional TV narrative genres; and programming drawn from archives and the internet. Telestreet thus cross-pollinates with the internet, print media, video, and even local gossip. This diversity of content raises an important issue for my examination of Telestreet: the medium is not restricted, in theory or in practice, to politically radical broadcasters nor to original content. In fact, Telestreet is a popular way of distributing pirated pay-per-view soccer games and other forms of commercial entertainment free of charge. An anonymous journalist (under the *nom de plume* Luther Blisset) claims that there is at least one Christian station. Telestreet thus poses a crucial question for radical media: can a media practice be radical by virtue of its form alone?

Telestreet seems to be poised between alternative and tactical media. Telestreet is relatively mobile, spreads easily, has the ability to engage with current political issues, and flouts the law to capture unused channels within a mass medium (qualities that have all been associated with the tactical); yet stations most often take the form of identifiable, relatively stable, local sources of information (often associated with the alternative). Perhaps the best way to articulate the tactical and alternative elements of Telestreet is to say that tactical interventions become possible within an alternative media source. Telestreet provides an opportunity for tactical practice that can be easily accessed by turning a TV to a certain channel.

Telestreet does not offer any guarantee of political radicalism. Indeed, Luther Blisset argues that one of Berlusconi's television stations, like Telestreet, is operating illegally, only using a much more high-powered trasmitter. But herein lies the difference between Berlusconi and Bifo: Telestreet takes consumer-grade materials and transforms them into broadcasting systems at a relatively low cost. Berlusconi, on the other hand, leverages his political and commercial clout to further saturate the television market. There is, I argue, something radical in the Telestreet form itself, but perhaps this radicalism has more to do with roots than with political ideology. Like a plant's roots, Telestreet insinuates itself in whatever space is available, forging connections. In some sense, taking broadcasting into one's own hands is political — perhaps a fundamental condition for media politics. But this act alone is not sufficient. The channels thereby opened are ambivalent, open to

The production methods of a telestreet are a little strange

in the sense that there is a mix of incredibly old technology

together with new technologies such as the internet.

I'm transmitting. We're going live at the moment.

This is the video mixer where we mix the different signals.

VHS, video camera, computer.

then it goes to the transmitter,

which is hidden behind here,

which has a cable that you can follow up there,

which then goes to the antenna...

which is what sends the signal out..

across this area..

..of San Lorenzo.

any kind of content. Perhaps the greatest potential of Telestreet is that opening new, grass roots channels within a traditionally "mass" medium provides an opportunity to shift the terrain of politics itself, to bring new issues to the fore and to experiment with alternative forms of political practice.

REFERENCES

video documentary
Telestreet: The Italian
Media Jacking Movement:
https://www.youtube.com/
watch?v=2EKQNtLXm4o

InsuTV's live feed
http://www.insutv.it/index.
php?sz=2&id=52

Telestreet: 'The Public Is Not
for Sale,' The street television movement in Italy (ca.
2003) by Matteo Pasquinelli.
Pasquinelli is a media activist
and critic based in Bologna,
Italy. He worked as a journalist
for the Italian public TV (RAI)
and has been involved in
several projects of media activism including Luther Blissett,
Indymedia and Telestreet.
He is editor of Rekombinant
(www.rekombinant.org), an
influential Italian weblog
focusing on media culture,
geopolitics, immaterial labour,
and creative avant-gardes.
Rekombinant is connected
to other international
internet-based critical-thought
communities such as Nettime
and Multitudes.] -- http://www.
servus.at/VERSORGER/64/
Telestreet.html

210

Franco Berardi (Bifo)
is an Italian media theorist
and a founder of "Orfeo TV",
one of the first Telestreets.

MACAO: Establishing Conflicts Towards a New Institution

Emanuele Braga

Macao is the name of a new self-organized centre for the arts in Milan, a city that until now has managed to create neither contemporary art museums nor community centres for experimental arts. Macao was born during a national uprising that led to the occupation of many public spaces. These answered a call for a more accessible culture through a radical process of reclaiming centres for the towns.

This is a widespread movement that involves citizens, performers, entertainers, artists and cultural workers, a movement that crosses, encompasses and describes a new map of political action of the last twenty years. The points on this map mark different political experiences: Teatro Valle Occupato, Cinema Palazzo, Angelo Mai in Rome, Sale Docks and Teatro Marinoni in Venice, Asilo della creatività e della conoscenza in Naples, Teatro Coppola in Catania, the Cantieri Arsenale and Teatro Garibaldi Aperto in Palermo. In the Milan area, many of the artists involved in Macao are active within the Isola Art Center, a grassroots movement that is fighting jointly with the local community of Isola to promote the creation of arts centers against the massive gentrification of the neighborhood.

THE ARTIST AS A WORKER: HOW TO ESCAPE THE DEBT TRAP

For a little more than a year a group of visual artists, critics, audio technicians, video editors, musicians, designers, arts managers, choreographers, and electricians from all over Milan have set up open meetings on a regular basis to discuss their social role as workers.

During these meetings we discuss some of the delusions which are the foundations of our exploitation and the direct cause of injustice. Show business, media, entertainment, fashion and design areas are the pillars of industry in Milan, with more than 66,000 new employees every year.

An army of overly trained and educated professionals who have invested big money in postgraduate courses, degrees and certificates land in a job market which is ready to exploit them, underpay them and subsequently eject them.

Capitalism captures and exploits the value produced by the risk that each worker is now forced to pay directly, because both the private and public sector are no longer willing to pay the price for it. All workers, more or less consciously, endure a general feeling of frustration due to a lack of artistic success. Both employers and the government teach us to stay humble because we supposedly owe them something each time they give us the chance to fill the void created by our incapacity of self-realization. Through this mechanism, we are considered isolated individuals, and we have lost rights and contractual leverage. Meanwhile the various monopolies, the stock market and government accumulate more and more economic and political power, exponentially increasing the equality gap and preventing the redistribution of wealth.

ART AS THE PROCESS OF TRANSFORMATION: FIGHT IS A LANGUAGE

Since the 1st of April, 2012, Macao has been online, as a new centre for the arts and culture in Milan. It began with a month-long countdown that was part of a viral campaign that would culminate in the occupation of Torre Galfa, a skyscraper that has stood abandoned for more than fifteen years in the heart of Milan.

Torre Galfa is the property of Salvatore Ligresti, one of the most

infamous real estate brokers in Milan, who was sentenced more than once for corruption and Mafia-related crimes.

The acronym Macao is a mock-up of the names of the various large art institutions: Moma, Macba, Mambo, Maxi, Macro, and others. It offers a new perspective on the idea of museum: a museum made by militant artists. Macao acts as an alternative to art as an autonomous concept, deprived of any potential revolutionary power, endorsed and enhanced only through the circuit of galleries and private collections, and evaluated only by critics on a leash.

Furthermore Macao rejects the wide-spread tendency to turn fights into something purely esthetic. Commercial distribution is mainly interested in critical contents and struggles only as long as they are out of real context, and entirely dignified as commercial products. Macao strongly asserts that any direct action intended to transform reality can be a performance that involves all our talents as artists, communicators, theoreticians, philosophers, architects. Sharing all our knowledge and talents in a radical fight is the only way Macao intends to produce arts and culture.

FINANCIAL BUBBLE, REAL ESTATE SPECULATION, POLITICAL IMPEACHMENT

In a few days Macao filled the skyscraper with thousands of citizens ready to give their time, abilities and goods to build a new museum. Self-organized teams of architects, performers, theoreticians, video artists, web developers, communicators, hackers, gardeners, electricians, plumbers, bartenders and the staff from the main universities and academies started planning their classes at Torre Galfa. Images of the skyscraper of 109 meters illuminated by blue lights, a true museum of art built by the public, circulated widely through the web. It was a product of collective consciousness, born from local communities, from day-to-day struggle, from pure political action.

What is the true meaning of an empty, thirty-two-story skyscraper in the heart of Milan, abandoned for fifteen years, even as new skyscrapers are being built at high speed in a neighborhood that clearly disapproves of them and doesn't need new threats to its scarce green areas? It means that in times of crisis, real estate speculation in this city directly serves financial speculation with no value whatsoever for the community of citizens that actually live there. It means that the owner of the real estate has no interest in renting or selling property because a real market would devalue it. He is more keen in keeping the property as a warranty for bank loans. So it goes: many buildings are useless to the city but are worth billions to banking funds through societies such as IMCO and Sinergia in partnership with the insurance company Fondiaria-Sai, main debtor to MedioBanca and Unicredit (two giant groups of the Italian banking system) and future acquisition prize to Unipol. These corporate alliances hide the interests of the main Italian political parties

WHAT'S LEGAL AND WHAT'S LEGITIMATE? THE CRISIS OF REPRESENTATION AND DIRECT DEMOCRACY

Despite the support of Nobel prize winners, international cultural institutes and countless others, we fight against very strong enemies. During the occupation of the skyscraper we wrote an official letter of caution to police forces and the public ministry. Together with the finest experts on the Italian Constitution we state that, based on article 3, 9, and 43, a political movement of citizens has the right to take charge of private property in cases of clear misuse of the space and proven damage to the community related to that misuse.

With this legal document we stated through the practice of struggle, that private property is not a dogma, but must submit to a larger frame of public utility, that sees in the building of a community and in the practice of direct democracy objectives that are as legitimate are those of private property supporters.

Repression was the immediate answer. The Minister of Domestic Affairs Annamaria Cancellieri gave direct orders to the Chief of the Police of Milan to evict Macao from Torre Galfa. A few days later we discovered that Piergiorgio Peluso, the son of the Minister of Domestic Affairs, is the manager of Fondiaria Sai, the very company that owns the skyscraper. A group of criminals who have been speculating for years in the city with direct damage to the citizens was teaching us what is legal through the use of force. Meanwhile a multitude of citizens found it legitimate to freely give all their time, effort and capacities to build a common good. Democracy needs people to rediscover the political value of self-organization, dismissing systems of representation which have proven ineffectual and insufficient, if not simply harmful.

COMMON GOODS: BEYOND PUBLIC, BEYOND PRIVATE

After five days of the occupation of Via Galvani—the street in front of the skyscraper—Macao called a press conference and officially launched an occupation of the building right there in front of newspapers and

215

journalists. The crowd at the press conference was led through two subway lines to mislead police forces. After a joyful move, hundreds of us entered Palazzo Citterio, a beautiful abandoned 700 meter building in the neighborhood of Brera. This building is the object of a renovation plan aimed at creating a massive museum complex based on the model of the Louvre. It has been empty for 40 years. The project has never been implemented, and two years ago, public managers stole 52 million euros in funds addressed to that project.

Macao invites everyone to build a new community museum involving citizens and asks for transparency and clarity from the public administration in regards to its project and how it will be funded. The Minister of Culture promptly replied: "My personal conviction, and I believe it's not just mine, is that no truly cultural movement, no truly cultural production can spring from an act of unlawfulness". A few days later Macao was cleared away with a massive display of police and military force.

To the well-doers who consider Macao just a deranged group of youngsters in need of space for arts and a bit of work, we replied with the occupation of the most important museum project in town, claiming justice and transparency for the common goods now managed by the private and the public sector.

Macao is currently occupying the former slaughterhouse of the fruit and vegetables market. We hold that a self-organized museum can be as legitimate as any institutional project. We are heating up the public debate on the subject of regulation and innovation as a solution to the effects of a financial and democratic crisis.

Common goods are not just given by Mother Nature: they are born from the daily struggle of citizens claiming their need for them, and finding ways to organize. These new forms of self-government are a concrete and real answer to the mass suicide organized by our system of neoliberal governance.

France

218

219

Situationism and its Influence on French Anarchist Squats

Margot Verdier

In France, artists' and anarchists' squats form two separated networks that only meet through exchanges between individuals. If this division is mainly due to their relationships with authorities, it also involves two different conceptions of the connections between art and politics. As other texts in this book speak about the artistic movement, I present here the anarchist conceptualization which is deeply influenced by the theories of the Situationist International.

The social changes which overwhelmed Europe throughout the 19th century also led to questioning of the role of culture in society. The arts had to emancipate themselves from the constraints of ancient codes and norms. Whereas the romantics defended the individuality of artwork as a reflection of the "genius" of the artist, another conception emerged. It established itself in socialist movements, and brought a new reflection on the link that unites culture and social organization. Anarchists in particular took a stand. In *Du principe de l'art et de sa destination sociale* (1865), Proudhon (1809-1865) supports the realism of his friend Courbet, and affirms the political function of an art designed to represent the real living conditions of the population. As for Kropotkine (1842-1921), he calls artists to "take the side of the oppressed", to fight "for light, humanity and justice" (*Aux Jeunes Gens*, 1880).

Finally, in *The Social Significance of Modern Drama* (1914), Emma Goldman gives a precise definition of the social role of the artist. For her, modern art is not only about aesthetics as it was in the "art for art" movement of the 1830s, but also aims to transcribe the intellectual and emotional implications of social life in a subjective vision of reality. Work is therefore a catalyst of transcendental truths. It is a shared language, and encourages the social transformation that is necessary to a real revolution.

In this way, anarchists distinguished themselves from the communists of the day by questioning culture as a pillar of any social system, just like economics and politics (Antliff, *Anarchy and Art*, 2007). Similar ideas developed throughout the avant-gardes of the beginning of the 20th century.

Born in 1957 from the junction of several artists' collectives, the Situationist International (S.I.) synthesized these theories into a strong ideological frame. Calling itself a critical Marxism, the S.I. thinks of culture as an intermediary. Through its transformations, the superstructure, constituted by politics and social customs, adapts to the new conditions of production, to the new economic infrastructure. In *La société du Spectacle* (1967), Guy Debord opposes representation which freezes a partial reality into an abstraction, and daily life, the order of present time and familiar space, that unifies reality throughout the experience of existence. Consumption society marks the advent of capitalist culture which regards these images as sacred. This supremacy of sight disconnects the individual from the immediate experience of life

Posters at the Atelier Populaire in the occupied Ecole de Beaux Arts

by turning him into a spectator of the show provided by the leaders of the society. Therefore, emancipation necessarily involves a radical questioning of contemporary culture. Daily life is to be collectively appropriated through the destruction of every specialized discipline that submits individuals to the expertise of the insiders. Art first.

In France, the theories of the S.I. constitute one the most important ideological influences of the 20th century. Like sociologists such as Henri Lefebvre, the Situationists especially tried to think the relationships between culture, social organization and urbanism as a specific kind of art. Thus, they accompanied the renewal of squatting practices. The history of occupation is long. With the uprising of new social movement in the late '60s, it became one of the main modes of action. Since then, squatting is not only about asking for land or housing, but it is also a means to create a balance of power with the authorities by opening interstices inside which new modes of being and new forms of relations can be experienced.

In anarchist squats, the collective operation depends on the horizontality of the decision-making processes to which every individual is invited to contribute; on the search for alternative modes of exchange, of goods and knowledge, and on the struggle against every kind of domination. Culture, in the larger sense, is politicized, and artistic practices are therefore socialized. They contribute to propaganda, serve expression and the sharing of social conditions (as in participation theater for instance), invite themselves into political actions (clown brigades and the percussion of Batucada have become classics in contemporary demonstrations), and join with craft (cabins of la ZAD de Notre-Dame-des-Landes create an anarchist urbanism based on individual and collective initiative and imagination).

Influenced by Situationism, French anarchists frequently refuse to merchandise their work or at least to do it inside the alternative spaces of the squat network. Art is offered as a means of expression and direct exchange between individuals. It is ephemeral, grounded in the desires and needs of present time. The figure of the "genius" artist, that imposed itself against the conservatism of the end of the 19th century, now serves the interests of capitalist culture through the system of art market. This contributes to the rejection of the title of "artist". Therefore, in most French anarchist squats people paint, sculpt, write or sing, but they refuse to call themselves artists.

In the Situationist conceptualization, culture appears as a system separated from daily life by the process of specialization. At first, this phenomenon affected politics and economics with the establishment of state and capitalism, which dispossessed individuals of the means of conceiving and producing their own lives. This contributes to the debate that divides French squatters into different movements. Artistic squats distinguish themselves from anarchists by claiming their specialization and their title, but especially because some of them decided not to take any political stand. This led to a separation between collectives who claim illegality as a means to build the conditions of a social war, a political and cultural revolution, and those who try to normalize their situation in order to build stable workshops and galleries.

Since 2001 and the introduction of the "conventions d'occupation précaire" (precarious occupation contracts), these issues are even stronger. Municipalities use these contracts to submit collectives to their needs (bring cultural activities into gentrified neighborhood for instance) and conditions (no housing, no public events, no smoking, etc.), as it is the only alternative to eviction. Thus, they distinguish a few "good squatters" that respect the deals from the "bad squatters" that must be repressed. The way authorities manipulate the insecurity of squatters so as to differentiate and set up oppositions between legitimate cultural practices and political activism, only reinforces the influence of Situationist theories on anarchist squats.

Emergence and Institutional Recognition of Artistic Squats in Paris

Vincent Prieur

Artistic squats developed in France, and especially in Paris, during the 1980s because of a lack of ateliers and the precarious situations of artists, most of whom live on public welfare.

MEDIATED EMERGENCE OF ARTISTIC SQUATS AND CREATION OF THE INTERSQUAT PARIS

Certain collectives such as the occupants-rénovateurs in the 19th arrondissement, active between 1981 and 1983, sought to avoid the marginalisation affecting political squats or those exclusively devoted to housing. They attempted to open up to neighbourhood associations, develop cultural and entertainment activities, and negotiate with the government for legalisation. They were the first of many to develop a mediated strategy of legitimacy to present a respectable image of their squats.[1]

From the late 1970s to the mid-1990s, media coverage of squats was diffuse, a result of the distrust squatters held towards the outside world and its media.[2] But in 1990, the first meeting of Parisian artistic squats, called *Coordination des articulteurs des lieux en friche d'Ile de France* openly claimed the right to exist in the city.[3]

In 1997, a former high school in the Belleville district was occupied by the Yabon Art collective whose leader Franck Hiltenbrand (aka Yabon) adopted a very open attitude towards the media. The Pôle Culturel Pi was open to the neighbourhood, representing a turning point.[4]

In 1999, two squats opened in the central districts and met with success in terms of attendance. The squat Chez Robert-Electron Libre at rue de Rivoli and the squat La Bourse on the square were located close to the headquarters of major newspapers. This encouraged media coverage of the phenomenon, offering an ideal subject for soft news portraits and life stories.

The demands of squatter-artists are as follows: recognition by the government, places to exhibit and cheap workshops in Paris, contracts with owners to legalise their situations, and for most, the development of alternative artistic practices and a greater closeness between art and public.

Parisian artistic squats were coordinated in 2002 as *Interface*, with a charter bringing together all the common demands of the collectives involved.[5] Active from 2002 to 2004, including the organization of a festival, Interface was reconstituted in 2008 under the name Intersquat Paris around the *Festival des Ouvertures Utiles*[6] (the FOU), which brings together the Parisian artistic squats in a common programming event that represents a moment of high visibility. The Intersquat Paris holds regular meetings, debates, and organises the festival.

INSTITUTIONAL RECOGNITION AND DEVELOPMENT OF LEGAL AGREEMENTS

The early 2000s marked a turning point in the institutional consideration of artistic squats in France.

In 2001, the Secretary of State for Decentralisation and Heritage, for the Minister of Culture in Jospin's government, ordered a report on the "new territories of art" that were currently being developed in France, in which artistic squats were considered extensively.

The same year, the Paris City Council turned left, and Bertrand Delanoë, mayor of Paris and his deputy for culture, Christophe Girard, took measures to save the iconic squat Chez Robert-Electron libre. The Haussmann building was bought for five million euros and brought up to standard in order to maintain it as artists' studios. The initial occupiers retained their management rôle.[8]

In 2002 the Palais de Tokyo contemporary art centre opened its doors in the chic 16th arrondissement of Paris. The building deliberately kept the raw concrete look and could be visited late at night, exactly like the artistic squats. Squatter artists mobilized to accuse the institution of stealing their methods while the evictions of Parisian artistic squats was still going on.[9]

A few months later, a collaboration was organised between the Palais de Tokyo and Interface to achieve the first *"Festival Art et Squats"*. The exhibition at the Palais showed documents telling the history of

225

Parisian squats – maps, photos and documentary films, but no artworks. Visitors were invited to discover the work of squatter-artists in their squats; this link was an important step for institutional recognition of artistic squats.[10]

A proactive policy towards artistic squats continues in Paris. When safety standards permit, the city of Paris legalizes the occupation of its own abandoned buildings with short period agreements.[11] Artist collectives have to produce activity reports and financial statements, and must ensure a minimum of rotation among users. They also have to organise entertainment and cultural activities with the neighborhood.

These agreements are a standard tool for these places. The project commissioning policy represents a form of governance to regulate illegality which might emerge in these empty spaces if they were not contracted.

Successive coordinations have led to the current Intersquat Paris which unites various Parisian squats around a common artistic festival. This dynamic has contributed to the institutional recognition of artistic squats and their needs. Nevertheless, the recent development of temporary agreements represents a possible institutional intrusion in the collectives' activities and the sustainability of the community project among artistic squats.

EPILOGUE

Tensions between political squats and artistic squats in Paris have several reasons. From the point of view of the entertainment industry, political squats develop a Situationist and anti-capitalist critique of art, as heirs of the 1980s autonomous movement philosophy. Squatter artists are considered to be involved in this world.[12] So far as the practice of squatting itself, artistic squats are accused of favouring gentrification of neighbourhoods and supporting the urban policy of excluding the poor.[13] Finally, occupancy agreements could contribute to criminalising political squats and residential squats that cannot benefit from them. However, judging by their event programming, artistic squats are likely to be involved in militant movements related to the problems of the squat itself, to the ZAD rural resistance movement, support of migrants and the undocumented, LGBT movements, green movements, anti-capitalist/ autonomist and anarchist tendencies.

Thanks to Beth-Anna

France

NOTES

1 Cécile Péchu, Squat, Paris, Presses de Sciences Po, 2010, p. 102-106.

2 François-Xavier Drouet, Conditions et effets de l'émergence des squats d'artistes parisiens dans la presse écrite, Sciences Politiques, Rennes, Institut d'Etudes Politiques, 2001.

3 Péchu, op. cit., p.109.

4 François-Xavier Drouet, op. cit.

5 Anonyme, "Interface ou Intersquat, une Histoire de Charte", éditions Un rat qui rit, Grenoble, 2003, in Infokiosques [http://infokiosques.net/spip.php?article66]. The website inter-face.net is no longer active, and this is in the website infokiosque.net that we can find traces of this charter , this website regularly publishes downloadable and printable anarchist texts. The texte in question paradoxically offers a political criticism and an anarchist version on the charter. This document is characteristic of the gulf that exists in France between political squats (anarchist/autonomous) and artists whose speeches squats, objectives, plans and practices are different. There are different types of squats. See Hans Pruijt, "Squatting in Europe", in Miguel Martinez Lopez and Ramón Adell, eds., ¿Dónde Están las Llaves? El Movimiento Okupa : Prácticas y Contextos Sociales, Madrid, la Catarata, 2004, p. 35-60, cited by Cécile Péchu, op. cit..

6 Lauriane Pasdeloup, « La ville vue par... L'Intersquat de Paris », Mouvements, n° 74, 2013/2 p. 89-90.

7 Fabrice Lextrait, "Friches, Laboratoires, Fabriques, Squats, Projets Pluridisciplinaires... Une Nouvelle Epoque de l'Action

Culturelle," Rapport au secrétaire d'Etat du Patrimoine et de la Décentralisation Culturelle, 2001.

8 "Le 59 rue de Rivoli invente l'after-squat", Le Parisien, september 8th, 2009.

9 "L'art des squatters s'explose dans tout Paris", Libération, september 14th, 2002, Marie Lechner et Anne-Marie Fèvre; "La fronde des squartistes", Libération, february 14th, 2002, A-M. Fèvre.

10 Frédérique Dorlin-Oberland; Palais de Tokyo, « Festival Art et Squat »; Marc Sanchez, Festival Art et Squat; see References for citations. Nicolas Bourriaud, the first director of the Palais de Tokyo, developed his theory of relational aesthetics that judge works of art based on human relations contained, produced or generated. This theory, elaborated around this time, is likely influenced by the artists' squats' conviviality (N. Bourriaud, Esthétique Relationnelle, Paris, Les Presses du réel, 2001).

11 Thomas Aguilera, "Innover par les Instruments? Le cas du gouvernement des squats à Paris", in Charlotte Halpern, Pierre Lascoumes, Patrick Le Galès, (under the supervision), L'Instrumentation de l'Action Publique, Paris, Presses de Sciences Po ,2014, p. 417-444.

12 See these texts on the autonomous and anarchist French website Infokiosque [www.infokiosque.net] : Thomas Genty, Art & subversion, deux pôles antagonistes ?, 1999, in Infokiosque, [https://infokiosques.net/spip.php?article11] and anonymous, A mort l'artiste, 2005, in Infokiosque [https://infokiosques.net/lire.php?id_article=273].

13 Elsa Vivant has shown that artists' squats are more

indicators of gentrification than triggers or catalysers. They are part of a wider process that revalorises centrality and its resources (especially cultural ones). See Eric Charmes, Elsa Vivant. La Gentrification et ses Pionniers: Le Rôle des Artistes Off en Question. Metropoles, 2008, pp.31-66.

REFERENCES

Books

Thomas Aguilera, "Innover par les instruments? Le cas du gouvernement des squats à Paris," in Charlotte Halpern, et al., L'Instrumentation de l'Action Publique, Paris, Presses de Sciences Po ,2014, p. 417-444.

Nicolas Bourriaud, Esthétique Relationnelle, Paris, Les Presses du réel, 2001.

Cécile Péchu, Squat, Paris, Presses de Sciences Po, 2010.

Cécile Péchu, "Squat", in Olivier Fillieule, et al., Dictionnaire des Mouvements Sociaux, Paris, Presses de Sciences Po, 2009.

Periodicals

Lauriane Pasdeloup, "La ville vue par... L'Intersquat de Paris," Mouvements, n° 74, 2013/2 p. 89-90.

University Studies

Thomas Aguilera, Gouverner l'illégal : les politiques urbaines face aux squats à Paris, Mémoire de Master Stratégie territoriales et urbaines, under the supervision of P. Le Galès, Institut Français d'Urbanisme, Institut d'Etudes Politiques, Paris, 2010

Frédérique Dorlin-Oberland, Squats d'artistes, perspectives d'un mode d'action. Usages et politiques, Sociologie Politique, Paris, Université Paris 1, 2002.

228

François-Xavier Drouet,
Conditions et effets
de l'émergence des squats
d'artistes parisiens dans
la presse écrite, Sciences
Politiques, Rennes, Institut
d'Etudes Politiques, 2001.

Documents

Anonyme, « Interface ou
intersquat, une histoire
de charte », éditions Un rat
qui rit, Grenoble, 2003, in
Infokiosques [http://infoki-
osques.net/spip.php?article66].

Websites

Palais de Tokyo, «Festival Art
et Squat, du 10 septembre
au 2 octobre 2002», in Archives
du Palais de Tokyo, [http://
archives.palaisdetokyo.com/fr/
docu/tokyonews/tokyonews27.
html]

Marc Sanchez, Festival
Art et Squat 2002, in [http://
www.marcsanchez.fr/
festival_art_et_squats/]

229

Paris: with the Artists of La Générale en Manufacture on Their Terrace ...

Alan Moore

The artists of La Générale squatted a grand empty building in Belleville, central Paris some years back, and got popular. With wild parties attended by movie stars, they became hard to ignore. They were given short-term tenure in an abandoned ceramics school behind the sprawling state (formerly royal) manufactory of porcelain in Sèvres, and began La Générale en Manufacture. All is quiet now, as the artists tiptoe around the listed historical building, making art and music in the light-filled premises. The theater people waited a couple of years, and then were given a building to continue normally. This history—and the theories besides—was laid out in an interview several of the artists gave on their roof terrace in April, 2011.

House Magic

How did you decide that you are going to squat?

Vladimir Najman

I don't think that we choose to be in a squat or in an institution. We have just chosen something that is useful to us. The idea is more to try something and then to try to name it, instead of beginning with choosing something which has already a name. Of course we are not naïve. We know that the squat movement, even if it is not organized, does exist. And I don't think we can really be apart from that. But it is so diverse that everyone can find a place in that movement. In France, but also in Germany and in Denmark, you have social squats. We are not so different from them. Or political squats. That we are for sure. But if we have a political struggle or idea to put in front of everybody, I don't think it's as important as the struggle that a foreigner without legal documents in France could have. This is to say that you can find in Paris very important squats, and we are certainly less important.* But we can [act]

230

without always thinking what is the political or the social meaning, and maybe we are then stronger. It's a kind of a paradox. We are stronger because we feel more free. Are we really free? I don't know.

We have in France a great opportunity in that we have very weak institutions. This is very useful to us. When there are weak institutions, we may be working more for these institutions than they are really working for themselves. I think this is simply because they are not sustainable like we are. Institutions like the FIAC art fair, I don't say that they are bad or good, but they cannot take any risk. They are sclerotic.... They contribute to a reality which is weak as well. I don't think it's very interesting to see how much we are, or you are working from inside institutions, from outside, with them, against them, and so on. Simply because they have their own discourses, and this discourse is not an open one. It's very closed, and made for themselves rather than the ordinary people that we are.

The most sensitive issue in politics today is the empty spaces. I don't mean only the buildings, but the empty spaces of political thinking, of political actions. That's why I said we cannot oppose an activism such as ours and institutions simply because ideally the space where we work is empty. It's some kind of investment into empty spaces which are not only empty by chance. And I do think that one of the most difficult political issues today is the border of the political question, and the way let's say some political institution and including some alternative movement do agree to put a border between politics and something else at some point. So that is interesting, not to cross the border but just to be on the other side of the border, to try to see what's going on there. I do think that the artistic movement of those who recognize themselves in [social] movements is much more interesting than the pure political activism, even the very intelligent one. [To have] an interesting politics, we have to open it.

Béatrice

We went yesterday to *Radio Libertaire* and passed Rue de Rivoli 59, and walked by [the old] La Générale. Maybe there is someone who can say a little bit about from there to here? The walk from Belleville to here?

House Magic

That was my first question, to ask how you decide to squat and why, because it's so different from the U.S. decision—they never come close to this kind of idea. Okay, you have a tradition. Second, how you form your group that's going to do this action, and how it develops, because always the beginning when you have adrenalin, you are crashing this thing and it's growing

231

really fast like an inflatable—tell us that story.

Eric Minkkinen

Well, Belleville was kind of like a snowball you put on top of a mountain, and before La Générale Belleville, there was a bunch of smaller squats and a bunch of different people. We all come from different areas. Eric [Lombard] comes from Zomééé, and we all had some spaces, some experience with squats, and I guess La Générale was one of the biggest ones. Everybody glued up all together and stayed quite a bit. Vladimir was part of the team that opened it. Everybody wound up being there in the end, having a space to work in, or maybe not having it because somebody else took the space. It was quite chaotic organization. Whoever left for two weeks would probably not see their space again. It was a city in itself.

Jerome Guigue

For many of us La Générale in Belleville was really the first involvement in squatting.

Vladimir Najman

Again, the idea was to hide the fact that it was a squat. To hide it as a good surprise after a visit. I'm not sure that we would have have a group of good friends such as this one if it was clear that it was a squat, and a "we gonna defend the squat," political point of view and so on. It was important for the

artists that accepted to participate in La Générale in Belleville and here, but it was important for people just going there to have a cup of tea, to see a painting, to see something. We had three schools around at less than 100 meters. So to have the kids, also the parents, it was important not to use the term "squat" as a political term. "Squat" is a denomination from outside. It is nothing more than not-legal occupation of empty spaces, that's it. And it's not so terrible. The housing question in Paris is very difficult. But it can be more difficult to find a place that is nice for you for working than for living. We wanted a place to work. Now the other point is—to come back to what Erik said—there's not one or two or three or four which have opened the space and will have some legitimation.

Eric Minkkinen

Part of the team.

Vladimir Najman

It's not to critique, but to be precise. I think it's very important not to be in a historical point of view, but to be in a process where you are driven by some point somewhere in the future instead of always coming back to the roots of the beginning, who was the grandfather, and so on. Concerning the question how do we move from Belleville La Générale in the center city to some kind of rich bourgeois neighborhood. How do we move from an illegal space to some kind of legalization—well, the history is important. La Générale in Belleville became a very trendy place, with famous people coming there from TV and radio. Erik didn't watch TV, nor myself, and we did not even recognize them. But at some point we had to decide either we stay there and accept the fact that we are a trendy place or we move, we close that. We say, "Okay, we had three very nice years," and this is pretty rare in a life. The second part is that we had elections in France, and the squat issue was very politicized. It was important to close Belleville before it could be used politically. It's not a question of autonomy or independence, it's simply that it's not very nice to be used by a politician, and there were some who tried. Third, is that after a moment you have a lot of individual interests about keeping things as they are, and this is the beginning of the end. I mean some kind of museum of alternative way of thinking, acting, living and so on. That should not be. These three factors were very important in our decision not to move but to finish. When we said we're going to close it, the Ministry of Culture came and offered us something really nice. The agreement was simple, they said "yes" to everything that we wanted, let's say 80% of what we asked, so at this point we decided we take what is offered to us and

we keep what we have. Meaning that the people that wanted to stay in a trendy place, try something that might become some kind of alternative institution, they could stay there, but it will be their project, their thing, and those who want to move on this agreement can move. So each one decided either to stay or to move. And some people, quite a lot, decided not to stay and not to move.

House Magic

So there is now still La Générale in Paris?

Eric Minkkinen

The city offered a smaller space, mainly all the people who were doing theater and things like that, which today is the Générale Nord-Est.

Vladimir Najman

They had to stop their activities for two years before they get the new space. And for me it was not an option. If I really needed a new place I would try to open a new space somewhere not legally. I won't wait for two years.

Eric Minkkinen

But they did.

Vladimir Najman

That's it. And it was not sure. But even if it was sure, two years, it's a lot of time, you need to do all this bureaucratic work.

Jerome Guigue

And the space they got was much smaller, and they had many internal fights over who would remain in the end. It's a cruel story. Because there were many, and finally there are few staying now.

Eric Minkkinen

At the same time people went through a whole bunch of other places, and a bunch of people moved around. I see people from La Générale in all the other squats as well. The people who wanted to stay inside Paris ...

Published in House Magic #3, 2011

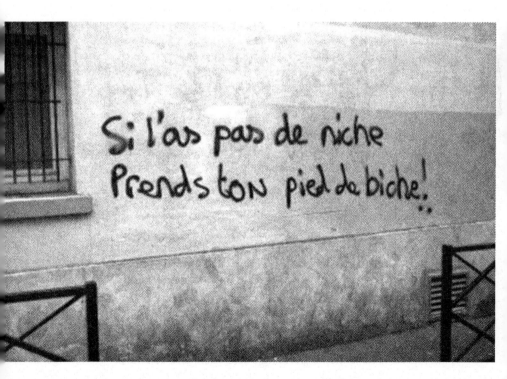

UX

Jon Lackman

UX is like an artist's collective, but — far from being avant-garde and confronting audiences by pushing the boundaries of the new — its only audience is itself. More surprising still, its work is often radically conservative and intemperate in its devotion to the old. Through meticulous infiltration, UX members have carried out shocking acts of cultural preservation and repair, with an ethos of "restoring those invisible parts of our patrimony that the government has abandoned or doesn't have the means to maintain." The group claims to have conducted fifteen such covert restorations, often in centuries-old spaces, all over Paris.

What has made much of this work possible is UX's mastery, established 30 years ago and refined since, of the city's network of underground passageways — hundreds of miles of interconnected telecom, electricity, and water tunnels, sewers, catacombs, subways, and centuries-old quarries. Like computer hackers who crack digital networks and surreptitiously take control of key machines, members of UX carry out clandestine missions throughout Paris' supposedly secure underground tunnels and chambers. The group routinely uses the tunnels to access restoration sites and stage film festivals in, for example, the disused basements of government buildings.

UX's most sensational caper (so far, at least) was completed in 2006. A cadre spent months infiltrating the Pantheon, the grand structure in Paris that houses the remains of France's most cherished citizens. Eight restorers built their own secret workshop in a storeroom, which they wired for electricity and Internet access and outfitted with armchairs, tools, a fridge, and a hot plate. During the course of a year, they painstakingly restored the Pantheon's 19th- century clock, which had not chimed since the 1960s. Those in the neighborhood must have been shocked to hear the clock sound for the first time in decades: the hour, the half hour, the quarter hour.

When UX members risk arrest, they do so with a rigorous, almost scientific attitude toward the various crafts they aim to preserve and extend. Their approach is to explore and experiment throughout the city. Based on members' interests, UX has developed a cellular structure, with subgroups specializing in cartography, infiltration, tunneling, masonry, internal communications, archiving, restoration, and cultural programming.

Its 100-odd members are free to change roles and are given access to all tools at the group's disposal. There is no manifesto, no charter, no bylaws—save that all members preserve its secrecy. Membership is by invitation only; when the group notices people already engaged in UX-like activities, it initiates a discussion about joining forces. While there is no membership fee, members contribute what they can to projects.

So what does the group do with all this access? Among other things, it has mounted numerous clandestine theater productions and film festivals. On a typical festival evening, they screen at least two films that they feel share a nonobvious yet provocative connection. They don't explain the connection, leaving it up to the audience to try to discover it. One summer, the group mounted a film festival devoted to the theme of "urban deserts"—the forgotten and underutilized spaces in a city. They naturally decided the ideal venue for such a festival would be in just such an abandoned site. They chose a room beneath the Palais de Chaillot they'd long known, and to which they enjoyed unlimited access. The building was then home to Paris' famous Cinémathèque Française, making it doubly appropriate. They set up a bar, a dining room, a series of salons, and a small screening room that accommodated 20 viewers. They held festivals there every summer for years. "Every neighborhood cinema should look like that," UX spokesman Lazar Kunstmann told me.

The restoration of the Pantheon clock was carried out by an UX subgroup called *Untergunther*, whose members are devoted specifically to restoration. The Pantheon was a particularly resonant choice of site, since it's where UX began, and the group had surreptitiously screened films, exhibited art, and mounted plays there. During one such event in 2005, UX cofounder Jean-Baptiste Viot (one of the few members who uses his real name) took a close look at the building's defunct Wagner clock—an engineering marvel from the 19th century that replaced an earlier timepiece. (Records indicate the building had a clock as far back as 1790.)

Viot had admired the Wagner ever since he first visited the building. He had meanwhile become a professional horologist working for the elite firm Breguet. That September, Viot persuaded seven other UX members to join him in repairing the clock. They'd been contemplating the project for years, but now it had become urgent as oxidation had so crippled the works that they would soon become impossible to fix without re-creating, rather than restoring, almost every part. "That wouldn't be a restored clock, but a facsimile," Kunstmann says. As the project began, it took on an almost mystical significance for the team. Paris, as they saw it, was the center of France and was once the center of Western civilization; the Latin Quarter was Paris' historic intellectual center; the Pantheon stands in the Latin Quarter and is dedicated to the great men of French history, many of whose remains are housed within; and in its interior lay a clock, beating like a heart, until it suddenly was silenced. *Untergunther* wanted to restart the heart of the world.

As soon as it was done, in late summer 2006, UX told the Pantheon about the successful operation. They assumed the administration would happily take credit for the restoration itself and that the staff would take over the job of maintaining the clock. They notified the director, Bernard Jeannot, by phone, then offered to elaborate in person. Four of them came—two men and two women, including Kunstmann and the restoration group's leader, a woman in her forties who works as a photographer—and were startled when Jeannot refused to believe their story. They were even more shocked when, after they showed him their workshop ("I think I need to sit down," he murmured), the Pantheon administration later decided to sue UX, at one point seeking up to a year of jail time and 48,300 euros in damages. Jeannot's then-deputy, Pascal Monnet, is now the Pantheon's director, and he has gone so far as to hire a clockmaker to restore the clock to its previous condition by resabotaging it. But the clockmaker refused to do more than disengage a single part—the escape wheel—that was the very part that had been sabotaged in the first place. UX slipped in shortly thereafter to take the wheel into its own possession, for safekeeping, in the hope that someday a more enlightened administration will welcome its return.

Vive la Miroiterie: A Preemptive Elegy

Jacqueline Feldman

"There is going to be a war," Anne-Sophie Devos says. She pulls beers
from a borrowed shopping cart, setting them on the outdoor bar before
us. She lives and bartends at La Miroiterie, a former mirror factory
in Paris's 20th Arrondissement that artists and others have illegally
occupied for 13 years, accruing a measure of fame. As I serve beer with
Devos, a punk band plays a concert, producing phlegmatic screams and
a steady, percussive drone.

After this month, police plan to evict the squat at 88 rue de
Ménilmontant. Punk, rap, and jazz concerts that have drawn thousands of
bands from several continents will lose a venue, and 13 squatters will lose
their home. The complex—two buildings sitting on a fenced courtyard—
measures about 1,400 square meters in total. An industrial room on the
ground floor accommodates about 150 concertgoers. Two hundred more
can crush into the courtyard. Upstairs, the factory's onetime offices are
bedrooms and a painters' workshop. Two Brazilian men who live at the
squat teach free capoeira classes three evenings a week. The residents,
artists, and concert organizers have worked together. Once they dressed
as spotted sheep and bleated as they marched downhill to City Hall. Look
what the system does to you, they were saying. Lately, though, eviction
weighs on La Miroiterie, and these people sort messily into factions.

Entering the squat is like entering a jungle. Thick layers of bright
spray paint cover the walls of the courtyard, depicting a blonde doll's
head, a pink-and-blue My Little Pony, and six-foot-tall penises arranged as
a waving hand. A three-legged cat prowls the courtyard. Strings of lights
and dried vines drape the courtyard walls. Black paper butterflies stud
them.

Devos serves beers to mostly men with gauged ears, scowls,
Mohawks. One man has improved his bald spot by shaving a stripe down
the back of his head that continues, skunklike, into his neck. In general,

Devos disdains these punks. They are just passing through. She hands them cans across the counter top covered in moldy stickers, and I follow her lead. Other times we serve mulled wine in quickly melting plastic cups. Someone's German shepherd curls on a low table adjoining the bar. Tonight's music is so loud; I wonder how the dog can sleep.

This concert is Michel Ktu's birthday party. He is 46. His girlfriend, who is 32, joins us behind the bar. She holds back a lock of my hair to whisper: Ktu is shy about his birthday. "He is a public figure, he gives interviews left and right, but it's the timidity of the artist," she tells my ear. "I find it touching."

Ktu, who organizes the punk concerts, helped found the squat in 1999. He spotted the shell of the factory. He had long moved in a circle of artists for whom vacancies were resources. He is prominent, too, among cataphiles, those who explore the city's catacombs. His father, he has explained to me, was an Egyptologist who traveled for fieldwork. Left alone, adolescent Ktu began his own excavations below the city. The name he took is a contraction of Cthulhu, the name of an undersea

241

demon in an H.P. Lovecraft story. I first noticed Ktu's eyes: they are light blue and very round and protrude from his head like those of fish in ocean valleys where the sun's rays don't reach. He widens them to tell me, "L'underground, c'est moi."

Ktu is widely quoted in newspaper articles about La Miroiterie, which attracts punks, students, adventurous yuppies, and support from politicians as well as journalists. "I would be very sorry if ever La Miroiterie disappeared," says Florence de Massol, deputy mayor for the 20th Arrondissement.

Devos has told me, dryly, "At the end of a squat that is well-known, everyone wants to have a hand in.... All these people are saying they lived at La Miroiterie when they never set foot inside."

One punk shoves another, toppling a beer, and scolds me when I rush to right it. As I take notes, the punks poke fun.

"You're writing your thesis?" They say.

I say, "Would you like a beer?"

They ask, "Are you inspired?

Over several months I spent visiting the squat, I verified several myths about its early days. A company called Bosch ran the mirror factory, but the property was divided among many owners. The building fell into disrepair and Bosch abandoned it in the 1990s. When I heard the factory's name, I was rapt. "It is a little like 'The Garden of Earthly Delights' here, isn't it?" I said to one squatter and artist, Andy Bolus. "Yeah, it is," he said fondly. "Full of freaks."

Ktu arrived there with two other artists who had worked in squats before. They named themselves after the mirror factory—miroiterie in French—and installed mosaics of shattered mirror, which resemble insect eyes and store many sevens of years of bad luck. Squatters in France who remain in a space for more than 48 hours cannot be immediately evicted but must be removed through a lawsuit. Some of the building's proprietors seemed not to care about their portions. They didn't sue, and the squatters stayed.

In 2009, a real-estate company called Thorel finished buying the parcels that comprised La Miroiterie and sued the squatters. It belongs to a businessman who owns a passel of similar companies. Its listed address is a spare Haussmannian cage for screaming phones.

A bailiff sent to count the residents and determine the uses of the space found in March 2009: "sculptures, paintings, and an empty mezzanine... a photography workshop... metal sculptures, musical instruments, and a drum set... a collective kitchen."

A February 2010 ruling said the squatters had to go, but Thorel needed to navigate appeals and delays. In September 2011, for example, a judge awarded the squatters a delay of six months in the eviction proceedings, finding the former proprietors had neglected the space, the squatters fixed it to be livable, and their projects were "artistic therefore useful." Because French law known as the "winter truce" forbids evictions between November 1 and March 15, the squatters weathered several winters. The truce technically does not apply to squatters but makes their wintertime eviction impolitic and rare.

The squatters requested another delay in the fall of 2012 and were denied two weeks before the start of the winter truce. Although they could stay the winter, they would have no legal recourse when spring came. They protested the decision outside City Hall, collecting thousands of signatures.

After a late-season snow, the government extended the year's truce to March 31, 2013. Wet, dense flakes caused the squatters to cancel a concert without entirely muting the squat. "It's a little anarchic, a little hellish," says Bernard Morlon, a painter there, laughing. "It's the end."

Thorel had the eviction order authorized. Police were set to carry out the order after the winter truce ended in April.

Before La Miroiterie was a factory, it had housed a painter named Daniel Pipard who hosted storied parties. He was called the Duke of Ménilmuche, which is local, affectionate slang for Ménilmontant, the Belleville neighborhood in the city's hilly Northeast where the squat is located. Belleville, a village covering the present-day 19th and 20th Arrondissements, was incorporated into Paris late and remained untamed. Here stood the last barricade of the Commune of 1871. The state's troops shot local rebels against a wall in nearby Père-Lachaise. Ktu tells me one of his ancestors died defending the Communards' barricade, which is not an uncommon story in this part of town. Eric Hazan writes, in *The Invention of Paris*, "Certain quarters of Paris have a character that owes most to history and architecture, others to their economic activity, and others again to geography. None of these criteria, however, is quite suitable for characterizing the hills stretching from Buttes-Chaumont to Père-Lachaise, and defining what makes Belleville and Ménilmontant unique. For my part, I am convinced that these are quarters whose identity is largely an emotional one ... Here these are emotions of affection for many people, but there are others as well."

When I asked her about squats in the 20th Arrondissement, one of the district's deputy mayors, Françoise Galland, prefaced each of her responses with the suggestion that a foreigner was not likely to understand it in any case. Over the course of a 400-page volume, Hazan never quite defines the "emotional" quality of the Parisian East more precisely. Similarly, Galland's characterization of the district that had charged her was surpassingly delicate. She said, "There are singers and a poetry you won't find in the 16th, you won't find in the 17th, in the chic neighborhoods. Often they forbid it, there. To say this in another way, the 20th is not under too much police surveillance. It's surveilled for its large problems, but it's not monitored for the little details. Which is to say, now, you don't have the right to sing in the street, but in the 20th, you can. And I don't want to say that everyone sings in the street in the 20th, but, still, as soon as it's nice out, there are people who walk around, and ask for money."

The squatters have developed other theories about their home. An old woman once knocked at the door to tell them she remembered dancing at a ballroom in the basement. Devos says a river runs far below La Miroiterie. Pipard would have wanted the place to remain artistic. They execute his wishes. "We preserve the patrimony of this old house," Ktu says.

Sylvain Dreyfus, the squatters' lawyer, has not heard this argument, but squat truth is relative. I imagine a will drawn in a more coercive magic than the normal legalese. Morlon, the painter, is the oldest person at La Miroiterie, and at his 66th birthday party, as Morlon smiled and spun, a guest told me, "He has made a pact with the devil. He has been dancing for three hours. He will turn young again. It will be a historic moment."

For Christmas, Devos and Morlon painted the second-floor workshop sea-blue and decorated it with ornaments and miniature candles, which the squatters used to light their joints. They were always repainting the workshop, as if to avoid capitulation. Now it shone, changing tone when Devos dimmed the lights. She danced in her chair, raising and hooking her arms, smiled so as to share the joke. An accordion played the Georges Brassens song "Belleville-Ménilmontant." We sang along. Devos shouted, "Vive la Commune!"

Ktu broke an ornament, but I couldn't hear it shatter—the room shook underneath tapping feet. "It's a miracle there have not been injuries or fires there over the years," Dreyfus said. Structurally the squat is not sound. Until recently bags of glass dust and pulverizing chemicals made a back room deadly. Stories rise from its past to startle me when I recall them: times the squat has reached a kind of fever pitch, a tumble down stairs, showing bone.

I reached Catherine Pipard, Daniel's daughter, who said she had

lived at 88 rue de Ménilmontant until 1982. She said her family had owned the place since 1830: "It was always artists." She called its current occupants "dishonest." She recently visited the building, and its decay alarmed her. "They are there completely illegally," she said. "I want nothing to do with these people."

"Artistic therefore useful," I remember. Devos says, "People ask if I am an artist. I say, I paint my life."

Bolus, who builds instruments, once looked for the ballroom where the stranger remembered dancing. He picked over the hollowed-out car in the courtyard. He felt about for a trapdoor. He found nothing but still believes in the underground room. He prefers his version: chandeliers, a red carpet, Belle Époque luxury, now choked with dust.

The squatters carry on the tradition of bohemian Paris, a city where artists can wait decades for a government-subsidized studio. They are a dying kind: among the last independent squatters in Paris. About 15 years ago, the City of Paris began awarding temporary leases to some artists who squat in buildings it owns. The artists pay rent and must not sleep at the building. The city typically helps to select the artists, who must provide projects or events for the neighborhood. "It's a kind of cultural dictatorship," Ktu says. The city has bought squatted buildings, afterward assigning leases that let the squatters stay. The first and most famous now attracts nearly 60,000 tourists a year. Marc Wluczka, a deputy mayor for the 20th Arrondissement, politically supports these leases, but they offend his sense of art: "Did Picasso ask for the help of the state?"

I have arrived too late to this Bohème. La Miroiterie still holds concerts but its major artistic accomplishments, which are venerable, lie behind it. Eviction hangs over the squat. Those who can leave soon have left. I visit two or three of the most determined squatters whose main art consists in keeping the squat open out of force of will, as if wrenching it open. What I see of their home is both emptier and more beautiful than its media image. Morlon uses watercolor to paint a building of gorgeous green glass and adds palms, fountains, knots of red blossoms, and a sign: number 88. "It's La Miroiterie in the future," he says.

Dominique Pagès, a councilor for the 20th Arrondissement, tells me a squat is a boîte noire, a black box, referring to its inscrutable inner working. As the mechanics of La Miroiterie become clear to me, I realize it is more similar to a void. Squatters occupied the empty building, and each filled it with whatever he or she required. I realize I am asking for a myth. Yet the squatters seem to need a chronicler. Devos tells me, "I say I paint my life" in a string of aphorisms she dictates. My notebooks are her canvas, I think in stupid pride.

She says the commissariat has promised to warn the squatters two weeks before the eviction. Dreyfus has advised them to leave before the truce ends. Devos, anyway, has been boxing up belongings since November: a matter of pride. "We are the ones who will choose the way of leaving," she says.

As the concert finishes, as Ktu's 46th birthday wanes, the German shepherd rises and walks across the bar, delicately stepping among beer puddles, plastic cups, ashes. I give a page of notebook to a handsome punk who asks for it. He returns lines from the Renaissance poet Pierre de Ronsard. I accept the gift politely but secretly am flattered. The studs on his leather jacket are taller than the other regalia I see, and I imagine this accords him alpha status.

I turn to Devos. She will stay at the bar long after the band has left. "You see the moon every time you enter La Miroiterie, through the trees," she has told me. Sometimes I catch it, sometimes it eludes me.

Ktu, who has opened squats before, is unbothered this one will soon close. He and Morlon spend nights roaming the city, eyeing vacancies. They want to open their next squat on the Champs-Elysées, for symbolic reasons. Squats are like phoenixes. Normally they don't last 13 years. "A squat is ephemeral," Ktu says. "If we open another squat, we'll call it La Miroiterie."

POSTSCRIPT

Months after this essay appeared, La Miroiterie was still open. I felt happy for the squatters and also a little sheepish. I searched and found multiple articles like mine written over the years, carefully studied in eviction proceedings, tolling the end. But the squat remained—in part, I thought, because each eviction menace generated popular buzz.

I walked by the squat many months later with a sometime squatter who had helped to open it. We were marching against the eviction of another Belleville squat, La Cantine. The Jourdain market, disassembling nearby, gave off a smell of fish on melting ice. A tawny dog with spotted paws leapt about and lay down in the road. We stopped before La Miroiterie. The façade had been re-painted into a version of the Looney Tunes last card in which the rabbit was scarred and smoked and looked challengingly at passerby, inquiring, "Is that all, folks?"

"The artists I knew have aged," said my companion, a juggler known as Snoopy, really named Stéphane Bourotte. "Then, we were all

247

outlaw squatters, and maybe now, those who have been rehoused someplace are happy to have a little place to sleep and not be evicted the next day … That's human." He had long lived in Belleville and helped to resist the neighborhood's razing in the '90s. His building was to be destroyed. Talking heads termed the protests a "second barricade." The neighborhood resistance held meetings at a since closed squat called La Forge de Belleville. "Now it's beautiful there," Snoopy said, "because they've let the vines grow."

Like many others, Snoopy smiled knowingly when he heard La Miroiterie was to close, this time from a concerned woman who was marching with us. "They always say that," he said.

He explained La Miroiterie would never be evicted because no one could build there. There were holes and caverns in the ground below the squat. I started, remembering Devos's river. La Miroiterie was not untouchable for its legend. It was untouchable because its foundations were unfit. Now he showed me where the stone wall buckled outward. The old factory was slowly collapsing. Two men nailing beams to prop it up saluted us.

Snoopy mentioned the catacombs. "They dug out all the stone from underneath Paris, and then used it to build the city on the holes. Smart, right?"

His tone was wry and fond, not mocking. This was his city. He loved it even for its faults. Still, the implication seemed to be all Paris would buckle and fall one day, its underground reclaiming it. We walked to Belleville Park and could barely make out the Eiffel Tower. The next day, the city would waive public-transit fees because of the pollution. A fine white mist covered its buildings. They faded into the contours of the valley.

During a concert April 20, 2014, a wall of La Miroiterie caved in. Ktu blamed pressure from the growth of a nearby tree. Police evicted the squat April 26, 2014, though Devos told a news website that La Miroiterie would live again. .

A version of this essay originally appeared in different form in Guernica magazine, March 26, 2013.

Spain

250

251

Urban Movements and Paradoxical Utopianisms

Miguel Ángel Martínez López

In the mid-1980s, hundreds of activists had undertaken to live in and transform empty buildings in every major Spanish city, very often in sites central to the urban core. These activists borrowed models from earlier movements and maintained connections with contemporary ones taking place elsewhere in Europe.[1] Since then, the squatters' movement in Spain has kept itself alive by squatting, protesting, gathering and creating ways of expression and social relations for more than three decades. Where the movement has remained close to its original form and image, as in cities such as Barcelona and Bilbao, its members are now seen as an inherent part of the urban landscape that contributes to cultural diversity, and sometimes even constitute a point of pride for the civic authorities who, more regularly, repress them. Wherever squatting took place—Madrid, Seville, Valencia, Palma de Mallorca, Vitoria, Saragossa, etc.—they revived practices adapted from the influential citizen movements of the late '70s (during the so-called "transition to democracy") and more broadly influenced the political attitudes of new generations. For instance, squatters protested not only against social housing cuts and real estate speculation, but also in support of illegal immigrants, and in opposition to media censorship. Squatting has been concentrated in the historical centers of big cities and other urban areas (former industrial districts, harbors, old public facilities, etc.) undergoing rapid restructuring processes. These areas have offered spaces that fit with the aspirations and capacities of young people wanting to do things at the margin of mainstream culture, politics and social organization.[2]

In resisting the oppressive conditions of life every social group produces a particular culture with its own variable boundaries: ways of talking and dressing, norms of loyalty and courage, shared values and identities, shared friends and partnerships. In the case of squatters, it can also be said that they create a kind of "university of life" in which the radical project of the squatters' movement compromises the whole of everyday life for the people most involved in it. Squatting in Spain has primarily taken place in the context of an alternative or "post-leftist" urban movement[3] that, for many, has been also incorporated as a day-to-day lifestyle.[4] In comparison to Germany, the Netherlands and elsewhere in Northern Europe, cooptation of activists and legalization of squatted buildings has been much less prevalent in the Italian and Spanish contexts, in which squatters have often been opposed to negotiations with local, regional or state governments, or with most private developers—at least until the protest wave 2011, after which there have been many more cases of squatters taking a favorable view of legalization.[5] Nonetheless, a transnational network of shared experiences and material-spatial infrastructures supporting diverse social movements has been established through squatting that, simultaneously, integrate with local culture and enhance the global character of cities in which they take place.

Political conflict has usually been manifested at the local level, often involving confrontation and ongoing struggles between municipal authorities and squatters.[6] In addition to conflicts with police and other official state actors, squatting has necessitated a constant commitment to self-protection against extreme-right, neo-fascist gangs and intimidators and thugs paid by private developers threatening squats from without. In parallel, squatters are devoted to a continuous work of internal self regulation and conflict resolution in domestic and social activities that requires constant mindfulness of the feminist claim that the "personal is political." Around a solid core of committed activists, the Spanish squatters' movement has coalesced as a flexible community with soft boundaries comprised of thousands of people of different types including

sympathizers, activists, residents and "users" of the social and cultural activities launched from the self-managed and squatted social centers. Historically, this community has, in fact, proven to be a much more powerful engine for the movement than full-time squatters of residential buildings could have created on their own. Since 2011, however, exactly the opposite has been the case, as occupations for housing purposes have been able to mobilize supporters and gain legitimacy on a greater level than even some long lasting squatted social centers.

Throughout the 1980s and 1990s, Spanish squatters increased both in their number and in the number of groups and initiatives they were able to organize. Legal and police repression of the movement intensified since the late '90s, but laws have not been homogeneous or consistently applied. Some intellectuals, lawyers, judges, and political leaders have even supported squatters' demands and projects. In some cities, the crisis of squatting during the early 2000s motivated changes in strategy with many squatted social centers turned into rented ones. In other cases, public activism has been combined with individual action in squatting houses. Selective enforcement of laws has not, however, been limited to squatting. Speculative practices in urban land and housing are forbidden in the Spanish Constitution, but are, in fact, wide spread and a common method of profit generation in private investment schemes using capital both domestic and international. With widely variations between cities, house prices in Spain have grown at an average rate of 18% per year since the end of the '80s until young people and renters in general have been unable to afford a reasonable access to market-rate accommodation, and public housing resources have become insufficient. Or, in the words of a movement slogan: "when living is a luxury, squatting is a right."

In one sense, squatting serves as a form of protest, giving visibility to such economic problems, and publicly manifesting urban conflict. Countercultural squatting, however, is not limited to struggles over specific issues, such as the scarcity of social and affordable housing. The movement combines macroeconomic criticisms with microeconomic management of houses, the production and transmission of knowledge, political organizing, the development of interpersonal relations and cultural production. As anarchists and autonomous communists, squatters work to create utopias located in the practices of the here-and-now rather than those projected into the future by the urban growth machine that sells dreams of the ideal city and chimeras of prosperity for the wealthy few. They think that no utopia is achieved without struggle or contestation.

URBAN COUNTERCULTURE

The right to the city is not merely a right to access to what already exists, but a right to change it after our heart's desire. The right to remake ourselves by creating a qualitatively different kind of urban sociality is one of the most precious of all human rights.
David Harvey, "The Right to the City"

The "alternative scene" to which squatters belong tries to go beyond necessity: it is most significantly about collective and individual desire. This desire is materialized and articulated primarily through channels of independent media that reject conventional and formal organization, and instead works through the strength of solidarity ties to negotiate between different personal and ideological cleavages inside the movement. External representations or squatting are usually either negative or marginal (see, for example, *Leo*, directed by José Luis Borau, 2000, for one of the few times that squatters have appeared in Spanish films). Squatters themselves, however, produce films, books and documents that present a different narrative of their actions (more active,

constructive and positive) and their enemies (accusing police of abuse of power and arbitrary repression of social and political activists, as in the documentary *Ciutat Morta* by Xapo Ortega and Xavier Artigas (2013). And of course, walking on the edge of life, as squatters do, involves a great deal of creativity, resistance and wise management of alternative temporalities. Indeed, *everything could end tomorrow.*

In remaining active over more than three decades, the squatters' movement has confronted dozens of trials and hundreds of evictions but, at the same time, showed a great capacity to resist (more than ten buildings were squatted for more than fifteen years, and many trials ended with squatters being acquitted) and to introduce new fields of political and social disobedience. This has included not only civil disobedience directed against the state but also to the laws that protect private and dead property, such as the advocacy of free software and the setting up of hacklabs, or demonstrations against mega projects involved in urban speculation such as the International Exhibition (Seville, 1992) or the Forum of Cultures (Barcelona, 2004). In referring to the squatters' movement as a countercultural lifeworld, it is not easy to get rid of received conceptions of the "spirit of an era" — whether May 1968, hippy communities escaping from alienation of abundance through music and drugs, etc. — but a lot has changed in three decades and squatting occupies a much different cultural position. Squatted social centers across Europe became platforms for the expansion and support of the Zapatist rebellion (from 1994 to the present) and the indigenous rights in Mexico, settlements for independent infrastructures of communication by means of the internet (such as Indymedia), and spaces for a huge circuit of underground music and artistic performances. Some squats have also maintained extensive, specialized libraries and documentation centers. Community projects are organized by specific co-operativist initiatives and an ethos of share-all-you-have rather than according to for-profit principles. Nonetheless, the rapid turnover of activists and constant evictions and displacements have had the practical and cultural effect of creating a high degree of nomadism in the movement that is not always intended or gladly accepted by all the squatters.

UTOPIA AND ANTI-UTOPIA

Utopian speculations can help free us from the habit of taking the status quo for granted, get us thinking about what we really want and what might be possible. What makes them "utopian" in the pejorative sense that Marx and Engels criticized is the failure

*to take present conditions into consideration. There is usually no
serious notion of how we might get from here to there. Ignoring
the system's repressive and cooptive powers, utopian authors
generally envision some simplistic cumulative change, imagining
that, with the spread of utopian communities or utopian ideas,
more and more people will be inspired to join in and the old
system will simply collapse.*
Ken Knabb, *The Joy of Revolution* 1997

Foucault called 'immediatist' those movements that criticize the immediate
sources and impacts of power while rejecting utopias and ideologies
which project liberation from the existing forms of domination onto a
distant future.[7] This applies accurately to the squatters' movement. Most
squatters explicitly rejected classical revolutionary projects and parties,
especially when these look to the formation of new state structures. In this,
progressive utopias are rejected as well. Nonetheless, many squatters
consider themselves 'revolutionaries' and emphasize their commitment
to ideas and ideal spaces beyond the places squatted. This is to say:
they look to temporary, provisional utopias, specific projects of urban
transformation, and especially, the transformation of their own everyday
lives. This is is partially informed by conceptions drawn from broadly
considered "new left" political discourses such as the Situationist "policy
of desire" and autonomist concepts of "communism here and now."[8]

If these discourses locate the squatters' movement within schemas
of leftist "post-modernism," it is also possible to trace connections
between the political ideologies of Spanish squatters and the traditions
of classical anarchism and radical modernist tendencies in Spain and
elsewhere. If squatters consider themselves revolutionaries, it is in the
sense of desiring to catalyze a social revolution in the short run, and
because they criticize and contest the present situation of alienation,
individualization, bureaucratization and censorship so pervasive even in
liberal-representative democracies. That is to say, they do a political work
within the myriad dimensions of their everyday life. This is particularly
important in the way they illegally occupy the buildings in which they live
and produce culture and counterculture.

Squatting also implies communication with neighborhood
communities and the local population arguing for the legitimacy of direct
action and the need for solidarity and mutual support in making demands
for decent housing and self-managed spaces. Just as squatters do not
put trust in the coming of revolution or utopia that will transform the
current conditions of global capitalism, they are also skeptical of political

parties—who are seen as being made up of professionals pursuing their own interests—and of old political traditions that give privilege to a sacrificial style of activism. The unique utopia they see as possible in the present locus of their resistance is based on the combination of direct action, teaching and learning techniques of self-organization, and the enjoyment of life as much as possible while protesting—as was popularized by the Global Justice Movement and groups such as Reclaiming the Streets. This is not, however, hedonism and individualism. Rather, in both partying and protesting, a challenge is made and an alternative posited to the excess and shortsighted individualism which is so useful for the uneven development of urban capital. Thus, in the material practice of opening empty buildings to common use, a dynamic tension is always established between creativity and protest, party and social criticism, that opens up spaces for both personal freedom and individual expression, as well as for the creation of new forms of sociability and collectivism.[9]

NOTES

1 Wates, N. et al., 1980. Squatting, The Real Story. London, Bay Leaf.

Koopmans, R., 1995. Democracy from Bellow New Social Movements and the Political System in West Germany. Colorado, Westview.

Mikkelsen, F., Karpantschof, R., 2001. "Youth as a Political Movement: Development of the Squatters' and Autonomous Movement in Copenhagen," 1981-95. International Journal of Urban and Regional Research 25 (3), pp. 609-628.

Moroni P. et al., 1998. Centros Sociales: ¡Qué Empresa! Más Allá Del Guetto: un Debate Crucial [www.nodo50.org/ laboratorio]

Pruijt, H., 2003. "Is the institutionalisation of urban movements inevitable? A comparison of the opportunities for sustained squatting in New York City and Amsterdam." International Journal of Urban

and Regional Research, vol. 27-1, pp. 133-157.

2 Adell, R., Martínez, M. (eds.), 2004. ¿Dónde Están las llaves? El Movimiento Okupa: Prácticas y Contextos Sociales. Madrid, La Catarata.

3 Kistschelt, H., 1992 (or. 1990). "Los Nuevos Movimientos Sociales y el Declinar de la Organización de los Partidos Políticos." In Dalton, R., Kuechler, M. (eds.). Los Nuevos Movimientos Sociales. Un Reto al Orden Político, Valencia, Alfons el Magnànim, pp. 247-286.

4 Bookchin, M., 1998. Social Anarchism or Lifestyle Anarchism: An Unbridgeable Chiasm, San Francisco, AK Press.

5 Pruijt, H., 2003.
6 Martínez López, M. (2007). "The Squatters' Movement: Urban Counterculture and Alter-Globalization Dynamics," South European Society & Politics 12, 3, 379-398.

7 Foucault, M., 1986. "Por qué hay que Estudiar el Poder: la Cuestión del Sujeto," In VV.AA. Materiales de Sociología Crítica, Madrid, La Piqueta, pp.25-36.

8 Deleuze, G., Guattari, F., 1997 (or. 1977). Rizoma, Introducción, Valencia, Pre-Textos. Bey, H., 1996. T.A.Z. Zona Temporalmente Autónoma. Madrid, Talasa.

Knabb, K., 1999 (or. 1997). El Placer de la Revolución, Madrid, Radikales Libres. Holloway, J., 2003. Cambiar el Mundo sin Tomar el Poder, El Significado de la Revolución Hoy, Barcelona, El Viejo Topo.

9 Mckay, G., 1998. "DIY Culture: Notes Towards an Intro." In Mckay, G. (ed.). DiY Culture.

Adapted from a paper presented at the 8th International Utopian Studies Society Conference, Plymouth, 2007.

259

Managing the Image: Squats and Alternative Media in Madrid (2000–2013)

Julia Lledin

In Madrid, the relationship between squatting and alternative media is complicated. Squatter ideology is built on "do it yourself" culture, autonomous practice, horizontality, self-management, anti-capitalism, feminism, anti-fascism, and anti-speciesm. Squatters try to create an alternative life in the city while alternative media tries to transform social communication, working for free to build a different society. But the relationship between them has not always been good.

In the case of Madrid between 2000 and 2013 we find two different tendencies: 1) those who reject technologies; and 2) those who propose that new technologies could be a way towards freedom.

These are both connected with different positions regarding social movements in relation to society. The squatter movement in the city has several branches, and each of these can be identified with one of two positions: "radicals"/anarchists vs "reformists"/squats 2.0. In addition, the development of new technologies, is paralleled by hacktivism and copyleft as expressions of freedom, but also by the development of consumer society. Criticism has been made concerning personal security, the loss of contact between people, and the fact that there is bias against squatters in mass media. On the other side there is the possibility to reach all of society, control communications, and provide ways to make information freely available.

We can identify three moments in this relationship: 1) the beginning of new technologies and hacktivism; 2) the period of contra-information and alternative media; and 3) the diversification of the use of technologies and communications.

The second moment is when squatter activists tried to fight the negative effects of the technologies of social control. They created their

CONTRA LA PRIVATIZACION

LIBERA LA CULTURA

ØKUPA LA RED ©

www. hacktivistas .net

hamlab. hacklabs.org

own media with the idea of security paramount, also managinng their own public image, and overcoming their initial prejudices. The 15M movement produced a deep change. With the emergence of social networks, the immediacy and simplicity of tools like Twitter and streaming video superseded the security, self-management and political projects of communication.

Squatted projects in Madrid in general lack strategies of communications. Most projects do not have a consolidated strategy which allows them to build the image of the movement they say they want to build. Also, the reach of the alternative media is limited and the codes of squatters are completely different from codes of the mass media: no leaders, no public faces, no names (as a way to protect horizontality and also their personal security).

Even if the information is not systematic, we can identify ideological elements throughout the period, with three different periods of boom and decline between 2000 and 2013. The movement is fast-changing and intense, and always influenced by the political context.

The information about squatters that we can find on alternative media is limited. Mostly it is about: evictions (29.9%) and announcements of new squatted buildings (15.64%). Other topics are repression, like trials or detentions (9.8%); campaigns for squatting, especially in the second period (5.3%); and related with anniversaries or the history of the movement (4%). Most communications are about social centres. The fact that in Spain squatting for housing is a crime, but not squatting to create a social centre, is one of the reasons that explains this difference.

Also, between one and two years after the big mobilization of 15M, the number of squatters increased and new social centres appeared. This could be as a consequence of their participation in other movements. or because of their strong anti-capitalist and autonomous discourse, which easily attracted recent arrivals to political activism. Especially after the 15M occupation of Puerta del Sol, and the social movement against crisis austerities, squatting has become the answer.

Squatters in Madrid today are located in specific neighborhoods. These are 1) old neighborhoods undergoing gentrification with empty houses as a result of speculation; and 2) industrial areas that were abandoned in the economic transformation of the city (from industry to service).

The most contentious question in the movement is negotiation with political authorities, or at least this is the question which sees the largest and most intense discussion on alternative media. In the case of Madrid, in the 2000-13 period, only four social centres have tried to negotiate. Two achieved their objective more or less (CS Seco and Eskalera Karakola), and another two were defeated and finally evicted (Labo3 and Patio Maravillas, although Patio re-occupied). The two which achieved their objective did so through consolidated social support, a long lifespan, and greater connection to other struggles (for example neighborhood activism or feminist struggles) and strong alliances. The social center assemblies took the initiative to negotiate with the authorities. The two defeated social centers did not have these qualities, but they tried to force the process in the same way. Finally, as an effect of these agreements, the legalized social centres became more cultural and easier to access, but less combative.

Ciclocostura: from the Engine to the Body, Collaborative DIY Textile Crafting

Elisabeth Lorenzi

Two years ago our group began a collaborative crafting lab called "*Ciclocostura*" (cycling-sewing). We gather together and host labs at some cycling events and in collaborative open places. We try to copy, make, remake and create accessories and clothes related to urban cycling life. Each lab experience has been registered, elaborated and published as a tutorial on our website in order to share the experience and push the copy-left process of our experiments. We also promote the prototyping of the lab itself.

Our aim is to encourage people to make their biking activity more comfortable, beautiful and affordable. Our project is free and open to the people, and we register and publish our development on a website: ciclocostura.wordpress.com, and on our Facebook page, Ciclocostura.

Before each workshop, we propose a topic: for example, how to transform a jacket into a more comfortable garment for cycling, or how to repair a worn crotch. During the workshop, we hack and experiment, copying ideas and also producing new solutions. In this process the participant also learns how to use a sewing machine and other device of this field.

Why cycling clothing? Because cycling culture is a field that is permeable to social initiatives and creativity. It is usual to find tutorials, and "how to" accounts of experiences related to bike repair, bike design, devices, accessories and also clothes. It's an open area, widened and developed by social initiative. Paul Rosen reflects on the tendency to experience change and appropriate technology in the social environment of cycling, which is associated with the dynamics of counterculture. Our project connects directly with this environment.

The philosophy of our workshop is "do it yourself", and is connected with the intense emergence of self-managed bike workshops in Madrid. (Lorenzi, 2012) These workshops emerged during the growth of the Critical Mass movement of bike riders in Madrid (*Bicicrítica*). The regular public expression of this movement is through spontaneous monthly meetings of cyclists in the streets in a way that the regular flow of motor traffic is interrupted. Madrid is one of the cities in Spain, and even in Europe, where this collective action is the best known and the most crowded. An average of 2,500 cyclists respond to the summer calls.

The monthly encounter is closely linked to an internet network of fluent communication, and a spatial network of "workshops" or "bike kitchens", most of them located in squatted and self-managed social centres. These are places of mutual aid, common learning about recycling, and how to make bicycles work.

People who promote Ciclocostura have these bike workshops and Bicicrítica as common places. They are our main references about how to run a collaborative and experimental project. We have also shared our experience in other cycling environments, and in forums about crafting itself. For two years we met two days a month, and have had the opportunity to participate in other cycling events, like the Brighton Bike Festival in England, and the Ciemmona in Rome.

Our experience is well known in Madrid and has been rich in outputs. Now we are developing more accurate digital tools to publish our outputs, and to facilitate more extensive and collaborative developments of this experience online. This is the best chance to make our experience replicable. The future of Ciclocostura is to develop a collaborative digital tool in order to amplify the interactivity of the creative process and widen its impact.

REFERENCES

Elisabeth Lorenzi, "'Alegria Entre Tus Piernas': To Conquer Madrid's Streets," in Chris Carlsson, et al., eds., Shift Happens! Critical Mass at 20 (Full Enjoyment Books, San Francisco, 2012)

Paul Rosen, "Up the Vélorution: Appropriating the Bicycle and the Politics of Technology," in Ron Eglash, et al., eds., Appropriating Technology (2002)

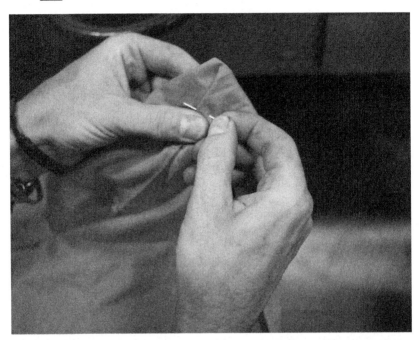

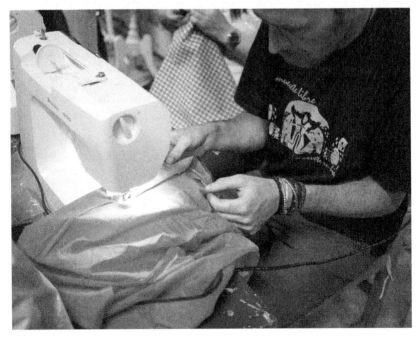

Ciclocostura: from the Engine to the Body, Collaborative DIY Textile Crafting

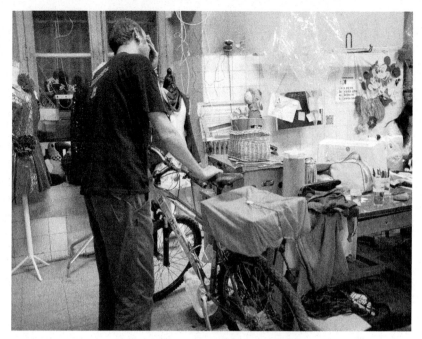

¡Porque sin Nosotras no se Mueve el Mundo! La Esclavitud se Acabó
(Without Us, the World Does Not Move. Slavery is Over)

Julia Lledin

Important feminist initiatives around questions of precarious labor and the labor of care have developed out of the Eskalera Carakola, in the Lavapiés neighborhood of Madrid. Originally squatted in 1996, Eskalera Carakola (the name means "stairway of the snail") is now a legalized place based on feminist, autonomous and self-management principles and open to feminist projects. It is the home of the feminist militant research project "*Precarias a la deriva*". It was the first squat by and for women in the country and it became the centre of the autonomous feminist movement in the city; their path shows the importance of feminist speech in the squatting movement of Madrid.

In November of 2014, as part of the Reina Sofia museum's exhibition "Really Useful Knowledge," a workshop was organized at Carakola introducing a new initiative, "*Senda de cuidados*" — the name is a play of words between Spanish for "citizen" and "care" — which seeks to build a dignified alternative for the labor of care. (The Argentinian researcher María Laura Rosa later performed an action at the museum. She works with feminist art groups, among them *Mujeres Públicas*, "public women," whose matchbox with the image of a church on it caused a controversy in the museum exhibition.)

268

The initative was introduced by a group within the Carakola, Territorio Doméstico ("domestic territory"). They define themselves as "a meeting place, for relationship, care and the struggle of women for their rights." Most are migrants—from Dominican Republic, Colombia, El Salvadora, Ecuador, Romani, Senegal, Nicaragua, Bangladesh, Bolivia, Morocco, etc.

Care—work with children, older people and the infirm—and reorganizing the labor of care in society has been one of the main points of the feminist movement in Madrid. In 2006, the Red de *Cuidados de Madrid* (Care Network of Madrid) organized the first conference about care. After this meeting, some groups working on the same subject started to talk about the necessity for the creation of a common group.

During this time, they worked in different ways. On one hand, *Territorio Doméstico* is a kind of trade union defending the labour rights of domestic workers, especially of foreigners whose labour conditions are really insecure, both regarding employment and administrative status. But they try to go further, understanding that these conditions are not only a result of the law, but also because of the global system. In this way it is absolutely necessary to transform social relationships. They created a group based on mutual support, care, self care, struggle and empowerment. From a feminist point of view, they propose a deep transformation of the system, including economic and social relationships, into a system based on human needs rather than market forces.

Reorganizing care means placing it at the centre of the social and economic system. Also, it means also transforming the responsibility of care, and the way that which is relegated to women in society.

Everybody needs care and everybody is able to care for others so, their proposal also directly confronts patriarchy. But not only this, since the responsibility for care is especially laid upon poor women—which usually means foreigners in our European context –the perspective of *Territorio Doméstico*, is then also anti-capitalist, anti-nationalist and anti-racist.

The coordination and daily work of the collective, they are organized horizontally around an assembly where decisions are taken. They also have working groups. In addition, they give legal assistance and support to women who want to protest their labour conditions, even if they are not in the group. No less important is the work they do with a the long-term objectives of organizing workshops, performances on the street, events and demonstrations, direct actions, producing texts, creating alternatives All of this relates to asserting the rights of both women and migrants, and trying to bring their reality and their lives into a visible place in society. They do not want to just be part of the landscape anymore.

Although they still have further to go, *Territorio Doméstico's* work over the eight years of life has been important and intense, fighting daily against a complicated set of problems. *Territorio Doméstico* is also an important experience in self-organization and empowerment that relates to a larger feminist and anti-capitalist network, through both political discourse and direct action.

REFERENCES

www.territoriodomestico.net

Precarias a la deriva, A la
Deriva: Por los Circuitos de
la Precariedad Femenina
(Traficantes de sueños, 2003)

Silvia Federici, Caliban and
the Witch: Women, the Body
and Primitive Accumulation
(Autonomedia, 2004)

¡ÚLTIMA HORA!
¡SE ACABÓ LA ESCLAVITUD!
MANIFESTACIÓN

EMPLEADAS DOMÉSTICAS

Las mujeres de SEDOAC (Servicio Doméstico Activo), el grupo Cita de Mujeres de Lavapiés y la Agencia de Asuntos Precarios, quienes juntas damos vida al Taller Territorio Doméstico, les CONVIDAMOS ...

a todas las empleadas domésticas
a todas las empleadoras y empleadores
a todas las feministas
a todas las inmigrantes, trabajadoras, precarias, estudiantes y paradas
a todas las cuidadoras
a las personas con diversidad funcional que luchan por ser atendidas
de otro modo
a todas las trabajadoras invisibles que sostienen la vida
a todas las personas, colectivos, grupos y asociaciones que apoyan la
lucha de las empleadas domésticas
... a salir a la calle

DOMINGO 28 DE MARZO 2010. 13 HRS. PLAZA JACINTO BENAVENTE. METRO SOL

ORGANIZA   APOYA

SEDOAC

CITA DE
MUJERES
DE LAVAPIÉS

AZIEN

FERINE

izquierda
anticapitalista

Patio Maravillas' Anti- gentrification Campaign against the TriBall Group

Stephen Luis Vilaseca

Here I will compare two urban spaces: the privately funded renovation of a zone of central Madrid known as the Ballesta Triangle and the second-generation squatted social center Patio Maravillas located in the adjacent neighborhood of Malasaña. These two spaces represent two distinct approaches to the city: one that conceives of urban living as highly normalized and directed; and one that fosters the notion of co-authorship with the city. Through this comparison, I hope to show how the reimagining of contemporary Madrid in terms of co-production is redefining certain citizens' relationships to the built environment, specifically affecting the lived urban experiences of activists, artists, social movements, and neighborhood associations.

TriBall, the soon-to-be-gentrified Ballesta Triangle consisting of the Gran Vía, Fuencarral and Corredera Baja de San Pablo Streets, is aggressively marketed as the first "concept neighborhood." Like a concept album, the songs of which are connected by a unifying theme, TriBall is claimed to be a concept-neighborhood in which the various spaces are connected by a modern, bohemian, ecologically friendly aesthetic. According to Pablo Carmona—cultural critic and member of the social centers Seco and the *Observatorio Metropolitano* group in Madrid— TriBall is able to generate a neighborhood with a vanguard brand almost for free because 95% of what comprises that brand is produced not by multinational companies with copyrights, but by small autonomous cultural associations, cooperatives, and squatted social centers (*centros sociales okupados*). Through the publicity campaign known as "*Okupación Creativa ¡Ya!*," the TriBall group arrived at an alliance with 45 of these autonomous, cultural producers and invited them to "squat" thirteen locales– among them, four sites formerly used as brothels. For one month from April 10 to May 10, 2008, these artists were given free rein to rehabilitate the spaces and to sell their artwork.

In the fifth edition of *InnMotion*, the biennial festival of performance and applied visual arts which takes place in Barcelona, Conservas criticizes artists who, willingly or not, participate in such campaigns. They argue that the transformation of physical space by artists results in increased property values "without the need for developers or city councils to make social investments ..." (*"Para qué sirven"*). This is known as the "bohemian" effect. Indeed, the forty five artists of *"Okupación Creativa ¡Ya!"* converted the Ballesta Triangle into a veritable gallery of squatter art, and in so doing, they attracted consumers back to the neighborhood. *"Okupación Creativa ¡Ya!"* was a brilliant marketing action that channeled the creative energy of the squatter artists and used the aesthetic environment that they produced to incite desire and consumption. It was not a celebration of street art or of urban artists, but, rather, a celebration of the power of capitalism. It is simply not the case that real estate developers suddenly see the altruistic value in promoting

urban artists. Instead, the driving factors were the consumers that the
squatter artists attracted to the zone, and the economic externalities that
they generated.

In contrast to the TriBall approach to the city—which supports
the privatization of public space, the city as normalized code—and
the appropriation of culture to produce monopoly rents for a few, the
creative squatting occurring in Patio Maravillas attempts to create spaces
in which to experience what Ava Bromberg calls "publicness." In an
interview with cultural critic Nato Thompson, Bromberg elucidates her
concept of "publicness":

> To create a place where strangers can develop or discover a
> new interest or engage deeply with people and concepts they've
> never encountered—this is what I think 'publicness' is all about
> ... To me, 'publicness' might be best measured—if we had to
> measure it—by the depth of interaction that takes place between
> unfamiliar entities." The disorder and spontaneity that Bromberg's
> "publicness" embraces as a source of urban social creativity is
> precisely what urban plans like the TriBall model strive to manage.

The possibility of a commons is facilitated by the move from an industrial
economy to an information economy and the increased availability
of inexpensive computers. According to Yochai Benkler, these changes
have collapsed the separation between the owners of capital and the
laborers, and have produced a new category known as "users": "Users
are individuals who are sometimes consumers, sometimes producers,
and who are substantially more engaged participants, both in defining the
terms of their productive activity and in defining what they consume and
how they consume it."

Benkler's new definition of "user" is a useful concept because it
stresses how technology is changing daily life patterns in the city. In this
new economic-technological context, the user is a co-author and a co-
developer. Patio Maravillas advocates giving more freedom to the user of
both physical and digital space by fostering the notion of co-authorship of
software with software developers, co-authorship of culture through the
abolition of copyrights, and co-authorship of the city with city developers.

Two separate but interchangeable names given to the user that
have emerged from Patio Maravillas are the hacktivista and the copyrata.
The hacktivist is both hacker and activist. Hackers, according to Richard
Stallman, founder of the free software movement, are people who enjoy
"playful cleverness"—oftentimes, but not necessarily, with computers.
McKenzie Wark argues in "A Hacker Manifesto" that a hacker's "playful

274

cleverness" consists of figuring out how to produce new information from already existing information. It could be said, then, that hackers (or many of them at least) are more interested in the free circulation of information and culture rather than in creating exclusive rights.

The second term, "*copyrata*," suggests one who makes unauthorized copies of copyrighted content, coming to be vilified by the media and labeled as a pirate. Jolly Roger Morgan in "El Manifiesto Copyrata" [The Copyrata Manifesto] reappropriates the label "pirate" and liberates the term from its negative connotation. By combining the English verb "copy" with the Spanish word for pirate, *pirata*, and changing the "i" to a "y," Jolly Roger Morgan creates a visually loaded word whose meaning differs depending on how it is divided. Isolating the "co" from pyratas stresses the importance of community and joining the "co" to pyratas emphasizes the philosophy of copying as a catalyst for future creativity.

Squatters at Patio Maravillas who are both hacktivistas and the copyratas desire free access to culture, information, and the city.

REFERENCES

Benkler, Yochai. "Freedom in the Commons: Towards a Poltical Economy of Information." Duke Law Journal 52 (2003): 1245-276. Print.

Carmona, Pablo. "Espacios autónomos y su relación con las instituciones: ¿pactar, colaborar o habitar el margen?" Krax Jornadas 2008. Krax. RAI Casal Intercultural, Barcelona. 24 April 2008. Speech.

Morgan, Jolly Roger. "El manifiesto copyrata." Copyratas 28 October 2004. Weblog. 6 April 2009. <copyratas.blogspot. com/2004/10/somos-copyratas-v09.html>.

"¿Para qué sirven los artistas?" Conservas.tk. Conservas, n.d. Web. 28 August 2009 <innmotion09.conservas.tk/ en/dequeva>.

Stallman, Richard. "On Hacking." Stallman.org, n.d. Web. 16 February 2009 <stall-man.org/articles/on-hacking. html>.

Thompson, Nato. "Interrogating Public Space: Ava Bromberg, February 2008." Creative Time. February 2008. Web. 15 April 2008.

Wark, McKenzie. "A Hacker Manifesto." Subsol.c3.hu. Subsol, n.d. Web. 26 April 2009 <http://subsol.c3.hu/subsol_2/ contributors0/warktext.html>.

Málaga's "La Casa Invisible"

La Casa Invisible, translation by Milena Ruiz Magaldi

March 2015 marks the eighth anniversary of Málaga's La Casa Invisible ("The Invisible House"). It is a unique experience in Málaga, and a national benchmark in community-run initiatives (*"gestión ciudadana"*) and experimental culture. Its building—a beautiful, over 2,000 square meter construction from the 19th century—was falling apart when it was squatted in 2007 by a heterogeneous group of local creators and members of several social movements.

The idea had been born the previous year: during the famous *Festival de Málaga* (Spanish film festival). Many of the collectives that would later open La Casa Invisible carried out a 24-hour squatting at the old Cine Andalucía. During that day they held an alternative "festival" with screenings, theatre, circus, concerts, and debates—many political and social debates. As a result, the "invisible creators" got organised throughout that year.

From its beginning in the current Nosquera street building, La Casa Invisible managed to enter negotiations with Málaga's city council which owns the property. The leading political party was, and still is, right-wing *Partido Popular* (PP). With astonishing speed, La Casa Invisible became a lung for creativity and production in the very heart of Málaga. This was evidenced by an overwhelming cultural programme with educational seminars, theatre shows, dozens of workshops, performances by some of the best jazz musicians, and free culture festivals, etc. The dream had become a reality, established along two fundamental axes,with and idea as its backbone. One axis was clearly cultural, the other was clearly social, and the idea insured that the two could not be separated.

2007, was the year the crisis officially began. Very much like today, Málaga's city council supported a sort of 'storefront' cultural model: disproportionate investments that increased its incredible debt and overambitious constructions, mostly overlooking the fact that, more than form, content is what really matters.

Nonetheless, local creators found their place to rehearse, work, show, experiment, and share and, simultaneously, some of the most engaged collectives at the time operated at La Casa Invisible including

276

Coordinadora de Inmigrantes de Málaga and Precari@s en Movimiento. It's difficult to understand the closing of the Centro de Internamiento de Extranjeros de Málaga (Detention Centre for Migrants) or experiences such as the MayDay Sur without mentioning these collectives.

Between these axes, the backbone idea was clear: community-run initiatives ("gestión ciudadana"). Faced with the idleness of the institutions or their asphyxiating regulation of public resources, and the market interests of the big private companies, La Casa Invisible showed that it was in the public interest ("procomún") to escape from those models, and that community-run initiatives—such as those of its members—were the only fair method of doing this.

In 2011, after a laborious negotiating process (during which an eviction notice in the summer of 2009 was stopped), and as a result of the strong social and cultural legitimacy achieved by the project, Málaga's city council, alongside other public organizations such as Diputación

Provincial de Málaga, Junta de Andalucía and *Museo Reina Sofía* (Spanish Ministry of Culture), agreed to sign a *"Protocolo de Intenciones"* (memorandum of understanding) with La Casa Invisible. The agreement was clear: if La Casa Invisible met a list of requirements within a twelve month period, the city council would grant the right of use on the building for a minimum of five years.

Shortly after, La Casa Invisible was settled as the headquarters of *Fundación de los Comunes*, which gathers related experiences from all across the country. That legal status, *"fundación"*, was the last of the requirements. In January 2012 the 12 month period stipulated by the *"Protocolo"* ended. Despite that each and every one of the requirements was met, the city council's representatives refused at the last minute to approve a cession agreement, and further negotiations have since been rejected.

During those three years La Casa grew in every respect: dozens of weekly workshops, music performances, theatre shows, educational seminars, conferences by activists such as Ada Colau (*Plataforma de Afectados por la Hipoteca*, the PAH), *"libre"* software creator Richard Stallman, culture managers such as Manuel Borja-Villel (current director of *Museo Reina Sofía*), and theorists like Silvia Federici. Furthermore, it has become a refuge for the most relevant social actors of these times of political transformation that the country is living. Its rooms have witnessed the consolidation of movements such as *Democracia Real Ya*, *Plataforma de Afectados por la Hipoteca*, *Marea Verde* or, more recently, the community-organised group *Ganemos Málaga*.

The main political lines of La Casa were set up during that period. These include free culture versus a model of storefront culture and disproportionate investments, mostly set aside for ailing museums conceived for tourism; and citizen participation and intervention in issues that concern the community. At La Casa, members of the community were directly involved in management, creating programmes and designing strategies for negotiations with the city council. La Casa fights for the right to the city and to turn its environment into habitable spaces, where the word "citizenship" (*"ciudadanía"*) can recover its true foundations. La Casa perseveres, as previously mentioned, in confronting the two prevailing models of public interest—the public sector's patronising tutelage, and the private sector's extraction of profit—with collective aggregation, resulting in many organizations that breathe at La Invisible or have been born there. It is an effective instrument for social transformation as opposed to solitude and individualism, etc.

An inseparable part of the project is a proposed rehabilitation plan that would allow a collaborative recovery of the building, which is part of the city's heritage, while respecting and protecting its integrity. The plan would be implemented in phases so that rehabilitation can coexist with the project's activities, while using green construction materials and traditional techniques.

Despite the city council's refusal to meet the terms of the agreement, and the impossibility of startiing the rehabilitation plan without a permit for the space, a huge amount of cooperative work has been invested, sharing knowledge and economic resources to maintain and preserve the building following the criteria of utmost respect for its original form.

On December 23, 2014, and under the pretext of a technical report from the city council's *Gerencia de Urbanismo* after an inspection coordinated by La Casa Invisible (once again facing the local government's abandonment of its own heritage), the council sent a police unit to close down La Casa Invisible. Only one day after, on Christmas Eve, the police cordon was withdrawn thanks to public pressure. Thus, La Casa remains open for meetings and activities of all the organizations that form it, but not for public activities.

As a result of public support, which culminated in a massive demonstration and the launch of a successful crowd-funding campaign to raise money to meet the requirements for developing public activities, the city council has been forced to resume negotiations with La Casa Invisible. The aim of this negotiating process is to obtain permission to use the space for La Casa Invisible's collectives, in order to continue with the project and carry out the comprehensive rehabilitation of the building that will enable its recovery as patrimonial heritage of the city. If the city council had any doubt, today La Casa Invisible is untouchable (*"no se toca"*).

The Wall Poem

Stephen Luis Vilaseca

*Ya que tenemos que morir
que sea pues
después de haber vivido
no solos y
desesperados
como viejos
románticos
sino como hombres y mujeres
híbridos de ser mortal
e inmortal que somos.*

Given that we have to die,
may it be after we have lived,
not alone and
desperate,
like old people
like romantics,
but as men and women,
hybrid beings that we are, of mortal
and immortal essence.

Sardenya 43, Miles de Viviendas
Vicente Escolar Bautista[1]

Near La Barceloneta Beach in Barcelona at the corner of La Maquinista Street and Joan de Borbó Avenue, there is an empty lot where the squatted social center *Miles de Viviendas* (Thousands of Houses)once stood[2]. Before the demolition of the building on June 12, 2007, the squatters had gone from room to room and floor to floor of the five-story edifice writing in oversized letters the verses of Vicente Escolar Bautista's poem, seen in the epigraph above. The interior walls, where the verses were written, became the exterior walls of the adjacent apartment building after the demolition. However, the towering wall poem was soon covered with metal siding by city employees. Just five months after the razing, on November 23, 2007, journalist Agustí Fancelli noted in the Spanish

280

Miles de Viviendas wall poem before the placement of the metal siding.

newspaper *El País* that the poem had been concealed. He lamented the disappearance of the poem, and wrote the newspaper article in order to prevent the poem, its author, and the circumstances surrounding why it was penned from being forgotten. He explained that the building had been the property of the Port of Barcelona where customs officers used to inspect the shipments that entered and left the city. Customs clearance had been moved to a different location years ago, and from that time on the building had remained abandoned. On November 25, 2004, the public property was squatted. Two years and seven months later, the squatters were evicted, the building demolished, and the parting words of the squatters soon concealed.

Although Fancelli was interested in remembering the poem and the events leading up to the eviction, he does not ask why the Barcelona City Council would be so concerned about the poem as to consider it worth the trouble and expense of putting up metal siding. I do. The shared walls of demolished buildings are usually left exposed. Empty lots or *solares* are notorious for being filled with graffiti and urban art because these abandoned sites are often the result of exploitative practices of property speculation, and, as a result, are ideal spaces for urban artists to critique such practices. Some examples in 2009 include the empty lots in Barcelona on Carrer de les Floristes de la Rambla and the future site of the Plaça de la Gardunya. In the second case, the Barcelona City Council erected a sign announcing the renovation and, by doing so, recognized that it had been in the space and had seen it. Nonetheless, the Barcelona City Council did not even bother to paint the graffiti grey let alone put up metal siding. What made this site different? As mentioned, the demolished building had been squatted, but more important than this fact alone was who the squatters were, namely a group of politically motivated squatters known as *okupas*. The *okupas* from Miles de Viviendas on Joan de Borbó Avenue were evicted because of the threat they represented to capitalism and the notion of private property. But it was not just their physical, bodily presence that was threatening. Their words were also apparently deemed just as threatening. City officials clearly considered it necessary to erase any trace of the *okupas* that might serve to remind, or worse, inspire neighbors or passers-by.

The massive wall poem on Joan de Borbó Avenue brings to my mind the imagery of a famous Simon and Garfunkel song in which graffiti, sprayed on subways and inside housing projects, is a "sound of silence." Those who write graffiti are marginalized and have no authoritative voice. Similarly, as explained by theorist Gabriel Rockhill, French philosopher

Miles de Viviendas wall poem after the placement of the metal siding

Jacques Rancière's notion of a writing that introduces lines of fracture into the norms of society "is the silent speech of democratic literarity whose 'orphan letter' freely circulates and speaks to anyone and everyone precisely because it has no living logos to direct it."[3] Normally, orphanhood does not carry a positive connotation. However, in this case, when the "parent" is the dominant discourse of politicians, economists, and multinational corporations, writing and speech that is emancipated from the constraints and predetermined rules of free market capitalism and social and linguistic laws enjoy a freer and less abusive environment.

Escolar Bautista's verse, as it stood on Joan de Borbó Avenue, served as an example of orphaned words. What made these orphans more threatening (read: more able to effect change) than the random graffiti and urban art that one finds in empty lots was that these orphans formed a family. These orphans combined with one another according to the rhythmic patterns produced by bodies that learned to be with one another in a different way, and that imagined a different style of life and urban environment. This different style of the *okupas* gives abandoned houses poetic space. In other words, squatted houses and social centers are not spaces of belonging, but spaces of continually repeating encounters. They are spaces in which to share experiences and to participate in a "doing with," a commoning[4]. During the process of commoning, the inner space of the *okupas'* consciousness empties into the world space of squatted houses and social centers, and overspills the limits of not only the physical space but also the limits of what can or cannot be said, thought, believed, desired, made or done within society. The power of expansion characteristic of poetic space generates new virtualities that have the potential to be actualized in reality. In squatted social centers, new words, sounds, writings, images, and bodies drift and disconnect from the pre-established program of free market capitalism and consumption-based strategies of urban growth and design.

NOTES

1 All translations are those of the author unless otherwise noted.

2 Reprinted from Barcelonan Okupas: Squatter Power!, Stephen Luis Vilaseca, "The Wall Poem," pp. x-xv, 2013 with permission from Fairleigh Dickinson University Press.

3 Jacques Rancière, Slavoj Žižek, and Gabriel Rockhill, The Politics of Aesthetics: The Distribution of the Sensible (London: Continuum, 2004), 92-93.

4 I am employing Louis Wolcher's concept of the commons as he defined it in his talk "The Meaning of the Commons" given at The Law of the Commons conference in Seattle, 2009. As he explains, commoning is an unscripted form of life in which people take their rights into their own hands instead of waiting for them to be granted.

REFERENCES

Fancelli, Agustí. "Poema de pared." El País, November 23, 2007, Cataluña ed. [http://elpais.com/diario/2007/11/23/catalu-nya/1195783662_850215.html]

Rancière, Jacques. The Politics of Aesthetics: The Distribution of the Sensible. London, Continuum, 2004.

Empty lot on Carrer de les Floristes de la Rambla.

The future site of the Plaça de la Gardunya.

285

Everywhere Transnational Movements and Continu

286

Networks,
ties

287

Puerto Rican Occupations in New York City

Alan W. Moore and Yasmin Ramirez

A 16th century colony of Spain, Puerto Rico has been a territory of the United States since 1898. Its people are U.S. citizens. Nevertheless, Puerto Rican migrants to U.S. cities after World War II faced discrimination and cultural marginalization. The barrios where they lived were among the poorest and least well served in the nation. As a wave of housing abandonment and arson swept through these neighborhoods in New York City during the 1970s and into the '80s, Puerto Rican nationalist groups took over vacant buildings in a series of coordinated campaigns.

Some of these actions were short-term occupations intended to draw attention to the problems of the community, while others were longer term attempts to establish what Europeans would recognize as social centers. These large building occupations began with the taking of the Christodora building in 1969 by a coalition of Black Panthers and Young Lords, which immediately turned it over to community groups to run. The building had been built as a charitable service center for the Lower East Side, and later abandoned. The squatters were forcibly evicted by one of the first New York City police SWAT teams. The building was later re-developed as luxury condominiums.

Originating in Chicago, the Young Lords organization was the most visible Puerto Rican/Latino group that arose on the East Coast in the late 1960s and early 1970s. They came to national attention in June 1969 when the Black Panther Party newspaper announced the formation of a "Rainbow Coalition" between the Panthers, the Chicago Young Lords, the Brown Berets (comprised of Chicanos, or Mexican-Americans in the west) and the Young Patriots, a mainly white organization which grew out of a project by the new left SDS (Students for a Democratic Society).

The formation of the Young Lords Party in New York was announced on July 26th, 1969, the anniversary of the Cuban Revolution, at the Tompkins Square Park bandshell. Built in 1966, many free concerts were held there, including the 1980s "Squatter Mayday" rallies and concerts.

288

The bandshell was demolished by Mayor Rudolph Giuliani in 1991 during his campaign of repression against the squatting movement.

Unlike the Chicago Lords, which was largely comprised of reformed gang members who had become politically active in their communities, the New York Lords were founded by Puerto Rican college student activists. Many later became prominent journalists, poets, actors, artists, photographers, and political organizers.

The Marxist-Leninist group *El Comite* was instrumental in leading occupations of buildings first on the Upper West Side and later some on the Lower East Side. The Third World Newsreel collective's film *Rompierdo Puertas/Break and Enter* (1971) documents their work in addressing the housing crisis of Puerto Rican people as they resisted urban renewal.

The New York Lords understood the value of spectacle and used it as a way to affirm the power of the people and the street culture of the slums. They adopted a paramilitary uniform that echoed the Panther's radical black power garb: camouflage pants, combat boots, black leather jackets, and afros topped by a little tropical color—their signature purple berets. The Third World Newsreel film, *El Pueblo se Levanta/The People Are Rising* (1971), shows the Young Lords' takeovers of the Spanish Methodist Church in December 1969 and Lincoln Hospital in July 1970.

Found painting promoting black and latino unity, exhibited in the COLAB (Collaborative Projects) Real Estate Show

These were carnivalesque happenings where people sang songs, listened to poetry, and sat through teach-ins. The group even had a poet laureate, Pedro Pietri, later a co-founder of the Nuyorican Poets Café.

The Young Lords' affirmation of the Black and Native American roots of Puerto Rican identity fostered the creation of a new aesthetic among New York-born Puerto Rican artists, who began to work with symbols of the enduring presence and oppression of African and Pre-Columbian peoples in Puerto Rico and the Americas. This stimulated consciouness and pride in the hybrid nature of Puerto Rican/Latino identity.

While the Lords disbanded in 1973, their community based ethos and activism continued. Another important occupation was carried out by CHARAS, a group which, like the Chicago Lords, included ex-gang members. They worked with architect Buckminster Fuller, artist Gordon Matta-Clark, and the University of the Streets free education project. In 1979, CHARAS took over a large former school building on East 9th Street, which they ran for nearly 20 years as a multi-service center including theater, cabaret, and film screening programs. Poets of the Nuyorican school, most notably Bimbo Rivas, were closely involved with the center, called El Bohio. Skilled in obtaining grant monies, CHARAS was more pragmatic than the avowedly revolutionary groups. After occupying buildings, they worked with the city through programs like Adopt-a-Building and organizations like UHAB.

Another Lower East Side occupation was CUANDO, a building on 2nd Aveue which featured the first solar power array on a commercial building in the USA. In the South Bronx, where apartment buildings were occupied during the 1980s, the Casa del Sol apartment complex was squatted into the 21st century. One of the South Bronx movement's leaders, Frank Morales, transferred his attention to his native barrio in 1985. The squatting movement on the Lower East Side during those years took some 30 buildings. Many artists participated. The ABC No Rio cultural center became a node of that movement, and was itself briefly squatted to defend it from eviction. ABC received the core collection of its current zine library when that project was evicted from its South Bronx home.

published in
House Magic #6, 2014

Clayton Patterson, Joe Flood,
Alan Moore, et al. eds.,
Resistance: A Radical Political
and Social History of the Lower
East Side (New York: Seven
Stories Press, 2007)

Adam Purple's garden, East Village 1982

Fake Tabloid Headlines

Gregory Lehmann

These "faked tabloid headlines" were made in order to be distributed outside of a large mid-town Manhattan hotel where then Mayor Ed Koch was being celebrated upon the occasion of his birthday. I played the role of a newsboy yelling out "Extra! Extra! Read All About It!"

I was later informed that the episode involving me and the faked headlines made it into an article that was published in the NY Daily News dealing with the then mayor and his birthday bash.

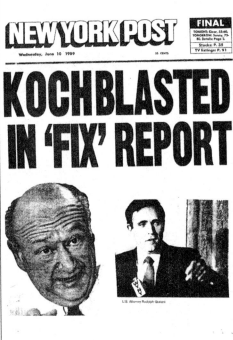

DAILY ⊡ NEWS

| 35¢ | NEW YORK'S PICTURE NEWSPAPER® | Wednesday, February 12, 1989 |

KOCH RESIGNS

Squatting as an Alternative to Counter Migrant Exclusion

Sutapa Chattopadhyay

Historically, like Europeans, Asians, Africans and people from Oceania have migrated all over the world. During pre-colonial, colonial and post-colonial times, the movement of people in the Global South has been higher than that to and within Europe and to North America. Why then, this emphasis on the Global North's burden from the inflow of immigrants from precarious locales?

Repressive immigration policies, costly naturalization and legalization procedures, immigration raids and tightening of economic policies did not deter employers from hiring undocumented workers instead created a shadow informal industry and an industry of fraudulent documentation that further increased migrant workers' precarity. Although there is no connection between migration and terrorism they are lumped together to justify the increased spending on securitization and the militarization of borders, which are transforming the migrant receiving nations in the West into 'carceral', 'gated', or 'fortress archipelagoes'.

Arguably following these trends, I was motivated to look for alternatives that can counter anti-immigrant policies, the dominant repressive processes of regularization, and their implications for the social acceptance and integration of migrants. Therefore my project analyses migrant illegality-legality-precarity and simultaneously looks into the relationships between migrants and autonomous Social Centre activists, who collaborate, cohabite, co-manage and co-exist with migrants. The project explores how squatting, as an alternative strategy of existence, and (migrant-led) autonomous movements can offer an alternative to dominant anti-immigrant policies and practices. The project therefore follows narratives from different kinds of clandestine migrants (those who are detained at detention centers/jails, any migrant street peddler, migrant women, and those involved in organizing or collaborates with Social centers) to understand: 1) their challenges while crossing borders, and 2) coping mechanisms with everyday repression from the state and police, economic marginalization, and societal exclusion. From the perspectives of the migrants, I confirm squatting as an action and a collective political apparatus that can shape horizontal-sustainable-creative networks with unwanted migrants through mutual aid, direct action, and solidarity.

MIGRANT SITUATION IN THE WEST

Liberalizing immigration masks significant restrictive features of policies, while restrictive immigration laws ostensibly intend to prevent migration, simultaneously sustain migration by keeping the status of classed and gendered migrants illegitimate. While some scholarly works and popular discourses have problematized migrants as commodities, weeds, criminals, burdens; others have perceived them as despoiling the cultural integrity and purity of Western nations. Though illegal migrants work, attend schools, contribute to social and economic good, yet stay in absolute anonymity. Paradoxically affluent societies cannot stand economically without the unskilled or semi-skilled immigrant workforce, their statuses are kept illegal with expensive and painful regularization processes – these repressive policies have not reduced the movement of people, both with and without documents across borders but have increased their economic marginalization as they are effortlessly used, devalued, expropriated, disposed of and deported. Like, the horrors of border crossing, this seldom catchs the attention of popular media, and news on the increase of state expenditure on securitization and militarization of borders, border patrols to execute raids, growth of prisons, increased detention and deportation, and harassment of illegal migrants are rarely communicated.

Over the past few decades unjust and discriminatory policies to control 'crime' and manage migration are made feasible by state-capitalist corporates, bureaucrats and politicians by drawing linkages between the movements of people with or without documents from Global South with the question of security of Western nations. The term 'immigrant-industrial-complex', has emerged from 'prison-industrial-complex', following the militarization of borders, police responses to terrorism and crime, and the social and cultural criminalization of immigrants and immigrant-phobia. The Spanish government for example has responded to pressure from the European Union with the gradual fortification of the North African exclaves of Ceuta and Melilla from 1990 onwards, which has extended to the Canary Islands, such as 'Fuerteventura'. Those who are arrested on the basis of illegal entry are first detained for three days, and if their national origin cannot be determined, an expulsion process is initiated. Then they are interned for 40 days (in Italy it is 60 days and in Greece it is 90 days), and if their nationality remains unknown, or if the country of origin or transit does not readmit them during this period, they are released. The authorities cannot send them out of the country but the expulsion order keeps their stay illegal and prevents them from taking up any legal employment.

Under these circumstances paperless immigrants are left to fend for themselves within the informal or shadow economy. Although described as illegal, most times the income-generating activities of migrants are neither illegal nor criminal. Rather they are forced to accept difficult trajectories to find livelihood in the host countries, in which they are effectively banned from living a normal life.

SQUATTING AS AN ALTERNATIVE TO COUNTER MIGRANT EXCLUSION

Squatter activists and Social Centers align to help clandestine immigrants evade the hegemonic polity. They autonomously establish a reality within which minority people can fight against other-ization, containment, and exclusion. Squats can provide spaces for activists belonging to different social movements and political ideologies. The important political element in squatting is the rich combination of different types of squats and activities. Some are occupied, some are non-squatted Social Centers, while some squats are legalized. Heterogeneous groups like squatters, migrants, visitors and locals, who share similar anti-capitalist eco-friendly concerns, strategies, and ideologies use run-down or unused spaces to work in solidarity. Squatted Social Centers stand on collective principles of horizontality and direct democracy, self-management, non-bureaucratic regulation, and spontaneous militant resistance. It is the productiveness and the diffusion of power from below that is useful.

Recalling from the writings on Social Centers and from the following experiences with Social Center activities and migrant narratives, I suggest that Social Centers can serve as a platform where paperless migrants can curve a niche or can serve as spaces where migrants might feel accepted:

1. The radicalism, autonomy and solidarity of the squatting movement is creative and persistently accepts new circles of

people, especially those socially and economically deprived and excluded by the mainstream society.

2. Squatting is a collective political mechanism for rightless and paperless people to claim their rights and access basic necessities.

3. Squatting validates their political situatedness and public visibility in the neoliberal West. Squatter activists and other immigrant rights and justice organizations actively collaborate to resist anti-immigrant politics, detention, deportation and border deaths.

4. Squatted Social Centers can serve as a network or a platform where clandestine migrants can practice their creativity through making and selling food, staging theatre, taking language lessons, and initiating and participating in dialog on politics and policy.

5. Most Social Centers re-cycle, share resources and promote low-cost living in an environmentally sustainable manner. Through these practices, new meaning, user value and alternative ways of living are created within squatted spaces that enable economically vulnerable people to experiment outside of the mainstream culture that exploits them.

6. Squatting can be passive or active protest, a form of social disobedience and non-cooperation against the unfair distribution of wealth, and the exploitation of resources, material or natural. It challenges unfair state politics and policies, and supports a gender-egalitarian and environmentally-sustainable society.

Standing at the interface of augmented western militaristic interventionism, heightened incarceration of the marginalized people (of color), robust neo-liberal capitalist initiatives and global ecological de-generative development projects it is vital to put in practice horizontal and gender-egalitarian practices such as squatting in order to halt rapid immigrant *apartheid* in first world nations and rest of the world.

Metelkova, Mon Amour: Reflections on the (Non-) Culture of Squatting

Jasna Babic

In some circles in Slovenia the name Autonomous Cultural Center Metelkova City is considered to be almost a synonym for squatting. Although Metelkova was not the first public squat, it is the oldest of those still around. In this text, comparisons are drawn with the international squatting movement, and the squatter community in Metelkova is analyzed on different levels—to what extent it nurtures the culture of squatting, and what was and remains the role that Metelkova plays in a wider Slovenian context in terms of developing and sustaining the squatting culture. The conclusion is reached, however, that the squatter movement in Metelkova (and elsewhere in Slovenia) has also failed so far to fully develop, nurture and maintain strict guidelines and principles, and that this can be attributed to the lack of squatting tradition, the large number of people involved in the project, and internal divisions among on issues of legalization.

If the Network for Metelkova, formed in 1993, had quickly and successfully concluded the dialogue with the city and state authorities, then the social-cultural center, which stands on the location of the former military barracks in the center of Ljubljana would have been legalized and discussion of its autonomy would, be but one of many theoretical concerns. However, events took a different turn. The reckless and aggressive autocracy of the then-owners of the abandoned barracks forced the initiators of *The Network* and its supporters to occupy the premises. Hunger—in a positive sense—for the physical space and for fulfilment of creative expression since then has led to vividly imaginative content and programming. The Network has struggled constantly—in

298

impossible living conditions without electricity and water—to demonstrate the importance of their existence to the neighbourhood, to the public, and to city and state institutions.

Today, in its middle twenties, Metelkova remains a synonym for squatting in Slovenia. Chronologically speaking, this was not the first public occupation, but it is certainly still a living one. It is a continuous social experiment embedded into informal structures, a fortress of unconventional social practices and a bulwark against the invasion of institutional culture. And most importantly, it demonstrates that occupied space can survive in Slovenia.

Squatting is living in or using empty, unoccupied and unused land or premises for the long term without legal rights or consent of the owner. Squatting is not a new phenomenon. It is an integral, albeit marginal, part of the history of the development of housing. It was not until the post-war era however that squatting moved beyond the mere need for permanent residence. Modern urban squatting is divided into five basic configurations, which encompass a variety of reasons for occupation (Pruijt, 2013): first, squatting that solves mainly housing problems due to deprivation, and second, squatting as an alternative strategy for obtaining housing. In the former, squatters occupy residences for themselves as an alternative to renting real estate. In the second, they occupy them for the most vulnerable social groups. The third form is conservational squatting, with the purpose of maintaining and preserving certain buildings, public areas or a part of the city. The fourth is entrepreneurial squatting—although I prefer the term "project squatting"—that embraces social centers and/or autonomous zones. This gives the opportunity to establish institutions with major potentials and without bureaucratic complications, such as studios, rehearsal rooms, concert venues, restaurants, cinemas, workshops, galleries, bookshops, libraries, infoshops, printing rooms, 'second hand' shops, 'give away' shops, help centers for migrants, etc. Many, if not most, are associated with alternative music and music production.

Such real-estate occupations may also be converted into living quarters, but not necessarily. The last kind of squatting is political squatting, where the squat is not a goal, but a tool for rebellion against the government per se.

In recent decades, squatting is no longer just a solution to housing deprivation, but has become a unique way of life. In conjunction with progressive social movements, squatter communities formed. Based on strong common identity, these make up the dispersed, yet communal squatting movement, characterized by common myths, heroes, rhetoric, symbols and stories. Under the common symbol of the squatter movement—a circle with a broken arrow—a number of stories about occupations or evictions, clashes with the police, martyrdom etc. are intertwined. Cities and/or countries where squatting is booming are idealized; squats that are well organized or have long lives are admired; and songs celebrate the squatting life and international squatter solidarity from which certain values and principles, like reciprocity, self-organization, equality, etc., have developed. So where can Metelkova Mesto be placed?

According to the Pruijt typology, Metelkova can be classified as an example of urban project squatting in conjunction with social movements. Today, the southern part of the complex of the former barracks hosts six venues and two bars, three galleries, a recording studio, an info shop, open kitchen and a number of studios, workshops and offices. Squats however are not just spaces, but the people who breathe life into these spaces, those who maintain and use them, their mutual relations, and the working and ethical principles they live by. What sort of community has been established in Metelkova and to what extent does it maintain the squatter culture? This text aims to sketch an overview of Metelkova through the prism of the squatter movement. I will examine what role squatting has played in Metelkova in the past and the present; to what extent Metelkova has developed and maintained the culture of squatting in relation to the wider Slovenian context, and what has been the relation of squatting culture to the local environment, the visitors and active participants within the Metelkova.

BETWEEN THEORY AND PRAXIS

Squatting, regardless of content, is primarily connected to the need for or lack of space. Although there are numerous factors influencing the origin of Metelkova, from the revival of grass-roots movements, the initiatives for a comprehensive conversion of the military barracks to peaceful civilian purposes, etc., at its core is a need for space, particularly to acquire artistic and cultural social space to fill spatial shortages, and to simultaneously allow many cultural creators, artists and groups to start creative work.

In the case of Metelkova, the occupation was definitely not the originally selected method for achieving this objective, but it was the only remaining means after the agreement for the legal takeover of the building was finally interrupted by a one-sided decision of the Municipality of Ljubljana to suddenly demolish the abandoned military

300

complex. Skipping over the fence around the barracks was necessary, yet the occupation could not have survived without the organization of the previously formed Network for Metelkova. During the period of the lobbying with the municipality, the Network prepared the basic distribution of facilities and defined the beginnings of a common principle of action despite the culturally diverse crowd of occupiers.

Just as the DIY principle is not only a type of production, squatting is not the mere act of obtaining more space. It entails a surplus of action in long-term voluntary commitment, which is reflected in (or through) manner, that is, lifestyle. The structural affiliation or internal diversity of the participants is not as important as the cultivation of explicit attitudes and/or ideology, direct political action, and the formation of certain alternative institutions, which sometimes become formalized. The main way the culture of resistance is defined in contrast to the culture of the majority is through the construction of its own zone, a pre-condition for forming the communities through which one seeks to realize a vision of an alternative reality.

Zones may vary, depending on the subcultural elements of music or lifestyle, yet they are all "liberated", "temporary autonomous zones".[1] Within the TAZ, and at the same time on a wider global level, the cultures of resistance horizontally form an informal and loose network of collectives, with mutual information and cooperation. Individual collectives are organizing music events, festivals and parties, distributing fanzines and musical productions, and forming communes. Travelling or squatter communities and groups connect on the basis of their mutual political and social interests. Relations between the different parts of the network are based on the principles of donation, volunteer work, co-operation, exchange and friendship, but this does not exclude cash contribution (e.g. entrance fees) when necessary.[2] Activities are not limited to leisure or hobby time, but go on the whole day. They are linked to self-interest (financing) in relation to the common good, and not to the creation of profit. Activities are self-organized, with a high level of reciprocity and mutual assistance. This forms the foundation of a kind of hard-to-describe inner strength. Mafessoli calls it *puissance* (Maffesoli, 1996), a lever that acts as a collective enthusiasm, and maintains the passion and love for the realization of ideas and beliefs.

Puissance plays a vital role in the squat's life path, from the occupation, the maintenance of the occupied status, through to the possible outcome and changes of the squat's status.[3] Its level of intensity affects the longevity and development of the squat. It may exceed the initial squatting enthusiasm and provide durability, even long after the first enthusiasm of all those who would like to be involved fades and they leave, while the handful of remaining people deal not only with program of activities but with additional infrastructural deficiency and maintenance, problems with the owners of the premises, etc.

Photos of squatters jumping fences immortalized the moment of the occupation of Metelkova. On the basis of this first enthusiasm, a community formed spontaneously, almost overnight, and immediately started with the program of production, which lasted until winter. The initial enthusiasm, however, wore off with first frost in buildings without electricity, water and heating, and was replaced by perseverance and the commitment of a few. They found the poor living conditions of secondary importance, and made sure Metelkova wintered until spring, and gradually began to challenge its marginal status.

The fear of otherness and the allegations of ghettoisation, according to B. Bibic (Bibic, 2003: 65), were overcome between 1997 and 2001: first, with the gradual "normalization" of utilities, i.e., gradual water and electricity supply and waste disposal. This coincided with an increase and regular organization of cultural, artistic activities and other programs, gradual renovation and maintenance of the buildings, and transformations of the visual appearance of the facilities and the surroundings. These improvements made Metelkova increasingly popular, and heavily attended. Secondly, an increased political engagement raised the issue of its cultural and artistic character and the social function of its "users", directly and indirectly addressing the function of Metelkova City itself. Metelkova, partly due to the influence of many other activist-oriented groupings,[4] became a legitimate public space of free association and expression of non-conformist political views, independent of political parties. As the millennium turned, the symbolic and practical expression of political Metelkova was embodied in the short-lived collective UZI (Office for Intervention). The name of the place—*Social-Cultural Center Metelkova Mesto* (SKC MM)—which for many expressed transparency, was changed into the more ideologically and politically suitable Autonomous Cultural Center Metelkova Mesto (AKC MM).

Outgrowing ghettoisation has had far-reaching consequences. Opening the space gradually led to the inclusion of a large number of external program producers, a wider range of available programs and, consequently, the arrival of many different audiences that unify the space on weekends and turn Metelkova into one of the most visited weekend night entertainment providers in Ljubljana.

The 1993 occupation of Metelkova was seen by the residents of Ljubljana, and the broader population, as something revolutionary, new, different, even strange. But after twenty years, as not only the crowd attending, but entire generations of squatters have changed, Metelkova remains a mystery for many, even today, despite its apparent obviousness,. (That is leaving aside the folkloric belief of those who never had any contact with Metelkova, and still see it as only a shelter for the social margin and social problems.)

Twenty years later it is surprising how few people are familiar with the status, processes and principles not only in Metelkova, but in squatted spaces in general. This is especially true of visitors, as well as many who want to cooperate, or are already operating within the Metelkova. Meanings of the notion of 'autonomy' are markedly different, sometimes even exclusive. Despite the debates on alternative, DIY culture, squatting and such are always vivid and dynamic (both formally and informally, in the theoretical 'tavern'). How could it come to such a divergence between theory and practice?

A SET OF DIVERSITIES

Slovenia does not have the tradition of squatting[5] as it is in other countries. Before squatting the barracks, there is only one example of public squatting in Slovenia, and even this was during the time of the former Yugoslavia. A house on Erjavceva street was squatted, primarily as an experiment, a few days' symbolic occupation with the aim of raising awareness on the issue of housing deprivation. (This was similar to the couple of hours' occupation of the cinema theatre Triglav in April 2014.) There were some occupations after Metelkova, established with

similar aims. Still, a lack of continuity, in regular occurrences of squatting, disabled any basis from which a culture of squatting could spring. Members of the Network originally anticipated that in order to 'acquire' the Metelkova premises they would need to squat them. They received help from Dutch squatters, who introduced them to the practical part of the occupation. The squatters-to-be, who were later joined by many outside the Network, did not, however, have experience or guidelines on which to act, except for the division of space, and a basic layout of their organization. This became clear shortly after the occupation, when two groups were formed within Metelkova. The first still intended to establish a formally organized cultural center, and share facilities and management. The second was "committed to direct democracy, the abolition of the division of labour and for sharing the premises, if necessary, from the inside" (Pirc, 2003)—meaning for the internal division of spaces according to needs, the position which ultimately prevailed.

Culture was the major marker of Metelkova, whether it be alternative, different, street, or any other type of creation. The place gained a political connotation somewhat later. This should be emphasized because the act of occupation of space itself is understood as political (as opposed to the provision of legal housing and workspace), and it predicts the establishment of the community (if it is not—and usually it is not—the act of an individual). However, the community which forms will not necessarily contain a high level of social capital, nor establish solid common values and rules of operation. For years, Metelkova has been pointing out that it represents a set of diversities and brings together different groups and individuals that are impossible to capture within a mould of formal structures as the Municipality of Ljubljana expects and anticipates. The whole project is community-based, as can best be seen in the monthly meetings of participants of the Metelkova Forum, in the work of cleaning, conservation and control of common external surfaces, and in occasional joint programs, like the annual anniversary and benefit events.

Metelkova has constructed a community, but the culture of community it has reared is insufficient. Squatting communities in general reflect a strong cohesiveness, self-organization, mutual assistance and respect. They set ground rules for functioning and for content and programs, and foster awareness of the fact that squatted places are not self-evident: they can only be used to the same extent as they are contributed to. Metelkova has always floated in a grey territory. Without any preliminary knowledge the squatters of Metelkova, considering the state of the military barracks, did the best they could in the situation required swift reaction. What the first generation of squatters considered self-explanatory, later generations are no longer taking for granted. Metelkova is no longer what it was 20 years ago. People change with the program (they provide). The lack of an explicit political stance, which could have provided clear conditions for the use and functioning of Metelkova, has already left its mark on the first generation of Metelkova squatters and visitors. Certain conditions have become established, and the lack of a political position has had far-reaching consequences.

Metelkova's loose structure has its advantages. It provides a high level of freedom for individuals, groups and collectives, and high flexibility in fixing last-minute events and situations, which could otherwise threaten the functioning or even existence of Metelkova as a whole. Its shortcomings can, however, be seen in a high drop-out rate in decision-making and the taking of responsibility, and low inflow of fresh forces, since certain spaces have been taken 'for life'. Also, club visitors and studio users become alienated, and there are occasional programs with politically questionable content. Organizers and producers of events who have personal commercial interests produce for their own benefit, and occasionally groups visit whose activities violate or damage Metelkova, such as organized pick-pockets, neo-Nazi groups, and dealers and users of hard drugs. The Metelkova community reacts too slowly to these situations, and often only when they are already beyond repair. Rules on how and how long spaces may be used by an occupant have never been set: for example, whether the use should be conditioned by results in the provision of creative artistic programs, or activity for the common good, rules on what is allowed and what can in no way be tolerated, etc.

CULTIVATING MEMORY

The motto 'a set of diversities' allows Metelkova to maintain the optimal position of democracy, but it also maintains stagnation and preserves looseness. The consequences of this situation cannot be immediately seen, but they are slow, thorough and far-reaching, eating into Metelkova's space. Why is this significant? Because the lack of common values and rules is producing the loss of Metelkova memory. With each generation, a certain segment of Metelkova's history falls into oblivion, increasingly putting Metelkova on an equal footing with for-profit cultural institutions and event venues, and not defining it as a separate political subject.

The highlight of Metelkova's political engagement was UZI (Office for Interventions), but it did not represent Metelkova as a whole. It did so to the outside, in the eyes of the media and general public, but upon a closer look, it was a group of individuals, who gathered at and were active in Metelkova. This continues to be the case today. Political theory and practice literally and metaphorically moved from the venues (clubs) and the courtyard to the attic of the Hlev building, into an info point founded by activists from the now-buried squats AC Molotov and Galicija. Although Metelkova is considered to be a political entity, which was self-evident to the first squatters, it never defined or strictly stood by certain political aspects and values. With the continuous surge of new creative forces, these have blurred. At the same time political values have given way to three considerations about the program and the visitors Metelkova sees: a consumer stance, uncritical comparison of different 'alternative' spaces of production, and a kind of generalization of the program.

One might think that visitors to the Metelkova zone would have some knowledge about where they are coming when they enter. Sadly, most do not know, and see Metelkova as one more visually unique and reasonably priced venue. And many who claim to understand Metelkova's mission and the way self-established spaces function, still enter with a consumerist position, expecting that the venues are going to be complete (with cloak room, excellent sound, etc.). While 'alternative' usually means free entry fee and low prices of drinks, the conventional discourse of work relations ('waiter', 'bouncer', 'staff', 'guests as clients') prevails. Visitors demand high-end service, including hospitality bonuses (straws, ice), and have low empathy towards the performers. This hardly differs from how the former Slovenian government treated artists.

Since the ownership of venues is not clearly legally defined (private or other), and the entire infrastructure is free, visitors feel they can do whatever they please, and regard warnings or prohibitions as personal insults. This is largely the fault of the Metelkova occupiers, since increasing beverage offerings has had a crucial effect on the understanding of a 'Metelkova bar'. In the past, this was kept on the sidelines, while today it occasionally overshadows the artistic program. It has also been solidified by government inspections, which have succeeded in turning drink sales from the status of support into consumerism.

This consumer mentality continuously reflects the general lack of understanding of the multi-layered practice of squatting and its conceptual foundations. The economic sphere is one of the key areas of alternative lifestyle practices. 'Alternative' means creating and bringing to life different, non-conventional lifestyle and production methods, which differ from the mainstream of social-economic relations and practices. While it can be easily understood at the macro-level, there is a continuous falling short of it in everyday personal relations, particularly in the 'underground' (sub)cultural scene. Due to the lack of an objective attitude towards, and understanding of non-profit status, debate around the economic sphere quickly turns into a repetition of prevailing market economy relations. On the one hand, there is a belief that the only measure of 'dedication', i.e., 'devotion to the alternative scene', is the provision of free and unpaid work. At the same time the labels and criteria of discussion are these of market economy relations. Very often the benchmark for such comparisons and confirmation of such practices is the squatted Tovarna Rog,[6] since nobody is familiar with any other squats in Slovenia. Those living outside the capital draw parallels with their local youth clubs, formal or informal. These comparisons can easily lead people in discussions to fall into a spiral of excuses and demonstrations of proof, without perceiving that both are unfounded. It is not about who is better or worse. Each debate on self-established spaces must contain not only principles of functioning, but also make a distinction about conditions which allow such functioning. Without this, comparison is impossible and can only lead to false conclusions, and create negative relations and divisions within an already small 'alternative' scene.

The main criticisms of Metelkova in recent years have been that it no longer provides alternative music content; it is becoming an entertainment center for the masses; it has lost the political connotation built up in the past. Presumptions of what is 'alternative' and what is 'popular' vary greatly, and can even be contradictory. Such a schizophrenic situation has a common foundation—aside from subjective preferences, the common point of criticism is that Metelkova visitors, as well as producers of its content, often generalize and put guidelines of all clubs on an equal footing. Thus the specifics of individual venues are blurred in the public discourse. What is more, as club activity becomes more identified with Metelkova itself, other parts of Metelkova are disappearing. In particular, the art studio activity is pushed to the limits of the seen, invisible. One of Metelkova's main ideas is that it is open to all who create in the area of non-profit culture, who organise and execute various social and activist activities. In practice this concept encounters a number of obstacles and limitations, from lack of space and appropriate technology, overbooking, and the appropriateness of content and quality. In answer to the criticism that the programming of venues has become loose, one has only to check the monthly programs of individual clubs to see that each has its own program policy, for a certain segment of visitors, and contributes to Metelkova's overall program.

Some older artists who have galleries at Metelkova criticize programs because they consider newer music genres like electronic, hip hop, and such to be commercial and non-alternative. Those who claim that Metelkova programs are not very diverse is either not familiar with the modus operandi of Metelkova, or wishes to stay ignorant in order to deny the legitimacy of modern urban culture, and to delegitimize newcomers by insisting that their work is untrue or worthless.

How can one love a place if one is not allowed to love it the way she wants to? And if, under constant pressure of criticism, one is denied the right to love, how can one be expected to unconditionally and passionately defend Metelkova in times of peril?

With all of this, which reflects the consumer nature of society in general, the larger picture is often overlooked. Metelkova continues to exist because some people are there every day, people who take care of it, often neglecting their personal lives, so that less illicit substances are abused on its premises, and that it is safe and clean. And because Metelkova people care about what is going on, because people care for the clubs and the equipment, this is why artists can still perform there, and why many get their first chance to perform or organise a show, learn how to use technical musical equipment, and start a musical career. As long as Metelkova lives, new self-organized spaces will continue to appear. Regardless of attitudes towards Metelkova, it remains the first and the last defender of alternative culture in Ljubljana and environs.[9]

CONCLUSION

While in its beginnings Metelkova aspired to break free from ghettoisation, it seems its main problem today is over-population. It is not the only place to experience this phenomenon. Many squats which have reached the respectable age of over 20 years are dealing with the question of openness: whether to maintain a certain level of counter-culture political identity and welcome only members of highly exclusive scenes, or to welcome a wide spectrum of users and risk eventually becoming a host for the cultural mainstream. There is no easy solution. The majority navigate between the two poles. Even though the majority of visitors come for music or other artistic programs, or merely to have fun, these spaces remain social and cultural meeting points within an activist network. We must therefore continuously repeat that these spaces are not to be taken for granted, and that non-institutional practices need to be nurtured and maintained. This is increasingly crucial given in line with the closing down or legalization of squats in the recent years. The motto

"Squatting is a right, not a privilege", one of the main principles of the squatters' movement, is increasingly becoming a privilege in the sense of the opportunities available to acquire experience, widen one's horizons and step away from established life practices and patterns.

Metelkova was unable to fully establish, nurture and maintain firm foundations in the principles of the squatter movement due first to the lack of a squatting tradition in Slovenia, and second to the large number of original squatters (some 200) and their initial division into two streams, one which supported legalization and the second, which supported an autonomous area. This division continues today. An ambivalence is ever-present about openness to the public, and about the classification of content. Within Metelkova itself, the situation is manageable, but this question will have to be assessed in the future. Legal venues with similar musical offerings are blossoming in Ljubljana, which makes it easy for visitors to no longer distinguish the particular status of Metelkova spaces.

Like other major cities, Ljubljana should have a number of autonomous cultural and political centers, which would complement each other's varied content. Unlike Metelkova, which truly is a product of a certain age—a mass public initiative with symbolic meaning—other spaces were occupied by smaller groups who could not protect them in the long run. That is why it is important that Metelkova nurture and give opportunity to various artists and groups, to motivate, and act as inspiration as a space of differentness and alternative culture. Now it is shadowed by the issue of legalization and the danger it will sink into conformity, in which the measure of success is the number of visitors

and events, performances by big names, etc. It requires responsibility from the programmers as well as visitors. Such an orientation requires united action, founded on mutual trust and respect for personal freedom and conviction, respect for agreements and mutuality, self-control during attacks of consumer mentality. Only in such an environment can idealism and conviction prevail.

NOTES

1 The concept of 'liberated', 'temporary autonomous zones' (ZAC) or TAZ in English was developed by Hakim Bey.

2 This connection method has symbolic value: it means resistance against the world, structured and regulated by global relations, dominated by market logic. They are justifying its action on two interrelated concepts, DIY and non-violent direct action, where DIY means to make something concrete by yourself in the cultural, social and political sphere, which in conjunction with the non-violent direct action goes beyond traditional protest rallies and offers a variety of actions and approaches of expression of resistance.

3 The life path of the squat takes from the pre-occupation, acts of occupation, the occupation of maintenance (life or functioning of occupied spaces) and usually predicts a three unravelations: first, the ideal, is the continued existence of squat, other two are more close to reality: eviction or legalization.

4 Villa Mara squat and AC Molotov squat, Dost je! (Enough!) collective and then growing protest movement in relation to Slovenia's accession to NATO and the EU.

5 At the time of Yugoslavia the housing problem was solved with social non-profit housing. With the independence of Slovenia there were individual cases of illegal occupation of empty military apartments. Examples of squatting may include 'black (illegal) construction', which can be found today. In the field of youth culture, youth clubs had an important role, especially in smaller towns, which make agreements with the local municipality to use a space to organize cultural events.

6 [See the text "Rog: Struggle in the City," by Andrej Kurnik, Barbara Beznec in the Transveral e-zine of the EIPCP, April 2008, in English, German, Spanish, Italian at: http://eipcp.net/transversal/0508/kurnikbeznec/en – Editor's note.] The social center Rog is just one small part of the Tovarna Rog squat. Nowadays Rog is more like a social and sport squat basically run by skaters, with yoga and kung fu practices there and so on.

The Universal Embassy: A Place Open to the World

Tristan Wibault, translated by Aileen Derieg

There is only one virtue: impotence.
Robert Desnos

A MICROPOLITICAL HABITAT

In January 2001 a group of "illegals"—*sans-papiers* fighting for regularization[1]—occupied the abandoned building of the Somalian embassy in Brussels to meet their urgent need for accommodations.

This place, abandoned because of the civil war in Somalia, property of a vanished state, was soon to become the Universal Embassy.[2] It is universal, because the individuals assembled here are conscious of the discrimination that is produced through ties to a nationality. Since then, the building has been inhabited solely by *sans-papiers*. The aim of the Universal Embassy is support and consequently autonomy. It helps the residents with their various administrative treks of a legal or social nature. It is a place that is open, where people that are illegal in their place of residence and can expect no support from the authorities of their countries of origin can exchange information, meet other communities, prepare battle plans. It has become the embassy of those who no longer have any embassy.

The Universal Embassy is a unique place in Brussels, where *sans-papiers* can share their experiences, mutually support one another and develop a public voice, where all kinds of encounters are possible, where different communities mix, where a social life can become manifest and diversity can be expressed. Today there are approximately thirty people living in the Universal Embassy: men, women and children of Algerian, Moroccan, Rwandan, Ecuadorian, Albanian, Iranian, Ukrainian origins.

Agency in the Universal Embassy is developed in articulation

312

between the misery of clandestinity and a political fiction. What is able to emerge in this is a new language. The language of a people to come.

The function of acceptance and care is fundamental. This makes it possible to grasp the development of the situation of migrants: the processes leading to clandestinity, the obstacles in the way of regularization. This is where the center of agency is found. From this point, an expertise in survival is developed together with the residents, a legal and political expertise, an everyday sensibility. The entirety of the activities is directed to preparing the *sans-papiers* for the battle for the recognition of their rights, to giving them confidence in their means again. Something beyond the horizon of survival slowly crystallizes—a place that is more than emergency accommodations. The residents are the political subject, they organize their life.

Social work retreats into an individual relationship between supporter and supported. This relationship is hopelessly incapable of helping the victims of clandestinity, who are by definition without legal security. The measure of the humanity of the policies that the illegals encounter is variable. On the one hand they have access to certain rights and to certain institutions: such as receiving medical treatment, enrolling their children in school, or even rights to carry out precarious activities. Other than that, they can be prey to a raid in the subway and end up in a *centre fermé*.[3] It is ultimately in this constrained juridical space that the *sans-papiers* conducts his or her battle. The arbitrariness and the lack of an overall vision constantly contribute to the isolation of migrants, to the development of rumors, to the reproduction of acts of subjugation to procedures with no future. The political dimension disappears. Almost all that is left in the end is to demand the minimal status of a human being ...

It is not enough to cry out the political dimension loudly. The *sans-papiers* are not a legal body that can assert certain claims. And yet mobilization work is all too often thought of in these kinds of terms. Clandestinity dissolves every life project. It is easy to accuse the *sans-papiers* of a corporatism of survival. It is time to go beyond the one-dimensional character of the battle.

CONSTRAINED EVERYDAY LIFE

The Universal Embassy is a star.

Clandestinity is an absurd journey, at the end of which there is the loss of identity. A resident from Somalia, that vanished country, wanders around in the city wearing a Zorro mask. In the centre fermé he

313

would have held incoherent speeches ... A migrant grandmother rings the doorbell of the neighboring building, convinced that her daughter lives there: the Embassy of Saudi Arabia. She has spent seven years on a journey, during which reality dissolves ... She is 77 years old. Clandestinity becomes a state of suspension in a parallel world, an evaporation of one's own substance.

The Universal Embassy is a concentration of weakness. When someone comes here to find shelter, then it is because the precariousness of their situation has become unbearable.

Fear is the clandestine's shadow. Fear of everything and everyone: of taking the bus, of working, of moving. One must take care not to be conspicuous, not to loiter in the shopping centers. Those who have nothing to buy, have no reason to loiter there ... Every action holds its own measure of risk.

It is the justice system that holds one together. The hope is minute, and everyone settles into waiting. Always, always waiting, everything concentrated on this waiting. Wearing out in wearing through the procedure, for months, for years. One seeks encouragement in thinking that it is still better than risking certain deportation. Obscene labyrinth.

20, 30 years old, with no future, no possible life plan. Clandestine migration extends the bitter experience of a lost youth. In order to flee from a leaden society or unemployment, migration becomes a life project in itself, the hope of a possibility. This dream retreats back to itself. The project becomes unreal. There is no more desire that could be articulated. The hypothetical day of regularization becomes devoid of meaning, none can be invested in it. The only constant is that there is no solution.

The loss of self is at work here. Becoming a driven, exploited animal, a criminal and a victim. No more reading, no more writing, earning three euros in an hour, even less as a woman.

Founding and building up the Universal Embassy means finding a concrete hope again. This is the articulation that is the point here: countering this constrained reality with something and moving beyond the nations and their desolate territories; being able to gain confidence in one's own means, to desire, to plan one's life.

The Universal Embassy is a facilitation. Initially it was a matter of accommodations that had to be renovated: cleaning from the top to the bottom, connecting water and electricity, furnishing a kitchen, repairing sanitary facilities, fixing the roof, etc.

Nevertheless, this place—which is open in every respect and exposed to all possible influences—can only be a place of crisis. The living space alone is not viable, if the entirety of the problems of its inhabitants are not covered. Without having any authority, without being able to delegate anything. Every difficulty requires finding ways to overcome it. Very often outside the realm of medicine, outside the realm of law, through the realization of a habitat. A heterogeneous mosaic of those involved gradually emerges, which is grounded in respect and the exchange of knowledge. At the same time that the habitat is enriched, it breaks through the social isolation that is so effectively organized through repression. It becomes autonomous.

One can read *"Ailleurs"* (Elsewhere) by Henri Michaux together, the story of the *Arpedres: The Arpedres* are the most obstinate people there are, obsessed with righteousness, with rights and even more with duties. Respectable traditions, certainly. All of it without a horizon. Expression liberates itself, steps out of the stigma, one can break loose, celebrate, and celebrating also means eating. It is possible to invest politics with meaning and derive a force of desiring from this, finding a place in the world again, where opinions are meaningful and actions are effective.

AUTONOMOUS MIGRANTS

As migrants with no protocol, the *sans-papiers* are driven by the evidence of law to have rights. They are neither victims nor criminals. The autonomy of their movements sounds the call for a new relation of the legal subject to the productive subject. What can the historical bond between the citizen and the worker still mean, if foreigners are enslaved here? Supernumeraries of bio-power, their existence in the transnational world today invents new diasporas without the original break and constitutes multifarious networks of solidarity and exploitation, in which origins, settlement and transit touch across several generations. The territory becomes the local that is linked with the journey.

What we have here is the immediacy of a legal subject that is transnational, because it transcends the small agreements between nations; an interest other than in changing citizenship or in (inevitably always suspicious) dual citizenship, the desire for something else: an autonomy of personal and collective constitution and the paths of new solidarities that are released from territories and borders.

Europe remains blind with regard to this essential foundation of the world to come. By insisting on a conception of nationality that has nearly run its course, the various European countries indulge in the illusion of being able to control and halt the migrations, whose motivations lie solely in the initiatives of the migrants. What is implemented here is a new landscape of war. And it was actually thought that the negativity of the wall had been overcome.

By accepting that human beings undergo existential crises because they have no papers, the states remind us of how identity is to be understood. The existence of an identity between states is a loss of identity, which can go as far as the loss of one's name, but can also become a place of the universal that recomposes itself where the paths cross. The Universal Embassy seeks to impel this transition: from the extinguished identity to the universal that is to be constituted; transgressing affirmation by power of the negation of an existence without papers and sowing the seeds of constitutive desire; leaving the obligatory mediation of the state behind, in order to invoke a direct effect on a transnational right. Like every embassy, the Universal Embassy is a place of representation, but without a figured state. What is represented is emerging. Its inhabitants, the *sans-papiers*, new pariahs of the free world, contest a national citizenship that is a blood relation of the nation. By intervening in the contours of state representations, the embassy abolishes the limitation of the border locally. Its inhabitants are those who have already arrived in terms of a local that is present in the world.

NOTES

1 The Verhofstadt I cabinet, the so-called "rainbow coalition" of liberal, socialist and green parties, had initiated a regularization campaign in 1999 for a limited period, which is meanwhile over. Roughly 30,000 sans-papiers were legalized in the course of this campaign. However, many applications still remained unprocessed after the end of the campaign, and many sans-papiers did not dare to submit applications to begin with (for fear of not meeting the criteria). (translator's note)

2 See also the Universal Embassy web site, where further information and documentation can be found, along with the "Declaration of the Universal Embassy": http://www.universal-embassy.be/.

3 In Belgium, as in a number of other EU states, there are so-called "closed centers" (centres fermés), i.e. separate camps, in which sans-papiers can be detained for months, before finally being deported or — in the case of those persons who cannot be deported, for example, for legal or administrative reasons — released into clandestinity again. [translator's note]

LE QUARTIER AUX RICHES

5000

Underground vegan rap - Wawa
+ AFTERPARTY

ROZBRAT {ROWEROWNIA} ul. Pułaskiego 21a

Le chômage   racis
la répression, la misère...

C'EST L'ÉTAT ET LES PATRONS

ANTIFA

2008
MERKEL

Chômeurs,
Étudiants, Salariés,
Sans-papiers, tous

C'EST LA SOCIÉTÉ QU'IL FAUT CHANGER

kolektyw **Rozbrat**

www.rozbrat.org   ul.Pułaskiego 21a P-

MIASTO
TO NIE
FIRMA

JESTEŚMY ZWYKŁYMI

Anywhere:
Media, Virtu
and Diffusio

lity,

319

Squatting, Mainstream Media Discourses and Identity

Galvão Debelle dos Santos and E.T.C. Dee

It is unsurprising that squatters tend to be "othered" when represented in the mainstream media. They present a challenge to the logic of capitalism, undermining the absolute right of the owner to enjoy his/her private property whether she/he actually puts it to use or not. Individual media accounts may on occasion represent fairly or accurately the squatting cases they refer to, but overall mainstream media stories retreat to easy good/bad stereotypes, characterizing squatters as "folk devils" who are deviant youngsters, foreigners, criminals, layabouts and so on.

In our work, based in critical discourse analysis of media portrayals of two distinct squatting movements, Dee analysed 235 media stories on squatting in eight English newspapers from January 1 2009 to December 31 2011, and Debelle examined the reporting by four newspapers of two cases where squatters made the news in Barcelona during 2006 (*El Forat* and *La Makabra*). We assessed the process by which squatters are othered and pigeon-holed as a threat. In England and Wales, where the squatters' movement is diffuse and fairly disorganised, a significant amount of news articles focused on "terrifying beasts from foreign lands", aka "bad" squatters, while sometimes mentioning a "good" squatter, who occupies an empty house and repairs it, getting along with her neighbors. In Barcelona, where the politicized squatters were the object of intense media coverage, this duality was re-created as the "violents" versus "pacifists", the "deserving squatters who claim their constitutional right for housing" versus "undeserving squatters who claim non-basic goods". This moral judgement, which adopts different forms in each situation, was found in most newspapers in both case studies.

We examined how squatters attempted to sidestep negative discourses. In Barcelona, where squats are known as *okupas*, the movement emphasizes its otherness by using the letter 'k' rather than a 'c'. Similarly, squatters in London claim to be occupiers or caretakers, to avoid negative connotations. Of course the danger here is that these squatters contribute to easy stereotyping by the media. The willingness of some groups to conform as 'good' squatters creates divisions within a movement and often ultimately fails. Mushrooming property prices almost always trump the needs of any squatted project.

We observed that it is hard to overturn the hegemonic viewpoint on squatting, but the tactic of shunning the media does not tend to help the movement. From this, our conclusion is that squatting movements are successful when embedded in the communities around them. In the recent example of Can Vies in Barcelona, several days of rioting and unrest followed the attempted eviction. After people power halted demolition, a campaign was launched to rebuild the centre. In a press conference with more than 15 TV channels present, Can Vies argued that it was the police and institutions who resorted to violence, while insisting on the legitimacy of self-defence.

This strategy is obviously not available for most squatting projects, where popular support is not as evident as in the case of Can Vies. Of course, much more attention was given to the burning barricades than to the appeasing, yet resistant, discourses coming from Can Vies. Still, as far as the unity of the movement is concerned, the pressure from politicians and the media was not successful. Thus, while it may not be possible to influence public opinion positively through the mainstream media, it seems that certain discursive strategies can be found to avoid internal conflicts. In short, what motivates some conflicts is the attempt of collectives to negotiate with authorities, more than the usage of a certain spelling or identity. Thus, our comments only begin to touch on several important issues.

It is important to note that the division between "good" and "bad" rests on a moral judgement. By blaming the authorities, Can Vies effectively subverted the moral division promoted by the elites by creating a new one, where "good" is self-defence of self-managed spaces, and "bad" is the violence exercised by institutions.

REFERENCES

"Examining Mainstream Media Discourses on the Squatters: Movements in Barcelona and London", by G. Debelle dos Santos and E.T.C. Dee.

"El Banc: Squatting as Urban Struggle in Barcelona", by E.T.C. Dee and Galvão Delle Rodrigues, [opendemocracy. net], October 9 2014.

Fair Trade Music

Spencer Sunshine

Few cultural movements have left more of a mark than DIY (Do-it-Yourself) punk. For the last four decades, the scene has had a tremendous impact on both music and radical politics. Best known for its anarchists, little attention to has been paid to its ideological contradictions. For example, even its most politicized form, anarcho-punk, proclaims anti-capitalist goals, yet economically ends up working through market mechanisms.

I'd like to propose a thought experiment, which illustrates two real impulses that participants in the punk scene will be readily familiar with. In my view, political DIY punk is essentially Situationist in its public proclamations, but in practice it is closer to something that could be called Proudhonist. This may be the cost of attempting to do the impossible: to live outside of capitalism without being able to destroy it.

This account is based on my own participation in US punk circles, from the late 1980s through the first part of the 2000s, in various cities; getting involved in anarchist politics after some years in the punk scene; and from living in Portland, Oregon in the 1990s. There, a large political punk community exists alongside a sprawling network of collective houses, as well as credit unions and cooperative businesses. Portland's punk scene established a multi-generational and highly politicized presence which mixed in with both the city's municipal culture, and the other local countercultures.

DIY punk takes a variety of forms, including those which are explicitly political (especially anarchist, feminist, queer, environmental, and occasionally Marxist-inspired politics.) These exist alongside, and overlap with, the parts of the DIY culture which shy away from direct political commitments. The latter is typical of the indie rock scene, but assimilates many other genres, including some kinds of punk (although one could argue that all DIY culture contains an implicit critique of the existing social order.)

PROUDHON: PATRON SAINT OF SMALL BUSINESSES?

Proudhon was one of the original European socialist thinkers who, from his first 1840 book What Is Property? (His answer was "Property is Theft!") until his death in 1865, advocated a model of small-scale businesses and cooperative enterprises which would produce for local needs. In particular, he aimed to reduce the role of finance capital by forming a People's Bank which would make extremely low-interest loans. These businesses would compete with each other on a market system. Local groups of producers would federate together, replacing the centralized state.

Although he was a supporter of the working class, Proudhon was an opponent of communism, unions, and violent revolution. The young Marx criticized him in The Poverty of Philosophy for championing the economic forms of the petite bourgeoisie (the small-business owners who at the time seemed about to be eliminated by the expansion of capitalism,) as well as promoting a pseudo-anti-capitalism that preserved the commodity form.

The anarchism of Mikhail Bakunin, Peter Kropotkin, Gustav Landauer, and others rely heavily on Proudhonism. Bakunin called him the "master of us all" and his own anarchism as "Proudhonism ... pushed right to its final consequences." Proudhon's views have an affinity with a number of other community-based economic systems, including time banks, social credit, local currencies, guild socialism, and distributionism.

SITUATIONISM: FOR THE ABOLITION OF EVERYTHING

The Situationist International (1957–1972), meanwhile, was a group that grew out of the post-Surrealist European avant-garde, and incorporated

various aspects of the Western Marxist critique. In *The Society of the Spectacle*, their main theorist Guy Debord drew upon concepts from Marx's early manuscripts, Georg Lukács, Henri Lefebvre, and the *Socialisme ou Barbarie* group, and combined them with avant-garde and crypto-spiritual conceptions of life and social change.

Debord claimed that all of society had become commodified and even turned into images (the "colonization of the lifeworld" by the "spectacle,") so that even our private moments no longer stood outside of this system. Everything had become dulled, alienated, and quantified. Anything that smacked of bureaucracy—such as political parties—were a target of contempt. An explosion of spontaneous resistance would overturn modern society, replaced by workers' councils; work and "dead time" would be abolished. Situationist ideas seemed to be verified by the uprising in Paris in 1968 (which the group participated in.) In the US counterculture, "pro-Situ" politics were widely disseminated in the 1970s and 1980s, and in the anarchist punk scene this peaked in the mid-to-late 1990s.

Proudhonism—and here I mean something akin to what Proudhon was advocating, beyond any special adherence to his specific views—can be seen today in those who advocate "buy local" campaigns, federated networks of co-operatives and worker-owned businesses, credit unions, community-supported agriculture programs, etc. It fits in well with urban planning programs focusing on livability and mixed use (anarchists such as Peter Kropotkin, Colin Ward, and Paul Goodman advocated similar schemas.) These practical projects and views appeal to a large variety of people, including anarchists, environmentalists, and activists around food issues. However, they're based on commodity production (or the purchase of real estate) and market exchange; therefore they do not question the fundamental structures of capitalism.

Situationism (here referring to both the original Situationists and others who were influenced by their critique) is entirely different. Its uncompromising and acerbic critique of almost every facet of the modern order (notably excepting questions of identity,) and use of striking visual imagery drawn from the European avant-garde, had a particular appeal to punks. (Malcolm McLaren and Jamie Reid, the Sex Pistols' manager and visual artist respectively, had both been involved in Situationist circles, and so punk's later incorporation of Situationist ideas may be actually reflective of its genesis.) Whereas Proudhonism, consciously or not, promotes a prefigurative strategy, there are few concrete actions that can be taken to promote a Situationist transformation.

The most popular is to pour gasoline on social antagonisms, in order to facilitate a climate of generalized revolt. On a more mundane level, one can "create situations"—a form of public performance art designed to provoke a change of subjective impressions on the unsuspecting audience—or go on a *dérive*, an aimless drift through the city that proposes to reconfigure a person's subjective experience of their geographic surroundings. Denouncing existing political organizations, especially if they're left-wing, is also a favorite pastime.

PUNK AS "MUSICAL SITUATIONISM"

The ideology of punk and hardcore bands is hard to quantify since there are so many, have such a variety of influences, and almost always have little specific articulation (they are, after all, bands and not political collectives—even if sometimes they have the same feel.) There are some that do have a critique that specifically incorporates Situationist ideas, including the Feederz, Submission Hold, J Church, and Catharsis (who are affiliated with CrimethInc, which began as a neo-Situationist propaganda outlet.) But political punk in general takes many things from the Situationist-style approach.

Unlike Proudhon and other anarchists who championed society (opposing its manipulation by reified forms like organized religion and the State), punk wants, as the Pist sang, to destroy society. It is openly antagonistic to the existing social order, and generally calls for its abolition (drop out of school,) rather than reform (better funding for, or community-control of, public education.)

The May 1968 Situationist slogan "Never Work!" certainly matches the punk ethos regarding the avoidance of wage labor, and the emphasis on traveling and train-hopping matches the dérive. Political punk's economic rhetoric, where it exists, is openly anti-capitalist, and rarely adopts traditional socialist positions for higher wages, job security, or safe working conditions. The glorification of shoplifting and communal sharing directly pits the punk against the commodity form. Dave and Stuart Wise, in 1978's "The End of Music," even proclaimed punk to be "musical situationism."

FAIR TRADE MUSIC

Paradoxically, the DIY punk scene uses a variety of Proudhonian structures to function, particularly in how bands, labels, and some music venues function. All of these forms engage in market-based production and exchange. The tendency is to try as hard as possible to make these productive forms based locally and/or in the punk community, so that bands will use other DIY companies to print their record sleeves, t-shirts, and buttons. The emphasis is on worker self-managed collectives, which have no direct economic exploitation from owners, nor hierarchical work structures with bosses.

But what actually happens is a kind of attempt at what might be called "commodity production for use values," with lower levels of retail markup. One Portland, Oregon project even calls it "fair trade music." Some clubs under "punk community control" have been started; 924 Gilman in Berkeley, California is a rare, long-lasting example. There is a lot of cottage industry production of craft items like jewelry (long predating Etsy) Some bands have tried to avoid this commodity-producing system by "moving directly into communism"—making shows and music free. Because there are actual costs involved in making music—paying for instruments, practice space, gas, studio time, pressing CDs, etc.—this is only an option if one is willing to pay for these expenses out-of-pocket (even if one assumes that playing music itself does not deserve financial compensation, a strange devaluing of the very labor that is most valorized by the punk community.)

PUNK ECONOMICS BEYOND MUSIC

There are other economic aspects of punk community beyond music, including running cooperative business such as groceries, free redistributive projects—like *Really, Really Free Markets* (RRFMs) and *Food Not Bombs*—and punk house collective living. The cooperative businesses wind up in the same bind as the labels: higher prices are required to pay living wages to employees, and products are still exchanged on a market basis which is mediated by State-backed currency. Some projects, like CrimethInc, charge money for some items (CDs and books,) but then produce free materials with the profits.

In others cases, one can find an attempt to create truly non-market structures, often through dumpstering food and the pooling of resources. Food Not Bombs and the RRFMs are attempts to redistribute surplus; but, ironically, they require an inefficient capitalist system to overproduce those goods they then redistribute them in a non-market fashion. Squats require that others put in the labor time and material resources to build the structures which are then taken over; the glorification of shoplifting follows the same lines. Nonetheless it is important to point out these elements in order to show that Proudhonist-style economics exist alongside other economic forms, in a common effort to live collectively in a different manner.

PROUDHONISM AS PREFIGURATION?

Finally, the question of prefiguration comes into play. Consciously or not, does DIY punk—which emphasizes the notion of production for use value and not exchange value, and a decentralized economic structure with worker control over both the production process and profits—"teach" people that punk rock is a model for a future anarchist society? The anarchist-punk magazine Profane Existence basically took this position. Even though many self-conscious radicals who are in the punk scene, or who have come into radical politics through it, may reject these Proudhonian political goals, the influence cannot be dismissed.

Martin Buber's *Paths in Utopia* is the best intellectual advocacy of the views of a self-conscious political counter-culture that I've run across in more mainstream political texts (Buber had been influenced by Gustav Landauer who, despite some conservative social views, is the true grandfather of anarchist counterculture.) Buber suggests that Marx's dismissal of the "utopian socialist" project was disingenuous: Robert Owen, Proudhon, and the others were advocating concrete, material forms (such as workers co-ops), and they based their projected future society on these "utopias" that actually existed. Marx and Engels's communism, on the other hand, was a possibility that existed only in their minds. Therefore, their supposedly materialist alternative was actually the idealist form of socialism.

Is DIY punk the really existing counterculture that convinces many that an anarchist-style society is possible? At least for some, it would seem that the answer is yes. But its existence inside capitalist society means that it cannot completely escape the very confines of the system that it is rebelling against—and it is forced to engage in commodity production, even while denouncing it.

But after all, who would even say that punk functions without contradiction? In fact, as we all know, it thrives on it.

This article originally appeared in **Souciant,** a online magazine of politics and culture, at souciant.com, in July of 2013. The author thanks Brett, James, Lawrence, and Morgan for their comments on this piece.

Hacklabs and Squats: Engineering Counter-Culture in Autonomous Spaces

maxigas

INTRODUCTION

Squatting as a social practice has engendered specific forms of life, producing a multiplicity of subcultures. Hacklabs have been the sites of an engineering subculture which developed in such milieus. Hacklabs were one of the first scenes where computer culture and political movements fused, forging embodied communities and fostering alternative practices of computing. While the history of hacking is crucial to understand these developments, here I focus on how this specific engineering culture fit into its social, political, and physical environment.

The lucid definition of Yuill (2008) is a good starting point for understanding hacklabs:

Hacklabs are, mostly, voluntary-run spaces providing free public access to computers and internet. They generally make use of reclaimed and recycled machines running GNU/Linux, and alongside providing computer access, most hacklabs run workshops in a range of topics from basic computer use and installing GNU/Linux software, to programming, electronics, and independent (or pirate) radio broadcast. The first hacklabs developed in Europe, often coming out of the traditions of squatted social centres and community media labs. In Italy they have been connected with the autonomist social centres, and in Spain, Germany, and the Netherlands with anarchist squatting movements.

RISE

Hacklabs have existed basically since the advent of the personal computer, but their "golden age" was the decade around the turn of the millennium. They have been most popular in Southern Europe (notably in Spain and Italy). Similar spaces in the North often had other names like "squatted internet work-spaces" or simply cybercafes. However, given the remarkable consistency between the actual activities and their social context, I discuss all of them under the hacklabs rubric.

The claim that hacklabs are a valid unit of analysis—i.e., that they hang together in reality enough to be studied empirically as a single phenomena—must in itself be substantiated. I argue that hacklabs have consistent engineering culture and material practices because they share similar social circumstances, and what I call a 'scene'. A scene is made up of self-referential circuits of cultural communication, and has vital online and offline components. It is not simply a common pool of knowledge but a common experience shared between people who mostly meet online but periodically gather in their bodies. The "hacker con" is a central ritual of hackers, where solidarity is built, meaning is negotiated and efforts are directed in a common direction (Coleman 2010). People involved in hacklabs and hackerspaces are clearly invested in the general hacker scene, and they turn out in massive numbers in hacker gatherings. All but one or two of the several dozen European hackerspaces I follow for my dissertation research sent a delegation to major gatherings. Informants often report that the idea of founding a hacklab or hackerspace was born at a particularly inspiring moment of a hacker gathering.

For the Southern European hackers these meetings have been organised annually in Italy since 1998 (Florence, CPA Fi-sud), and in Spain since 2000 (Barcelona, CSOA les Naus),[1] constituting the heartbeat of the scene. (anonymous 2010; Ferrer 2014) A common feeling among interviewees was that the Italian hackmeeting enjoys more prestige than the Iberian one: for instance, practices and participants move more often from Italy to Spain than from Spain to Italy. While there are no hackmeetings in North Europe, very interesting hackmeeting traditions exist in Spanish-speaking Latin America, especially Bolivia, Mexico and Chile, even though they are out of the scope of the present investigation.

North European hackers have a different circuit largely based on hacker camps, which like the South European ones, are bipolar. There the German node is somewhat more prestigious than the Dutch. The former is always called Chaos Communication Camp, and the latter has a different name each year, and often different organisers too.

According to legend, the first hacklab was founded in 1995 or 1996 in Catania, Sicily, of all places, hosted by the Auro squat. (ana 2004) Freaknet or Poetry hacklab continued to be an inspiration for hackers for decades (and is still active today). But at what point did hacklabs become a genre of initiatives recognisable in the scene? Oral history and a few texts pinpoint this moment at the concluding discussions of the 1999 hackmeeting in Milan, Italy. (ana 2004; Anarchopedia contributors 2006; anonymous 2010) After this hackmeeting many Italian and Spanish participants went home with the common understanding that they needed to found a hacklab in their home town. Indeed, empirical data based on domain registration years (maxigas 2012) shows a steady rise in the number of hacklabs from then on. The demise of hacklabs caused by changes in the social, political and technical context is narrated in a separate section of this essay. Few were founded after the year 2010. The majority of them are probably closed down by now.

HEYDAY

Often located in squatted spaces and occupied social centres, hacklabs were part of the toolbox of autonomous politics, on a par with such institutions as Food Not Bombs vegan kitchens, anarchist infoshops and libraries, free shops and punk concert halls. (maxigas 2012) For instance, Les Tanneries occupied social centre in Dijon housed all these activities under one roof, as did the RampART in London, the Rimaia in Barcelona, and Forte Prenestino in Rome. The largest network of hacklabs existed in Italy,[2] where influential hacklabs bloomed—from the LOA hacklab in the populous North (Milan), through the aforementioned Forte and Bugslab, also in Rome, to the already mentioned Freaknet. Today, notable examples exist in Amsterdam (LAG)[3] and near Barcelona (Hackafou).[4] Both operate in the context of a larger autonomous space. The Binnenpret[5] in Amsterdam is a legalized (ex-squat) building complex which houses an anarchist library, the OCCI self-managed music venue, a vegan restaurant and the Revolutions Per Minute record label, amongst other things like apartments. Calafou6 is an "Eco-Industrial, Post-Capitalist Colony" based on a cooperativist model, including a social centre for larger events and parties, freeshop, kitchen, library and many other "productive projects". It is telling that neither of those host spaces is an illegal occupation, like most of the houses which hosted hacklabs in their heyday. Since hacklabs themselves were spatially embedded in occupied social centres, and most of their participants lived in squatted houses, hacklabs were also socially embedded in this milieu. Hacklab participants routinely participated in other activities organized in these places or in the city, such as solidarity concerts, recycling food from markets and dumpsters (e.g. "skipping"), occupations and other direct actions.

Since squatters largely work from recycling trash, in a way it is inevitable that when computers and networking equipment turn up in junk piles, grass roots activists in squatted social centres will use them. Any kind of goods which can be recycled from refuse will be put to creative use in squatted social centres. In the beginning of the 1990s computers became household electronics, and by the middle of the decade modular IBM-PC compatible computers were not only ubiquitous in richer middle class homes, but were turning over quickly driven by regular hardware upgrades. While personal computers were still inaccessible for the lower middle class, "[m]embers of the collective scavenged and rebuilt computers from trash" (*Wikipedia* contributors 2014). Obsolete computers and discarded hardware would often find their way to hacklabs, and be transformed into useful resources — or failing that, into artworks or political statements. Blicero from the LOA hacklab in Milan says that "We built a classroom of i486 PCs recovered from the dumpsters of banks and other offices." (*Anarchopedia* contributors 2006)

In the decade before GNU/Linux adoption achieved a critical mass, installing a FLOSS (Free, Libre, Open Source Software) operating system was an art or a craft, not a routine operation. In this brief moment, free software was not yet established as a lucrative segment of the market, but had some characteristics of a movement, and hacklabs housed many developers. Software support was a main line of activity in hacklabs, with squatters, activists and some members of the general public coming specifically to get help, and hacklabs like LOA were organizing courses for beginners and intermediate users alike, while experts were collaborating in contributing to the software themselves.

While the hardware came from junk, and communities of practice formed around technical skills in occupied social centres, knowledge and software were shared over electronic communication networks. However, even access to these networks had to be established collaboratively and was tied to specific locales. At a time when modem connections were considered modern, it was sometimes only possible to connect to the Internet (or its predecessors, like BBSs and networks like FidoNet) by going down to a hacklab in your neighborhood. Building and cracking wireless networks has been a key skill of hacklab participants, often requiring substantial work on the physical layer, like installing antennas, routers and cables. Hacklabs then became grassroots communication hubs. In the times before mobile phones and well before popular voice-over-IP solutions like Skype, hackers from WH2001 (Wau Holland 2001), Madrid and bugslab, Rome set up telephone booths on the street where immigrants could call home for free. Therefore, these "squatted Internet work-spaces"—as they were sometimes called in the North of Europe—not only facilitated virtual connections between people and machines, but also contributed to the formation of embodied counter-computing communities. Internet use then brought people together in physical spaces.

At the same time media activists seized the new opportunity brought about by cheap ICTs (Information and Communications Technologies) to produce propaganda and build alternative networks. Halleck (1998) emphasizes that at least some activists started using ICTs as soon as they became available. However, access to knowledge was relatively scarce—especially outside academic and corporate environments—so autodidact users struggled to find associates. Marion Hamm observes that physical and virtual spaces enmeshed due to Indymedia activists' use of electronic communication media: "This practice is not a virtual reality as it was imagined in the '80s as a graphical simulation of reality. It takes place at the keyboard just as much as in the technicians' workshops, on the streets and in the temporary media centres, in tents, in socio-cultural centres and squatted houses." (2003) In the early '90s the largest media activist network was Indymedia (Halleck (2003); Pickard 2006a; Pickard 2006b), and according to my research most hacklabs were used by Indymedia activists at one time or another. Outside of big mobilisations like anti-WTO or World Bank counter-summits, hacklabs provided the "peace-time" infrastructures and the embodied communities which supported the Indymedia network and related activities.

One example of these four factors (1. junk, 2. FLOSS, 3. network access, and 4. media activism) coming together is the Ultralab in Forte Prenestino. Forte Prenestino is an occupied fortress in the heart of Rome renowned in Italy for its autonomous politics. The Ultralab is declared to be an "emergent pattern" on its website (Avana.net contributors 2005), which brings together various technological needs of the communities supported by the Forte. The users of the social centre have a shared need for a local area computer network that connects the various spaces in the occupied fortress, hosting server computers with the websites and mailing lists of the local groups, installing and maintaining public access terminals, having office space for the graphics and press teams, and finally having a gathering space for the sharing of knowledge.

Meeting these needs is not a light undertaking even by corporate enterprise standards. The Forte comprises 16,500 square meters of shifting flotsam and projects run on a no-budget basis. The point of departure for the hacklab was the server room of AvANa, which started as a bulletin board system (a BBS: a dial-in message board) in 1994 (Bazichelli 2008, 80–81). As video activist Agnese Trocchi remembers, *AvANa BBS was spreading the concept of Subversive Telematic: right to anonymity, access for all and digital democracy. AvANa BBs was physically located in Forte Prenestino the older and bigger squatted space in Rome. So at the end of the 1990's I found myself working with technology and the imaginative space that it was opening in the young and angry minds of communities of squatters, activists and ravers.* (Willemsen 2006)

AvANa and Forte Prenestino connected to the European Counter Network7, which linked several occupied social centres in Italy, providing secure communication channels and resilient electronic public presence to antifascist groups, student organizations, free radios, the T*ute Bianche* militant social movement, and other groups affiliated with the autonomous and squatting scenes. Housing servers inside squats had their own drawbacks, but also provided a certain level of physical and political protection from the authorities. While such setups worked for decades, it is a telling sign of the deterioration of hacklabs as an infrastructure for social movements that in 2012, a European Counter Network server was seized by the FBI not from an Italian occupied social centre but from a professional server farm in New York hosted by a social justice oriented non-governmental organization (*People Link* 2012). In fact, autonomous server projects have been the few components of the scene which survive to this day, and as the ECN case shows they continued to operate services, but in a more professional way. The active collectives Autistici/ Inventati from Italy, Poivron/Potager from France, Sindominio from Spain, and PUSCII from Utrecht started in now-defunct occupied spaces, and now host their servers in professional settings.

The descriptions given above serve to indicate how hacklabs grew out of the needs and aspirations of squatters, media activists, marginalised groups and the general public. In broad terms these activities could be treated under the rubric of access activism. Access activism in hacklabs had a number of characteristics which are important to explain.

First, hacklabs fitted organically into the anti-institutional ethos cultivated by people in the autonomous spaces. Just as free shops recycled clothes to serve as an alternative to commercial fashion shops, hacklabs recycled computers and taught and developed ICT knowledge as an alternative to computer shops, computer courses, and corporate research and development. They did so without any official or institutional support or backing, organized in an informal and horizontal way, along explicitly political aims and principles.

Secondly, hacklabs were embedded in the political regime of these spaces, and were subject to the same forms of frail political sovereignty that such projects develop. Occupied social centres typically have written and unwritten codes of behaviour which users are expected to follow, in and out of the hacklab. These informal rules typically state for instance that people who exhibit sexist, racist, or authoritarian behaviour should expect to be challenged and, if necessary, forcefully excluded. Such rules created what was called the activist ghetto, where many mainstream attitudes were effectively outlawed, but at the same time the same rules created a "safer place" for groups with limited access to social spaces like illegal immigrants or queers.[8]

Thirdly, the political dynamics of squatting, and more specifically the ideology behind expropriative anarchism[9], had its own particular consequences. A social centre is designed to be a public institution. Its legitimacy rests on serving its audience and neighbourhood, if possible better than the local authorities do, by which the risk of eviction is somewhat reduced. Thus the open-door policy of hacklabs and the low barrier of access in terms of credentials or skills is mandated.

Finally, the state of occupation fosters a milieu of complicity. Certain forms of illegality are seen as at least necessary, or sometimes even as desirable. These factors are crucial for understanding the differences between hacklabs and other shared machine shops like hackerspaces. For example in the latter case illegality is much less embedded in the social context of the space because it is rented and operated by a foundation, allowing for certain projects like spin-off companies which would be impossible in hacklabs, and making some normal hacklab practices such as stealing wireless Internet from the neighbors untenable.

During their prime days, hacklabs seamlessly combined three functions: providing a social and work space for underground technology enthusiasts to learn and experiment; supporting and participating in social movements; and providing open access to information and communication technologies for the public. In cyberspace, everything was still fluid and there was an overwhelming feeling, inspired by cyberpunk literature, that if the losers of history learned fast enough, they can outflank "the system". Paradoxically, cyberpunk stories describe a dystopia where corporate power incorporates state power, and runaway technology has become the scourge of civilization, without any hints that a real change through either technology development or social movements is possible. Such techno-optimism was not altogether unfounded, however. It is important to remember that before the dot com boom10 neither the state nor capital paid serious attention to the Internet, yet it seemed to offer unbounded possibilities to any young person familiar with sci-fi. While the autonomous movement in general was waning away, cyberpunk lived its golden age.

In conclusion, hacklabs were political projects that appropriated technology as part of the larger scheme of the autonomous (squatter) movement to transform and self-organise all parts of life.

FALL

The overarching historical process is the demise of the autonomous movement as a whole, in which hacklabs were but one component. In the 1970s the autonomous movement was strong enough to be called an extra-parliamentary opposition in core countries like Italy, Germany and the Netherlands. (Cuninghame 2005; Wright 2002; Geronimo 2012; Schultze and Gross 1997) In the 1980s the mass organisation of violence against the state and capital gave way to armed struggle in small clandestine groups like the Red Brigades (*Brigate Rosse*) and Prima Linea in Italy and the R.A.F (*Rote Armee Fraktion*) in Germany. (Aust 2008; Lotringer and Marazzi 2007) Hakim Bey's 1991 manifesto *T.A.Z.: The Temporary Autonomous Zone, Ontological Anarchy, Poetic Terrorism* captured the imagination of the next generation of militants, activists and hackers, who retreated from open confrontation with the state and capital. The slogan of the alterglobalisation movement of the next decade—"Another World is Possible"—follows the same logic of ontological ambiguity between imagination and reality. It is evident that the imaginary of cyberspace and virtual realities pervasive in hacklabs fitted neatly into such a strategy of retreat and self-valorisation, while the DIY spirit of the hacker ethics blended smoothly with the autonomous strategy of building your own realities ("the new in the shell of the old").

In fact many hacklab participants misinterpreted the open source movement as fighting for the same thing as them—a misunderstanding that took years to clear up. At the same time that peer production as an organizational form of digital labour rose to prominence in the technology sector,11 to some extent embraced by capital (Tapscott and Williams 2006) and some states (Bauwens and Kostakis 2014), peer production of political spaces and lives slowly declined. Recent years saw the abolition of "squatters rights" in the Netherlands (Pruijt 2013) and the

335

criminalisation of squatting residential buildings in the UK (Manjikian 2013; Government 2014; O'Mahony, O'Mahony, and Hickey 2015, 1). In my view criminalisation was merely the final nail in the coffin of a movement that had already started to decompose. Many participants retreated into cooperativist strategies, local initiatives of various kinds, and sometimes simply private life. The hacklab generation failed to reproduce itself.

Access activism as it was became largely obsolete when Internet connections and basic networking equipment like routers and IBM-PC compatible computers became so ubiquitous and affordable that all walks of society could partake of them. Similarly, common use cases of ICT like installing software, configuring basic networking, producing media and documents became much easier once technology stabilized, documentation was written and the social intellect of the general population caught up. At the same time the new wave of DIY technologies—physical computing,12 (Igoe and O'Sullivan 2004) computer aided manufacturing,13 (Söderberg 2014) and synthetic biology14 (Delfanti 2013) have grown relatively capital intensive—a development hacklabs could not follow on their own terms, while political applications of these technologies remained unclear despite "revolutionary" discourses around them. (Gershenfeld; Anderson 2014; Troxler and maxigas 2014) These technologies became the basis of the hackerspaces—the new wave of shared machine shops—and subsequently, progressively more and more heavily recuperated genres.

Meanwhile on digital networks, the community-run, self-managed, federated social media of the old Internet protocols like BBSs, Usenet forums, Internet Relay Chat rooms, Indymedia websites and later blogs, gradually gave way to Web 2.0 with its corporate-run and state-controlled, centralised "walled gardens" like Facebook, YouTube and Twitter. As the architecture of the web has been recuperated, so too has the architecture of the urban environment. Gated communities have been built in urban areas and squatting has been slowly criminalised. "Anti-squat" companies offer cheap rent to students in derelict houses, while art centres opened in industrial ruins are managed by the local government. (Dadusc and Dee 2015)

In summary, the demise of hacklabs can be attributed to the following four factors, internal and external. First, the autonomous movement lost steam, and thus the political context of hacklabs disappeared. Second, occupied social centres which hitherto housed hacklabs became less common. Third, the activities of typical hacklabs were rendered superfluous by socio-technical progress. Fourth, with their resource mobilisation strategies of expropriation and recycling failing, hacklabs were unable to appropriate and politicize the next wave of DIY technologies—physical computing, computer aided manufacturing and synthetic biology.

AFTERWORD

The demise of hacklabs closely aligns with the rise of hackerspaces. In the Netherlands the first hackerspace was established the year the last hacklab of the time was evicted. As I have argued (maxigas 2012), hackerspaces follow a similar tradition yet represent a different paradigm. They are rented clubs where technologically minded people can come together, socialize and work on projects. Hackerspaces are more squarely invested in hacker culture, and avoid political overtones in their public discourses. As self-organised and self-managed grassroots research and development spaces, they are generally open to the public with a liberal membership policy based on a monthly fee.

As the cultivators of the new wave of DIY technologies—physical computing, computer aided manufacturing and synthetic biology—they have grown exponentially, by now far outnumbering the hacklabs in their heyday. (maxigas 2012) Fitting into a hacker culture which is becoming mainstream, along with discourses of innovation and entrepreneurship, they have managed to cooperate with a wide range of organizations including schools, small and large businesses, even law enforcement, all while largely maintaining their initiative and independence. (maxigas 2014a; Hofman 2013) Hackerspaces are a form of shared machine shops which has broken out of the "activist ghetto", while building up institutional limitations which curtail their emancipatory potential.

Their impact can be measured by the plethora of genres they have engendered. Makerspaces distance themselves even from hacker culture which they deem too controversial. Fab labs (fabrication laboratories), often tied to institutions like universities or local governments, concentrate on design and manufacturing. Co-working spaces welcome freelancers and businessmen who want to share infrastructure and inspire each other. Tech shops provide machine use for commercial clients in a kind of hackerspace-as-a-service. As is apparent from this inventory, all these shared machine shops can be interpreted as progressively more recuperated versions of one another. They reprise paradigms of historical restructuration where state and capital absorb subversive subcultures and grass-roots organizations through neoliberal discourses and practices revolving around innovation and entrepreneurship. (Dardot and Laval 2014)

To be clear, the relationship between technology and politics is constructed in diametrically opposed ways in hacklabs and hackerspaces.

Hacklabs are conceptualized as explicitly political organizations embedded in a social movement which questions not only intellectual but also private property. (personal communication, Lunar 2013) The devotion to FLOSS (Free, Libre, Open Source Software) is continuous between the two types of shared machine shops, as well as the promotion of alternative licenses for the production of free culture (like Creative Commons) — and both of these legal techniques can be understood as a subversive critique of intellectual property. However, occupying buildings extends such a critique to private property in general. The expropriation of empty buildings points to the critique of a specific form of property: capital. For this reason it is not unusual for hacklab participants to engage in direct action against the state and capital in solidarity with other social groups even technology or culture are not at stake. Therefore hacklabs exhibit more coherence in their approach to property and politics, and do not confine their concerns to the realm of engineering. A hacklab participant is first and foremost a politically engaged person, who then acts on his conviction through her specialization.

Hackerspace members on the other hand owe their loyalties primarily to the hacker scene, an engineering culture. They defend the values and interests of that specific social group, mainly connected to user control over technology, including privacy, anonymity, open data, free technologies, etc. They question intellectual property through the critique of copyright and the development of free software and hardware — like hacklabs — but do not go so far as to take action against private property, and don't necessarily recognise capital as a problem. Hence spin-off companies arise from hackerspace inventions, while even cashing in on your skills in multinational corporations is looked down upon amongst hacklab alumni. It is not that the hackerspace scene does not occasionally mobilise strongly around political issues, even engaging in street protests as in the case of the campaign against the ACTA (Anti-Counterfeit Trade Agreement). It is that such engagement is confined to the professional ethos. A hackerspace member is first and foremost an engineer, who may engage in politics to defend her idea of technology.

Of course both groups include many hobbyists, lifestyleists and tinkerers who seek to stay away from anything which resembles political action. In a way shared machine shops in all their manifestations provide a shelter for self-centred or technology-centred individuals who do not want to be distracted from engineering either by bottom-up (social movement) or top-down (state and capital) pressures, but instead believe in "The Right Thing" or, theoretically speaking, pure technique. Nevertheless, even they shape technological possibilities and therefore the social *dispositif* therein, which is in itself a political activity. It goes without saying that their broader milieu has a profound effect on their ideas of what counts as a correct implementation.

However, these participants should not be dismissed. In the final analysis, the political potential of both genres of shared machine shops should not be measured by their instrumental contributions to social movements or the subversion of social order, but by the cultivation of an alternative vision of technology—call it cybernetic ontology (Pickering 2010)—that goes beyond the confines of capitalism, liberalism and even modernity. This is a bottom-up practice of engineering organized outside of the modern institutional grid, sustained through a semi-independent culture, and driven by the desire for unalienated labour. (Söderberg 2008; Himanen 2001) The difference lies in the consistency with which each genre of work can put forward such a vision.

Hacklab activities revolve around the desire for a widely conceived political technology, while hackerspaces pursue a more focused techno-politics: on one side technology is framed by politics, on the other technology frames politics. The tragedy of hacklabs is that they lack the resources to convey their message effectively. The comedy of the hackerspaces is that they have all the resources but lack a coherent message. Fortunately, the hacker scene has evolved into a movement of its own, and debates over recuperation, mainstreaming and politicization abound. (Toupin 2014; maxigas 2014a)

REFERENCES

ana. 2004. "Hacklabs: From Digital to Analog." Blog entry, translated from the Suburbia Telemacktical MediaZine. https://network23.org/ana/hacklabs-from-digital-to-analog/.

Anarchopedia contributors. 2006. "LOA Hacklab." Encyclopedia entry.

Anderson, Chris. 2014. Makers: The New Industrial Revolution, New York: Crown Business.

anonymous. 2010. "Storia." Wiki page. http://web.archive.org/web/20100613015928/http://hackmeeting.org/hackit09/index.php?page=storia&lang=en.

Aust, Stefan. 2008. Baader-Meinhof: The Inside Story of the R.A.F. London, Bodley Head.

Avana.net contributors. 2005. "Progetto Ultra Lab Al Forte." Web page. http://avana.forte-prenestino.net/ultralab.htm.

Bauwens, Michel, and Vasilis Kostakis. 2014. "From the Communism of

Capital to Capital for the Commons: Towards an Open Co-Operativism." TripleC: Communication, Capitalism and Critique 12 (1).

Bazichelli, Tatiana. 2008. Networking: The Net as Artwork, Ed. Simonetta Fadda. Aarhus: Aarhus Universität.

Benkler, Yochai. 2006. The Wealth of Networks: How Social Production Transforms Markets and Freedom, New Haven, CT: Yale University Press.

Bey, Hakim. 1991. T.A.Z.: The Temporary Autonomous Zone, Ontological Anarchy, Poetic Terrorism. New York: Autonomedia.

Coleman, Gabriella. 2010. "The Hacker Conference: A Ritual Condensation and Celebration of a Lifeworld." Anthropological Quarterly 83 (1) (Winter): 47–72.

Cuninghame, Patrick. 2005. "Autonomia in the 1970s: The Refusal of Work, the Party and Power." Cultural Studies Review 11 (2) (September): 77–94.

Dadusc, Deanna, and ETC Dee. 2015. "The Criminalisation of Squatting: Discourses, Moral Panics and Resistances in the Netherlands and England and Wales." In Moral Rhetoric and the Criminalisation of Squatting: Vulnerable Demons?, ed. Lorna Fox, O'Mahony, David O'Mahony, and Robin Hickey, 109–132. London: Routledge.

Dardot, Pierre, and Christian Laval. 2014. The New Way of the World: On Neoliberal Society. New York: Verso.

Delfanti, Alessandro. 2013. Biohackers: The Politics of Open Science. London: Pluto Press.

Ferrer, Mercé Molist. 2014. Hackstory.es: La Historia Nunca Contada Del Underground Hacker En La Península Ibérica. Barcelona: Self-published. http://hackstory.es/.

Geronimo. 2012. Fire and Flames: A History of the German Autonomist Movement Paperback. Oakland, CA: PM Press.

Gershenfeld, Neil A. Fab: The Coming Revolution on Your Desktop–from Personal Computers to Personal Fabrication. New York: Basic Books.

Government, Her Majesty's. 2014. "Squatting and the Law." Her Majesty's Government. https://www.gov.uk/squatting-law/overview.

Halleck, Dee Dee. 1998. "The Grassroots Media of Paper Tiger Television and the Deep Dish Satellite Network." Crash Media (2).

———. 2003. "Indymedia: Building an International Activist Internet Network." Media Development 50 (4): 11–15.

Hamm, Marion. 2003. "A R/c Tivism in Physical and Virtual Spaces." Republicart (9) (September).

Himanen, Pekka. 2001. The Hacker Ethic. New York, NY: Random House.

Hofman, Wilco Baan. 2013. "Alarm System Security." Research paper.

Igoe, Tom, and Dan O'Sullivan. 2004. Physical Computing: Sensing and Controlling the Physical World with Computers. London: Premier Press.

Lotringer, Sylvére, and Christian Marazzi. 2007. Autonomia: Post-Political Politics. Los Angeles: Semiotext(a).

Manjikian, Mary. 2013. Securitization of Property Squatting in Europe. London: Routledge.

maxigas. 2012. "Hacklabs and Hackerspaces—Tracing Two Genealogies." Journal of Peer Production 2.

———. 2014a. "Cultural Stratigraphy: A Historical Rift in the Hacker Scene Between Hacklabs and Hackerspaces." Journal of Peer Production (5) (July).

———. 2014b. "Use the Open Source, Luke!" Blog entry

on Open Thoughts, UOC blog. http://openthoughts-peerproduction.blogs.uoc.edu/use-the-open-source-luke/.

O'Mahony, Lorna Fox, David O'Mahony, and Robin Hickey, ed. 2015. Moral Rhetoric and the Criminalisation of Squatting: Vulnerable Demons? London: Routledge.

People Link, May First /. 2012. "FBI Seizes Server in Attack on Anonymous Speech." Press Release. https://mayfirst.org/fbi-attacks-anonymous-speech.

Pickering, Andrew. 2010. The Cybernetic Brain: Sketches of Another Future. Chicago; London: University of Chicago Press.

Pruijt, Hans. 2013. "Culture Wars, Revanchism, Moral Panics and the Creative City. a Reconstruction of a Decline of Tolerant Public Policy: The Case of Dutch Anti-Squatting Legislation." Urban Studies: An International Journal for Research in Urban Studies 50 (6) (May): 1114–1129.

Schultze, Thomas, and Almut Gross. 1997. Die Autonomen: Ursprünge, Entwicklung Und Profil Der Autonomen Bewegung Broschiert [the Autonomists: Origins, Development and Profile of the Autonomous Movement]. Hamburg: Konkret Literatur Verlag.

Shirky, Clay. 2008. Here Comes Everybody: The Power of Organizing Without Organizations. New York: Penguin Press.

Söderberg, Johan. 2008. Hacking Capitalism: The Free and Open Source Software Movement. London: Routledge.

———. 2014. "Reproducing Wealth Without Money, One 3D Printer at a Time: The Cunning of Instrumental Reason." Journal of Peer Production (4).

Tapscott, Don, and Anthony D. Williams. 2006. Wikinomics: How Mass Collaboration Changes Everything. New York: Penguin.

Toupin, Sophie. 2014. "Feminist, Queer and Trans Hackerspaces: The Crystallization of an Alternate Hacker Culture?" Journal of Peer Production (5) (October).

Troxler, Peter, and maxigas. 2014. "We Now Have the Means of Production, but Where Is My Revolution?" Journal of Peer Production (5) (October).
Wikipedia contributors, "ASCII (Squat)," Wikipedia, the Free Encyclopedia, 2014.

Willemsen, Merel. 2006. "Telestreet: Squatting Frequencies." Untitled Magazine (37) (Spring).

Wright, Steven. 2002. Storming Heaven: Class Composition and Struggle in Italian Autonomist Marxism. London: Pluto Press.

Yuill, Simon. 2008. "All Problems of Notation Will Be Solved by the Masses." Article in Mute: Politics and Culture after the Net.

Hacklab at centro sociale Bruno in Trento, Italy

Squatting in Media / Media in Squatting

Mujinga

SQUATS + PARTIES

Squat parties are an essential part of the squatting movement but are seldom written about, and sometimes disparaged by the political wing. A split between *politicos* and hedonists is traditional and perhaps even inevitable, but I've always had one foot set firmly in each camp. It's true that a lot of sound systems are anti-political, but for me that in itself has always been an intensely political stance. Without over-glorifying Temporary Autonomous Zones (since permanent ones would also be useful), some of the London multi-rigger parties of the past with twelve or fifteen sound systems spread across several different buildings in Brick Lane, Vauxhall, Hackney and Brixton, have had a massive impact on who I am and how I see the world.

RAVES

Growing up in London in the 1990s, squat parties invariably meant free parties where underground tekno music would be played. Later different styles like drum n bass, gabba, acid techno, speedcore, wonky techno and even disco flourished. Following on from the 1992 "summer of love" raves, and taking on influence from the punk squatters of the past, sound systems like Mainline, Virus, Jiba, Ooops, Insanity, Mayhem, Immersion, DV-ant and Unsound put on amazing parties in abandoned buildings. They did cinemas, libraries and schools, and invaded the dead warehouse zones of the capital—Acton, Stratford and especially the crumbling Victorian-era warehouses of Hackney Wick (now largely demolished for the 2012 Olympics).

The Criminal Justice Act pushed raves back underground, but it did not stop them. Next generation party people like Headfuk, Hekate, Panic and Pitchless kept the scene alive. Nowadays the scene may have eaten itself a bit, and the reluctance of sound systems to mobilise against crack

342

and muggers has led to some rubbish things happening, but I don't live in London any more and I'm sure banging parties are still happening. The Pokora crew do great speedcore events.

PARTY + PROTEST

Squat parties of course can be great fundraisers for political projects. The Reclaim the Future series of parties raised thousands of pounds for activist causes, and put on amazing nights full of different entertainments. The Brufut Education Project have raised money for a school in Gambia and the Anarchist Book Fair normally benefits from a squatted afterparty. When Freedom Books got firebombed I was really stoked to see a sign at the bar at the squatted Combat Wombat / Drowning Dog gig saying profits were going to the Freedom Books fund. Reclaim the Streets would not have been at all so good without the help of sound systems.

Spiral Tribe was an influential early sound system, alongside Bedlam, Vox Populi, Circus Normal, Circus Warp and Desert Storm. They had already left the UK and dissolved into other systems by the time I started partying. I remember watching thousands of people raving at the Castlemorton Common Festival on the TV news. Still, the virus kept spreading. Whilst the Spirals were travelling in Europe, heading always further into the industrial wastelands via Storm squat in Rotterdam, Tacheles squat in Berlin, Ladronka squat in Czech Republic and so on, they inspired native sound systems to put on teknivals, or week-long (illegal) free tekno festivals.

A whole tekno underground culture developed with a tribal dress code, live-in vehicles and hard underground music. The scene still continues, but *teknivals* are harder to do in countries such as England, the Netherlands and France. They are still happening further east in places such as Slovakia and Bulgaria. As the cycle of musical trends changed from hardcore to slow, maybe the way people choose to party has changed also. In any case, the UK saw a teknival near Brighton in 2014, and there are still illegal parties in France, where years ago already the movement forced the Government to permit three large parties of some 100,000 people every year.

BOOKS + FILMS

Teknivals and the travelling culture around them are celebrated in several books such as *No System* by Vinca Petersen, *Sonique Village* by Christel van Bezouw, *Overground* by Tomski and Bze, and *3672 La Free*

Story by Wilfrid Esteve and Sarah De Haro. Molly Macindoe released a book of photography called *Out of Order* focusing on London squat parties, mainly featuring Crossbones sound system. *Paname san dessus dessous!* by Frotte Canard shows how party people in Paris enter the catacombs for raves. All these books are great in different ways and they really capture the energy and movement of squat parties.

Finally, there are plenty of films on youtube about sound systems like *Heretic, Kierewiet, KX* and indeed the excellent five-part *World Traveller Adventurer* series following tekno travellers as far as Africa and India.

SQUATS + ZINES

When I first started making zines (hand-produced magazines, normally A5 in format) in the mid-2000s, the internet was awash with e-zines. These were being proclaimed as the future of publishing. But strangely enough, paper zines persisted and e-zines flopped. In fact the internet has only helped the movement of offline content, with sites like zinelibrary.info (mainly in English, now sadly on hiatus) and infokiosques.net (mainly in French) hosting loads of scans and pdfs of zines.

When I visited Les Tanneries, a big squat in Dijon, France, I was impressed to see a whole table full of zines, with a "*prix libre*" (pay what you wish) sign. Some were hand-drawn, many were produced on computer. The zines covered the same topics I was familiar with from English squats and social centres, such as consensus decision making, herbal health care, anarchist history, reports from demonstrations, perzines (personal zines) about activism and many other topics, but it was a completely different scene. While the excellent *Beyond Amnesty* zine was there, most titles were written in French and Spanish and were totally separate productions from the English language zines I knew. I found it fascinating that the information flows were running in parallel.

More often than not when you go to a social centre project in western Europe like Amsterdam, Berlin, Madrid, Milan, Paris or Rome, you will see a free/donation infotable with some zines. It's a part of the activist wallpaper. It makes me feel at home in the movement. Whilst I don't actually know so many zines with squatting itself as a subject, the squats themselves aid the circulation of knowledge and ideas through their events, and further through posters, zines, stickers and fliers. Many places also have fantastic archives.

I myself make a zine called *Using Space,* which focuses on squatting, social centres and alternative ways of living. I write about squatted places I've been to and what they made me daydream about, as well as reprinting news I find interesting. I try to leave some copies whenever I visit somewhere, both as a way of saying thanks to the people involved in the project and also as a means of keeping information flowing. I'm always happy to find zines other people have made. For example, that's how I discovered the *Super Happy Anarcho Fun Pages*, at Molli in Amsterdam.

The crossover between a zine and a pamphlet is always fluid, so here I'll claim the various squatters handbooks as zines. In most places where squatting is prevalent, squatters will make something to answer frequently asked questions such as "how do we get the door open?", or "how do we find out who is the owner?" The Squat.net website hosts a long list of such sites. In England, the Advisory Service for Squatters has been making a guide for decades. The 14th edition is in progress. In France, a new version of Le Squat de A a Z was just released.

Other zines focus on useful skills such as lockpicking, barricading and installing wood burners.

Last but not least, *Stressfaktor* deserves a mention. This Berlin-based A5 zine is produced with listings for radical and alternative events. The agenda is also online of course, but it really shows the strength and diversity of the Berlin scene that such a zine can be produced on a monthly basis.

Beyond Amnesty—http://325.nostate.net/?p=6144
Using Space zine—[http://cobblebooks.wordpress.com/tag/usingspace/]
Super Happy Anarcho Fun Pages—http://superhappyanarcho.tumblr.com/
Squatting manuals on Squat.net—http://squatting-manual.squat.net/
Advisory Service for Squatters handbook—http://www.squatter.org.uk/squatters-handbook/
Le Squat de A a Z—https://infokiosques.net/IMG/pdf/Le_squat_de_A_a_Z_version2014-cahier.pdf

SQUATTING MOVIES

There are lots of classic films about squatting and occupation in the Minority World. The archive at video.squat.net hosts many of them, mainly in English, Dutch and German. A lot of stuff is available on YouTube or Vimeo. There news clips and eviction footage, but also films (short and long) which stand in their own right as documents of local scenes. These would include:

Lipdub Kukuzta (no dialogue, just music in Basque) — To celebrate a social centre in Bilbao under eviction threat, Basque activists made this incredible one take 10 minute long journey through the building. Sadly Kukuzta was evicted, but a new iteration has since been occupied! [http://video.squat.net/lipdub-kukutza/]

De Stad was van Ons ("The City Was Ours", in Dutch, English subtitles) — A really interesting film about the 1980s Amsterdam squatter movement made by Joost Seelen and Eric Duivendoorden which serves as an accompaniment to the latter's book Een Voet Tussen de Deur ("A Foot in the Door", only in Dutch).
[http://video.squat.net/
nl-de-stad-was-van-ons-en-subs-70mins-708-mb-avi/]

More recent Amsterdam-based films are *A Chair, A Table and A Bed* (in English) and (confusingly) *Table, Bed, Chair* (in Dutch, English and Brazilian Portuguese subtitles). Plus a TV show exploring autonomy which spends some time at the now 17-year-old ADM squat.
[http://video.squat.net/en-a-chair-a-table-and-a-bed/]
[http://video.squat.net/nl-table-bed-chair-en-subs-avi-30mins/]
[http://video.squat.net/
nl-de-hokjesman-afl-5-de-autonomen-351mb/]

Rotterdam is represented in two local TV programs, *Kraken2000* and *Kraken in Rotterdam* (both in Dutch only).
[http://video.squat.net/nl-kraken2000/]
[http://video.squat.net/
nl-cineac-extra-21-feb-2013-terug-naar-kraken-in-rotterdam/]

A Dutch phenomenon which seems to be spreading like cancer is anti-squatting. [See text by Tino Buchholz in this book.] Abel Hejkamp's film *Leegstand zonder zorgen* ("Carefree Vacant Living" in Dutch with English subs) is a useful documentary showing the downsides of what might appear at first to be a very cheap way to live.
[http://video.squat.net/

leegstand-zonder-zorgen-nl-carefree-vacant-living-eng/]

69 (in Danish, English subs) — is a film produced by someone involved with Ungsdomshuset in Copenhagen who went on to be a professional film maker. This is a fantastic view into the struggle against the eviction of the Youth House and the eventual happy ending.
[http://video.squat.net/dk-69-694mb-60-mins/]

Battle of Tuntenhaus (in German, English subs) — a funny documentary about an early gay squat in Berlin, with a part two which revisits some of the participants.
[http://video.squat.net/de-battle-of-tuntenhaus/]

There are some great short films about various squats in Brighton, UK, (in English) including *Rhizomatic*, the *West Pier Squatters*, and "Temporary Autonomous Arts".
[http://video.squat.net/en-rhizomatic/]
[http://video.squat.net/west-pier-squatters-webm-1996-en/]
[http://video.squat.net/en-taa-brighton-2008/]

The *Bonnington Square* (in English) documentary is a great 20

minute film showing how a Victorian square in central London was rescued by squatters in the 1970s, many of whom still live there today.
[http://video.squat.net/en-bonnington-square/]

After the fall of Communism it was possible to squat some of the many empty buildings in Prague, Czech Republic. Now it is very difficult to avoid eviction. *Squat Wars* (in Czech, with Russian, English, German subs) documents some essential projects by interviewing participants. *Obsa a žij!* (in Czech, with English subtitles) shows that attempts at occupation are continuing into the present.
[http://video.squat.net/squat-wars/]
[http://a2larm.cz/2013/09/obsad-a-zij/]

Looking further afield, a view from the U$A is provided by Hannah Dobbz in her film *Shelter*. She later went on to write the excellent *Nine-Tenths of the Law* (AK Press, 2012) about squatting in the States.
[http://video.squat.net/shelter-a-squatumentary-2008-en-953mb-43mins-m4v/]

Another great movie is *Roses on My Table*, about a housing co-op in Richmond, Virginia.
[http://video.squat.net/en-roses-on-my-table-116mb-19mins-flv/]

Some recently produced films include *Rent Rebels*, about somewhat successful community activism against gentrification in Berlin, and *Give Us Space*, about housing struggles in London.

This quick overview only scratches the surface. The sheer number of excellent films about squatting all over Western Europe and beyond is a reflection of the amount of creativity which exists in different squatting movements. In any case, I'm looking forward to seeing and screening new movies about new projects.

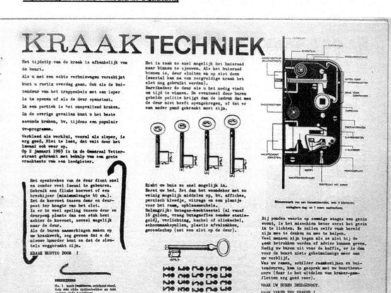

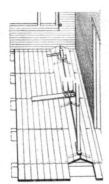

Handleiding Krakers (Squatters' Handbook) produced by the Amsterdam Squatters' movement in the 1970s. The handbook contains information on entering, securing and improving squatted buildings as well as illegal information and a presentation of the movement's political agenda.

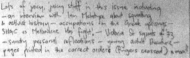

IMAGE CREDITS

p. 1: photo by Miguel Ángel Martínez López
p. 2: photo by Sutapa Chattopadhyay
p. 13, 21: photos by Alan Smart
p. 27, 29, 31: Illustrations for Universidad Nómada, by Mar Núñez, (noez.org)
p. 39: photo by Sutapa Chattopadhyay
p. 40–41, 45, 47, 51: photos by Alan Smart
p. 53 (top): photo courtesy of Andrew Castrucci
p. 53 (bottom): photo courtesy of Anton Van Dalen
p. 57: photo by Alan Smart
p. 63, 71: from the Bluf! archive at the International Institute of Social History (Amsterdam)
p. 73, 81, 82–83, 95: photos by Alan Smart
p. 97: http://www.christiania.org
p. 102–103: photo by Heb, Wikimedia Commons
p. 107: photo of Ungdoms poster
p. 109, 112–113: Creative Commons Attribution-Share Alike
p. 114-115: photo by Miguel Ángel Martínez López
p. 119: photo by Alan Smart
p. 121: photo by Miguel Ángel Martínez López
p. 123, 124, 125, 126: courtesy of Kasper Opstrup
p. 128–129: photo by Alan Smart
p. 135, 139, 141, 143, 144-145, 149, 150, 151, 152-153, 154, 155, 156, 157, 158, 159: photos by Sarah Lewison
p. 163, 165: photos by Alan Smart
p. 173, 175: photos by Franziska Holz
p. 181: Creative Commons Attribution-Share Alike
p. 183, 185, 187, 189, 191, 192-193: photos by Tobias Morawski
p. 194–195: photo by Alan Smart
p. 197: photo by Miguel Ángel Martínez López
p. 201: from Clash magazine, Interference Archive
p. 203: photo by Alan Smart
p. 207, 209, 211: stills from Telestreet: The Italian Media Jacking Movement
p. 213, 217: courtesy of MACAO
p. 218-219: photo by Miguel Ángel Martínez López
p. 221: Wikimedia Commons
p. 223, 234, 235: courtesy of Margot Verdier
p. 239: photo by Miguel Ángel Martínez López
p. 241, 245, 249: photos by Jacqueline Feldman
p. 250–251: photo by Miguel Ángel Martínez López
p. 259: Podemos posters appropriating illustrations by Seth Tobocman, courtesy of Miguel Ángel Martínez López
p. 255, 259, 261: photos by Miguel Ángel Martínez López
p. 263: poster courtesy of Miguel Ángel Martínez López
p. 266, 267: photos courtesy of Elisabeth Lorenzi
p. 269: photo by Brocco Lee, Creative Commons Attribution-Share Alike
p. 271: Creative Commons Attribution-Share Alike
p. 273, 277: photos by Miguel Ángel Martínez López
p. 281, 283, 285: photos by Stephen Luis Vilaseca
p. 286–287: International Institute of Social History (Amsterdam)
p. 289: painting by unknown artist, photo by Alan Smart
p. 291: photo by Tony Yarus, Wikimedia Commons
p. 292, 293: photo collages by Gregory Lehmann
p. 303, 309: Wikimedia Commons
p. 310, 317: photos by Miguel Ángel Martínez López
p. 318–319: still from Telestreet: The Italian Media Jacking Movement
p. 323: Anarchy No. 106, Interference Archive
p. 341: photo by Paolo Massa, Creative Commons Attribution-Share Alike
p. 347, 349: from Handleiding Krakers, courtesy of Alan Smart
p. 350–351: 'zine covers, Interference Archive

Making Room: Cultural Production in Occupied Spaces

**Editors
Alan W. Moore, Alan Smart**

**Editorial Assistance
Marc Herbst, ETC Dee, Art & Context, Vanessa Diehl**

**Translation
Milena Ruiz Magaldi, Jeannette Petrik**

Designed and Published by Other Forms

Colophon

ISBN 978-0-9791377-9-2

First edition published in collaboration with the Journal of Aesthetics and Protest, and printed in Barcelona by the self-managed workshops of Los Malditos Impresores. fotocopies@riseup.net, May 2015

This publication is a cultural report produced as an outcome of research project CSO-2011-23079: The Squatters' Movement in Spain and Europe: Contexts, Cycles, Identities and Institutionalisation (PI: Miguel A. Martínez), which has been funded by the Spanish Plan of Research and Development, between 2012 and 2014

CPSIA information can be obtained
at www.ICGtesting.com
Printed in the USA
LVOW04s0126140916
504493LV00018B/304/P